Praise for *Eight Bears*

Shortlisted for the Banff Centre Mountain Book Awards

"[A] timely survey." —*The New Yorker*

"[Gloria] Dickie's detailed, accurate, and holistic view of human-bear relationships is impressive. Even bear researchers can fall short in this regard." —Özgün Emre Can, *Science*

"A captivating and carefully considered mosaic of stories." —Jake Buehler, *Science News*

"A family album of the remaining varieties of bear." —Edward Posnett, *Guardian* (UK)

"I found wonder, awe, melancholy, and terror woven amid stories of the creatures being chronicled. . . . [L]yrical." —Gretchen Lida, *Washington Independent Review of Books*

"This book is not just a bear encyclopedia. Dickie wants to ask what it means to conserve a species, and in some cases how much conservation is 'enough.'" —Katrina Gulliver, *Spectator* (UK)

"Superb. . . . [T]he crisp prose will transport readers. . . . [A] winning combination of travel and environmental reporting." —*Publishers Weekly*, starred review

"A cleareyed view of the world's bears and the many threats they face." —*Kirkus Reviews*

"*Eight Bears* roars about the majesty and charisma of these remarkable creatures while illuminating their escalating vulnerability in a changing environment." —*Library Journal*

"Laced with climate change warnings as [Gloria Dickie] explores all the ways humans both love and endanger these creatures." —*BookPage*

"A definitive and magisterial account. . . . This book is essential reading about the ongoing Anthropocene collision between humanity and the rest of the natural world."
—James Balog, director of Earth Vision Institute and
A.D. White Professor-at-Large, Cornell University

"Written with deep compassion and striking humor, *Eight Bears* provides a deep and clarifying understanding of our history of ursine kinship." —Lyndsie Bourgon, author of *Tree Thieves:*
Crime and Survival in North America's Woods

"With deep, on-the-ground reporting and vivid writing, Gloria Dickie takes readers from the historic mythologies that have made bears the most charismatic of megafauna to the lairs and laboratories where the future for each of the world's eight ursine species is being written. Her book is as magnificent as the animals we meet in it."
—Michael Kodas, author of *Megafire:*
The Race to Extinguish a Deadly Epidemic of Flame

"In this insightful, absorbing book, Gloria Dickie not only introduces us to the eight remaining species of bears themselves but deftly connects the plight of each species to a much larger story: the story of our ancient, fraught, irreplaceable relationship with these astonishing animals."
—Michelle Nijhuis, author of *Beloved Beasts:*
Fighting for Life in an Age of Extinction

"Gloria Dickie takes us on an intimate global journey into our tangled and absorbing relationship with bears, where fur brushes close to skin, where the stakes are high, and in which the future of bears is our future as well." —Harley Rustad, author of *Lost in the Valley of Death:*
A Story of Obsession and Danger in the Himalayas

EIGHT
BEARS

EIGHT BEARS

MYTHIC PAST AND IMPERILED FUTURE

GLORIA DICKIE

W. W. NORTON & COMPANY
Independent Publishers Since 1923

For information about permission to reproduce selections from this book, write to Permissions, W. W. Norton & Company, Inc., 500 Fifth Avenue, New York, NY 10110

For information about special discounts for bulk purchases, please contact W. W. Norton Special Sales at specialsales@wwnorton.com or 800-233-4830

Manufacturing by Lakeside Book Company
Book design by Beth Steidle
Production manager: Anna Oler

Library of Congress Control Number: 2022303238

ISBN: 978-1-324-08699-4 pbk.

W. W. Norton & Company, Inc.
500 Fifth Avenue, New York, N.Y. 10110
www.wwnorton.com

W. W. Norton & Company Ltd.
15 Carlisle Street, London W1D 3BS

10 9 8 7 6 5 4 3 2 1

For Mom & Dad, better than the average bear, in every way

CONTENTS

PREFACE

I n the summer of 2013 I moved into a small, second-story condo in downtown Boulder, Colorado, a college town bordering the foothills of the Rocky Mountains. I was about to start a master's program in environmental journalism at the University of Colorado Boulder, and the city seemed like a fitting place for this field of study. Boulder, gently sloping toward the mountains, is located on the fractious edge of wilderness. It's the kind of place where people can hike up one of the five Flatirons—unique geological formations that resemble their name—before dawn and still make it to the office before the workday begins. Later, I'd learn that scientists have a jargony name for this: the wildland-urban interface.

The WUI (pronounced "woo-eee") presents all sorts of challenges to people and critters alike. Houses built in this zone are at greater risk of burning down during ferocious wildfires. Erosion and then flooding often follow, washing over charred soil and eating up riverbanks. And humans and wildlife fight for territory in the WUI; less than a mile separates some of Boulder's most extravagant homes from the black bears and mountain lions prowling the pine forest above town.

When I moved there, bears were frequent visitors. They could often be found eating apples in the North Boulder neighborhood, once a rambling orchard, and around University Hill, where hundreds of students lived in fraternity and sorority houses bordering the Flatirons. Dumpsters spilled their fermenting guts into alleys, drawing bears down from the mountains.

I'd come to Boulder from Canada, a place that the country's founders had once considered naming Ursalia, meaning "place of bears," for its abundant bruins. Except I'd grown up in southwestern Ontario, one of the most populated areas of the country, where humans had exterminated anything bigger than a white-tailed deer. There were black bears all around me—in the cottage country of northern Ontario and over the border in Michigan and New York State—but I was stranded in a bear desert. For a child obsessed with wild creatures, it was a tough break. Squirrels were the height of charismatic megafauna. The one chance I had to see a bear was during childhood trips to visit my grandparents, who lived in Calgary, Alberta, not far from Banff. But when we visited the Rockies, my parents kept me on a leash (humiliating) for fear that I would run ahead on the trail and be mauled by a grizzly. It was a bleak and tame existence.

Boulder promised to be different. I eagerly followed news of animal sightings in *The Daily Camera*, the local paper. There was the bear sleeping in the tree on campus; the mountain lion trading glares with a house cat; the bobcat roaming through backyards. Nearly every week that fall there was an article about a black bear wandering into town. Colorado Parks and Wildlife, the state agency tasked with managing wild animals, moved the bears away from Boulder. Often they drove them as far as the Wyoming border. But a few months would pass and I'd read that a relocated bear had returned to town. Living so close to wild animals wasn't nearly as thrilling as I'd expected. Boulder was no utopia for bears: Colorado officials were operating under a "two-strike" policy. If they caught a nuisance bear repeating so-called bad behavior, they killed it.

One early September day, a male black bear was dozing in the tall oak trees near Boulder's Columbia Cemetery. It wasn't the first time. A green ear tag drew attention to the bear's previous urban rendezvous. At 3 p.m., nearby Flatirons Elementary School went into lockdown. No student was allowed to leave the building with the bear hanging around. Wildlife officers were called. After three hours of waiting to see if the bear would return to the mountains of his own volition, officers shot and killed the animal. Parents of the pupils at Flatirons weren't happy. Their children were heartbroken to learn of the slumbering animal's fate. Three days later, another especially large black bear—590 pounds—was killed outside the elementary school. He, too, was known to wildlife wardens. A necropsy revealed that the fat bear's stomach was filled with two steaks (still in their wrappers), pasta, potatoes, eggs, avocado, paper towels, apples, lunch meat, and carrots—all scavenged from nearby dumpsters.

Outraged citizens flooded the city council meetings. It was clear the dead bears had been drawn into town by the endless availability of human food. They pushed council members to pass an ordinance that would require Boulder residents to lock up their trash in bear-resistant garbage bins—specially designed containers with complex configurations to keep bears out. Though trash ordinances already existed in small mountain towns, like Banff and those near Lake Tahoe, it was the first time a large city would pass such a law in the United States. That Boulder, a city with more than one hundred thousand residents, should need to implement this strategy to deal with black bears signaled a profound shift in the American West; as urban areas expanded, hungry black bears were no longer going to abide by arbitrary human boundaries.

So began my ursine odyssey. Halfway into my master's program, I zeroed in on reporting on bear-human conflict around the Rocky Mountains. On crisp autumn weekends, I tagged along with Boulder's Community Fruit Rescue initiative as dozens of volunteers armed with clawed fruit pickers and wicker baskets traveled among North Boulder's backyards, stripping apple trees bare at the behest of homeowners. Their mission was to remove any food source that might entice a bear to abandon its woodland home and end up on the wrong side of a rifle. I also started hanging around with the Boulder Bearsitters, a hodgepodge group of local citizens tasked with watching over bears sleeping in town, ensuring the bruins could safely make it back into the mountains at night.

Boulder wasn't the only place confronting an ursine insurgency. Across the American West, black bears were moving into towns and cities and grizzlies were expanding their range. In Aspen, Colorado, I accompanied enforcement officers patrolling the town for free-flowing garbage. Aspen was nearly overrun with meddlesome bruins. "Bears are all I do," one officer told me as he inspected a tipped-over garbage bin that had been secured with a piece of string. "Bears in trash. Bears in garages. Bears in cars. Bears in houses." An off-duty cop had even been attacked while walking through a trash-infused alley one recent summer night. Aspen led to Banff, Alberta, where the province's grizzly population was recovering following the end of a trophy hunt eight years prior and moving east into the foothills. And I followed the spine of the Rockies down to Yellowstone, where I met with ranchers worried about their own booming grizzly population; the population in the Greater Yellowstone Ecosystem had more than doubled since the bears were first protected under the Endangered Species Act in 1975. Now the bears were wandering out of the national park and getting into cattle and sheep herds.

Conflicts were surging in the wake of such ursine expansion. As I'd discovered in Boulder, people weren't exactly sure *how* to coexist with bears living next door. In New Jersey, where the black bear population has grown by a factor of thirty in just five decades, in 2014 a black bear chased and killed a hiker—the first documented fatality in the state's history. In Sierra Madre, California, near Angeles National Forest, a young woman was attacked by a black bear while napping in a backyard hammock; she escaped by hitting the bear on the face with her laptop. Meanwhile, grizzly attacks in the Rocky Mountain West have ballooned. In the summer of 2020, a mountain biker riding near Big Sky, Montana, was severely mauled by a bear. Too mangled to speak, he tried to explain what had befallen him by scribbling "bear" in the gravel where he collapsed. Near Yellowstone's Old Faithful geyser, a woman was attacked when she encountered a grizzly sow and cub. Five others in the Yellowstone area had been attacked by July of that year, obliterating past records. While most attacks in previous years had occurred on elk hunters in the late fall, most of the 2020 incidents involved other outdoor recreationists—joggers, hikers, cyclists.

It seemed our relationships with bears were nearing a tipping point.

The Rockies eventually led me to more distant ranges—I hiked through the Min Mountains of China, home to many of the world's remaining wild pandas. I traveled the Andes in search of South America's only surviving bear species. And I encountered feeding sloth bears in India's Aravalli Hills. But overwhelmingly, I encountered bears behind bars—pandas in captive breeding centers, caged moon bears on bile farms, and rescued dancing sloth bears. Those species I was fortunate enough to see apart from such manufactured landscapes were often living on the fragmented edges of wilderness. At the top of the world, polar bears are spending more time ashore as climate change melts their sea ice habitat. Scientists told me they expect almost all of the world's polar bear populations to crash before the end of this century. Some bear species I never witnessed roaming free. My journey would ultimately yield an unromanticized view of bears' tenuous position in the Anthropocene.

Though the conservation challenges ahead are many, I was often struck by the leniency and grace extended toward the bears I encountered, particularly when compared with other predators. Though state wildlife agencies in North America are tasked with killing so-called "problem" bears, many people strived to prevent such needless death. (I have never heard of any wolf or mountain lion sitters.) The gruff men with leathered hands and burnished Stetsons I met in Montana would never abide wolves or coyotes; a howl on the breeze had them reaching for their gun. But bears were another matter. The distinction puzzled me. Why were bears put in a different class from the other predators on the landscape? Perhaps it was because of our own social constructions. The first animal form we encounter in this world is often a bear—a cribside companion that accompanies us in our formative years. Later, in childhood, parents read bedtime stories featuring bears as fairy-tale heroes—Winnie the Pooh, the Berenstain Bears, Rupert Bear, Paddington Bear. By imbuing bears with a whimsical nature during infancy, had we unwittingly crafted a complicated relationship with the species?

Consider the fairy-tale antagonists. The Big Bad Wolf reigns supreme in *Red Riding Hood* and the *Three Little Pigs*. But I've yet to encounter a tale featuring a villainous bear, though brown bears likely still roamed Germany's Black Forest—the ground zero of fairy tales—when the Brothers Grimm were spinning their most famous yarns. In *Goldilocks and the Three Bears*, arguably the most notable piece of bear folklore, our ire is not directed toward the bear family, but rather the intrusive human. Robert Southey, the English poet who wrote the first printed version in 1837, describes three bachelor bears—"a little, small wee bear; a middle-sized bear; and a great, huge bear"—as good-natured, trusting, harmless, and hospitable, as polite as bears can be. In contrast, Goldilocks is characterized as impudent, foul-mouthed, ugly, and dirty. (Initially, he wrote her as a silver-haired old woman; later iterations would transform her into a blonde damsel or child.) This triumvirate of friendly bears is the unwitting victim of a narcissistic human who breaks into their home, eats their porridge, and splinters Wee Bear's beloved chair. Then, when all is said and done, she passes out in their bed.

Our modern reality does not differ much from this fabled world. We have entered the bears' home without permission and selfishly laid claim to what we found there. In the words of Wee Bear, "someone's been lying in my bed," and, well, here we are.

EIGHT
BEARS

INTRODUCTION

The family of animals known as Ursidae was once considered to be among our closest relatives. Indigenous stories and myths of antiquity spoke of an animal with profound similarities to our own kind—a being that shared the same core and thereby our journey through this world, or a shape-shifter switching seamlessly between human and beast. These perceptions live on in dances and legends wherein the bear serves as mother, protector, teacher, and medicine man. Along the western coast of North America, First Nations share the same estuaries with grizzlies and black bears, moving synchronously between sea and shore. Elders say that if a person ever becomes lost in the forest, to survive they should eat everything a bear does—salmonberries, silverweed, chocolate lily, northern rice root. Everything except the toxic skunk cabbage. Peruvian farmers tell stories of a bear-man who travels the Andes and steals away young women. In Scandinavia, Laplanders speak of the "old man with the fur garment." The Yakuts of the Russian Far East refer to neighboring brown bears as "grandfather" and "uncle."

Stories of a familial bear exist in almost every human culture that shares territory with the animal.

But why? The likely reason is that bears resemble and behave like people. Few living mammals are able to move on their hind legs. Primates, rodents, pangolins, kangaroos, and bears, which are scientifically dubbed "occasional bipeds," are the exceptions. When skinned, a bear's pale gleaming carcass exhibits a disturbing resemblance to the human body. (William of Auvergne, a medieval theologian, observed that bear meat also tastes considerably like human flesh, raising the unappetizing question of how he was able to draw such comparison.) A bear's footprint, equivalent to a man's size 11 shoe, appears in the soil much like our own five-toed impression. Shepherds in the French Pyrenees call the brown bear *la va-nu-pieds,* the barefooted one. Even American conservationist John Muir was known to wax poetic about our ursine doppelgänger. "Bears are made of the same dust as we," he wrote, "they breathe the same winds and drink of the same waters."

This likeness was not lost on the Greek philosopher Aristotle either, who made note of the bear's erect posture, single stomach, and five claws with three joints in his *History of Animals,* written in the fourth century BCE. In one Greek myth, the nymph Kallisto strolls through the forest and swears to the goddess Artemis that she will remain a virgin. When such a promise proves hard to keep in Zeus's presence, Artemis transforms Kallisto into a bear as punishment for her unchastity. Kallisto's son, Arkas, later hunts his mother, not recognizing the bear as his own flesh and blood. Zeus intervenes, sending Kallisto and her son to live on among the burning stars as Ursa Major and Ursa Minor.

The belief that humans and bears were of close relation, underlined by the writings of Aristotle and Pliny the Elder, persisted until the Middle Ages. Three animals were then considered to be our wild siblings: the monkey, the pig, and the bear. The monkey because it appeared to imitate human behavior and expression. The pig because, when dissected by medical students, it was found to mirror our own anatomical composition. However, the Christian church considered these two comparisons unsavory. By simulating our actions, the monkey proved itself a dirty trickster. It was a demonic creature. The pig, gluttonous and lazy, was similarly relegated to the devil's bestiary. "This is why, although doctors knew that the pig was anatomically a cousin to man," wrote medieval historian Michel Pastoureau in *The Bear: History of a Fallen King,* "[the Christian church] did not declare the fact too openly and allowed clerics to assert that the animal that most resembled humans was neither the pig nor the monkey, but the bear." Yet this did not stop people from subjecting the bear to cruel spectacle in a boorish attempt to dethrone the animal.

Paleontology and the advent of genetic analysis would eventually disprove any true relation. The March of Progress began not with a bear, but with a common ancestor of human and ape. The bear lineage diverged around thirty million years ago, when global changes in the environment spurred a compendium of carnivores to split off from a group of slinky mammals with sharp teeth, known as the Miacidae, that resembled today's civets or martens. The Miacidae served as the primitive precursor for the world's modern meat-eaters, giving rise to modern seals (science suggests that this is the bear family's closest living relative), wolverines, dogs, and bears. There were even bear-dogs before man's would-be best friend went extinct. The oldest known bear genus, *Ursavus*, emerged around twenty million years ago and, according to fossils dug up in Colorado and China, was roughly the size of a sheepdog. As such, the earliest bears are older than humans by an order of magnitude—the first human ancestor only appeared around seven million years ago.

Early bear species looked little like the animals we know today. Over the years, some extinct species have been unearthed or identified. *Ursavus elmensis*, the dawn bear, is considered the first true bear species. It was stout and not much bigger than a cat, with a doglike face and a long fluffy tail that it used for balance when it hunted from trees. Most of the modern bear lineages appeared in just the last five million years—extremely recently in terms of geological time. At the end of the Miocene, a minor extinction event caused most older bears, including *Ursavus*, to vanish. The world's modern bears evolved to fill the gaps left in the ecosystem. As jungles turned to dry forest, and dry forest to grassland, bears adapted their diets to thrive in new environments. The short-faced bear clade emerged on the plains. *Agriotherium*, which lived between twelve and three million years ago, was the only bear species to have ever roamed sub-Saharan Africa, with fossils unearthed in Ethiopia. Bears eventually spread from Africa and Eurasia into North America, and, around 2.7 million years ago, after the continents connected, walked down to South America. Polar bears appeared on northern seacoasts around five hundred thousand years ago, making them the world's "newest" bear species. By the advent of the Holocene, bears could be found on nearly every corner of the planet.

AROUND TWENTY-FIVE THOUSAND YEARS AGO, many bear species began to go extinct. The cave bear (*Ursus spelaeus*) disappeared from Europe. What drove the animal to extinction continues to be a topic of contention in academic circles, with a cooling climate and conflicts with humans offered as the two warring explanations. The latter theory has gained ground in recent years. Even before the onset of the Last Glacial Maximum some thirty thousand years ago, the genetic decline of cave bears had already begun. A 2019 study in *Scientific Reports* used genetic sequencing to reconstruct fifty-nine complete cave bear mitochondrial genomes from fourteen sites across Europe. The researchers found that cave bear populations began crashing around forty thousand years ago, coinciding with the spread of modern humans in Europe— not the spread of ice and snow. Neanderthals and modern humans were known to compete with cave bears for shelter as well as hunt the animals. Accordingly, the cave bear is likely the first bear species humans managed to push to extinction.

Arctotherium angustidens, a Honda Civic–sized giant short-faced bear that lived in South America, similarly did not make it out of the Pleistocene. At the time, it was likely the largest carnivorous land mammal on the continent and could top running speeds of 45 miles per hour. Most other species in the short-faced bear clade vanished during a period known as the Quaternary Extinction, when more than thirty species of large American mammals—horses, mammoths, giant beavers, and musk oxen—disappeared. Were humans to blame—again? The Clovis people who inhabited North America at the time have largely been exonerated from triggering the demise of ancient bears; paleontologists have never turned up any evidence to suggest the Clovis hunted short-faced bears. However, the Clovis *did* hunt other large mammals, leaving behind sharp stone spearpoints at sites across the Americas. It's possible that the Clovis appetite for herbivorous prey, combined with a changing climate, proved extinguishing for the bears.

Modern ursids are now exceedingly rare. There are thirty-five species of canines, from wolves to dholes, jackals to foxes. Felines number forty-one. Cetaceans—whales, porpoises, dolphins—are abundant with more than ninety species. And there are as many as five hundred species of primates. Bears don't even enter the double digits.

Today, we are left with just eight species of bears. Some are celebrated as icons of the natural world: the brown bear (*Ursus arctos*), the American black bear (*Ursus americanus*), the panda bear (*Ailuropoda melanoleuca*), and the polar bear (*Ursus maritimus*). The others are lesser known: the Asiatic black bear (*Ursus thibetanus*), the sun bear (*Helarctos malayanus*), the sloth bear (*Melursus ursinus*), and the spectacled bear (*Tremarctos ornatus*). Charismatic and unloved alike, these eight bears are all that remain of a family that has been our steadfast companion since time immemorial, shaping our cultures, our geographies, and our stories.

All of the world's living bears belong to the Ursidae family, which accommodates the subfamilies of Ursinae, Tremarctinae, and Ailurpodinae. In the Ursinae subfamily, we find what biologists consider the modern bears: the polar bear, brown bear, American black bear, Asiatic black bear, sloth bear, and sun bear. The cave bears were part of this group, too, before our ancestors wiped out the species. In the Tremarctinae subfamily, which once housed the short-faced bear clade, we're now left with just the spectacled bear of the Andes. Similarly, the giant panda is the sole living member of Ailuropodinae and belongs to the oldest bear lineage, diverging nineteen million years ago from *Ursavus*, the ancestral genus of the Ursidae family. *Ailuropoda microta*, the panda's ancestor, was alive around two million years ago, and according to scientific reconstruction, appeared much like the modern panda, but smaller at 3 feet long instead of 5. Beyond this, the panda's anatomy has hardly changed over millennia. "Pandas have been 'uniquely pandas' for many millions of years," Russell Ciochon, a paleoanthropologist, told the *New York Times* in 2007, following the discovery of this pygmy ancestor's skull in southern China.

Naively, many people refuse to believe the list stops at *just* eight. They point to the koala or the red panda in their rebuttals. The koala bear, the most famous of the not-a-bears, earned its misleading title because when Europeans arrived in Australia, they believed the tiny eucalyptus-dwelling creature was part of the bear clan. In 1816, the marsupial was given the Latin name *Phascolarctos cinereus*, meaning ashgray pouched bear. In actuality, the wombat is the koala's closest relative. Similarly, the Australian drop bear is also a not-a-bear, nor an animal at all. This fictitious creature, *Thylarctos plummetus*, is nothing more than a hoax designed to scare American tourists. Pandas are bears (despite what some think), but red pandas are not. The Chinese red panda and Himalayan red panda, recently discovered to be two distinct species, are the only living members of the family Ailuridae. Apart from their eye patches, they have little in common with the giant panda. Lastly, there is the water bear. These minute tardigrades—eight-legged micro-animals named for their bearlike gait—are extraordinarily resilient animals, able to survive from the deep sea to mud volcanoes to outer space. Alas, they are also not-a-bears.

Still, the eight true species are remarkable in their own right. They inhabit four continents and a wide range of environments. They can be found in the cloud forests of the Andes; in the bamboo forests of Asia; in the scrubland of India; in the sheep-dotted Pyrenees; and in the arid Gobi Desert of Mongolia. Cultural representation of bears, however, skews toward the north. Scholars refer to this phenomenon as the "circumpolar bear cult tradition": the notion that countries in the Northern Hemisphere are far likelier to foster an ursine obsession in iconography and oral history than equatorial nations. Bears, they posit, are "unique among other-than-human persons in being so honored throughout the circumpolar north, from North America across Eurasia." There are popular and long-standing festivals featuring bears, from Catalonia to Romania, and archaeological remains of bear ceremonialism have been unearthed across the region. Countries nearer the Southern Hemisphere, though home to four unique bear species, prefer to pay homage to big cats—tigers, leopards, jaguars.

Even with just eight species remaining, the physical diversity of bears is extraordinary. The world's bears come in all shapes and sizes. There are long snouts and short snouts. There are 150-pound bears and 1,000-pound bears. Some slurp up insects. Some eat meat. Others munch on fruits and nuts. Brown bears can be black. And black bears can be brown. Take this convoluted correction from a newspaper article, for instance: "A previous version of this story stated that the bear is a brown bear. While it is a bear that is brown, it is not a brown bear; it is a black bear (that is brown). The story has been updated to reflect this." Despite such variation in appearance and habit, all eight species are critical actors in their local environments. Spectacled bears and black bears are the gardeners of the forest, dispersing seeds in their scat. A single pile of bear poop in Colorado's Rocky Mountain National Park, for example, was found to yield twelve hundred seedlings after it was replanted in a greenhouse. In coastal areas, brown and black bears drag salmon from rivers into forests, allowing for the decomposing fish carcasses to fertilize giant cedars. And bears that feast heavily on meat help to keep populations of deer and moose in balance. Ultimately, because of the bruins' outsized presence, conserving bear habitat helps to protect all the species that fall beneath them in the food chain.

And yet, despite their profound differences, many of the world's bear species are united by a single, shared characteristic: They're in trouble.

WE HAVE NOT SHOWN MUCH COMPASSION to the animal we once considered our next of kin. Where humans have proliferated, bears have often declined in tandem. In 2007, the International Union for the Conservation of Nature (IUCN) Bear Specialist Group released a dire assessment: not only are there only eight remaining bear species, but six of the eight are now threatened with extinction. Only the American black bear is considered secure throughout its global range. At nine hundred thousand strong, black bears are more numerous than the seven other bear species combined. Admittedly, I'd been a bit naive in Boulder. The backyard black bears that had first piqued my curiosity were an indication of just how robust the population had come to be, not a failure of conservation by any means. Black bears are a conservation success story. It would require a global journey to uncover others.

Out in the real world, bears weren't much like how I'd imagined them to be. The first grizzly bear I saw in the wild wasn't surrounded by towering mountains and rushing streams filled with salmon. It was digging up roots near a construction site by the Trans-Canada Highway. India's sloth bears, too, were struggling to eke out an existence in a country where land was at a premium and conservation dollars were funneled toward charismatic tigers. In the subarctic town of Churchill, Manitoba, polar bears weren't leaping nimbly from ice floe to ice floe, their sopping wet yellow-white fur dangling from their bellies like icicles. Rather, they were being swarmed by a dozen monstrous vehicles full of tourists, eager to see the bears before they disappeared forever. In China, it was easy for me to see a panda—dozens are born in captivity every year to be shipped around the world as fluffy diplomatic bribes. And the moon bears and sun bears I saw in Vietnam were caged, often with furless skin marred by needle marks. Almost everywhere I went, bears seemed to be a shadow of what they once were.

Bears weren't always held in such contempt. In other cultures, the bear was seen as an admirable, useful, and trustworthy member of society. For example, the Viking berserkers who roamed the northern isles a millennia ago were said to draw their trancelike fury from the power of the bear when they went *berserk*, howling like beasts, foaming at the mouth, and gnawing on their iron shields in battle. The Old Norse word *berserkr* translates to "bear shirt."

As early as the twelfth century, troupes of Romani nomads led domesticated bears through the Byzantine Empire. The animal trainers traveling with the group were known as the Ursari. Just before the eve of the new year, they would stop in villages with leashed bears, said to embody powerful magics, to dance and chase away evil spirits from the outgoing year. For hundreds of years, the Ursari busked brown bears across Europe before many settled down in modern-day Romania in the nineteenth century. Even after some shed their nomadic ways, the Ursari continued to employ bears. Pain was treated with bear fat and bear hairs tucked into amulets. Though the Romanian government began to legislate against dancing bears during the twentieth century, it wasn't until Romania joined the European Union in 2007 that bear dancing finally came to an end. But the robust culture surrounding bears did not disappear. Every year, Romanians and Romani communities dress up as bears and parade through village streets. At the end of their trek, a designated "bear tamer" bleeds a faux bear with a knife, releasing the demon within and bringing good luck.

In the Far North, the Inuit say the polar bear—*Nanuq*—is worthy of fear and respect as he presides over whether or not a hunt will be successful. The Inuit strive to respect polar bears in death as in life. Elders believe that if a dead bear is treated well by those who took its life, the bear will share this news with other bears and they, too, will happily submit themselves to be killed.

Many Indigenous stories position the bear as human. By donning the skin of a bear, a person can become the bear itself. One of the most famous legends among the nations inhabiting the coast of British Columbia, including the Haida, Nisga'a, Tsimshian, and Gitxsan, is that of the Bear Mother. In this tale, a woman berry picker disrespects the bears who live in the cedar forests. They kidnap her and force her to marry the son of a grizzly bear chief. In time, she gives birth to two bear cubs who appear as half-breeds, stuck between human and bear. The story is used as a moral teaching to emphasize the importance of honoring and respecting animals, especially bears. Recent studies have shown that along British Columbia's central coast, the genetic diversity of grizzly bears mirrors Indigenous language groups, suggesting the two evolved in tandem, shaped by the landscape in a similar way. First Nations leaders and scientists have put forward the argument that the grizzly bear and polar bear are cultural keystone species with the power to advance reconciliation between Indigenous and non-Indigenous people through the bears' continued restoration and conservation.

Even in antiquity, bears were respected and honored. At Brauron, one of the twelve cities of Attica in ancient Greece, bears leveraged their bipedal status into galactic inspiration. Young girls would honor the Great She-Bear Artemis by participating in a rite of passage known as *arkteia*. Draped in bear skins, the girls—on the cusp of puberty—danced in slow, staggering steps, mimicking the movement of the bear. This tradition, and Brauron, were abandoned some time in the third century BCE. In 146 BCE, ancient Greece fell to the Romans, and a brutal set of ideals came to dominate human interactions with wild animals. The bear was no longer seen as celestial, supernatural, or familial, but as a brutish foe to be conquered in bloody spectacle. Gladiators were the first to be recruited to fight one another to the death in the pits of Rome as entertainment for the unwashed hordes. But when such novelty wore off, Roman emperors had begun seeking new thrills for their audiences, landing on the *venator*, "the hunter."

In 186 BCE, a Roman general staged what's believed to be the first spectacle of a man sparring with a group of panthers and lions. It was an overnight sensation. *Venator* fever gripped the empire. Julius Caesar even built a special amphitheater to host the bestiary bloodbaths. Emperors dispatched Roman dignitaries around the world to capture intriguing animals for the fights and a veritable menagerie returned to Rome; rhinos, crocodiles, lions, cheetahs, tigers, and hippos were all recorded to have passed through the city gates. Indeed, only the most charismatic animals would suffice, and bears soon emerged as a popular arena foe.

Another antihero also debuted during this sanguinary period: the *bestiarius*. He was often not a trained fighter like the *venator*, but rather a convicted criminal thrown into a pit of beasts as punishment. This was gruesome spectacle at its finest. The *bestiarius* did not live long, even by gladiator standards. Prisoners would sometimes kill themselves ahead of the games rather than be subjected to such a horrid death; the Roman orator Quintus Symmachus told of twenty-nine Saxon prisoners who agreed to strangle one another in their cells the night before they were scheduled to fight.

Bears appeared time and time again in these battles. Sometimes as many as one hundred in just one go-around. Bears, however, posed a challenge for Roman rulers. Not all were inclined to fight. Sometimes a lazy bruin just sat there, minding his own business, while crowds jeered. In one such instance, a leopard had to be called in as a half-time replacement when the bear refused to leave his cage. (A very bearlike thing to do.) The other problem was that the nearest bears lived in the Scottish highlands, which were not under Roman rule at the time. To meet demand, some dignitaries turned to North Africa for their ursine supply.

By the time Roman rule ended around 476 CE, thousands of *bestia-*

rii and *venatores* had expired. Far more wild animals were killed. Rome's bloodlust was so insatiable that some areas of Africa and the Mediterranean were almost entirely depleted of wildlife when barbarians seized control. The hippo disappeared from much of the Nile. Lions vanished from Mesopotamia. Elephants no longer roamed North Africa. And bear numbers had been decimated in both the British Isles and North Africa. Emperor Augustus bragged that he alone had held twenty-six shows during his reign that led to the death of thirty-five hundred "African wild beasts."

The mistreatment of bears persisted well beyond the collapse of the Roman Empire. As Christian scripture came to dominate European ideologies in the Middle Ages, bears fell even further from grace. The church promoted the belief that humans were created superior to all other creatures—a belief that persists to this day—and it was therefore important to distinguish themselves from the rest of the animal kingdom. The bear, with its humanlike posture, was a great threat to humankind's singular supremacy. Reverence was a dangerous game. So, bears were swiftly dethroned and recast as unintelligent clowns, subjugated to all sorts of cruel human behaviors. In Britain, brown bears were also trained as dancing bears. Chained bears were dragged from town to town and made to perform tricks in front of cajoling crowds.

Bearbaiting found even greater success as a form of street entertainment. Not unlike the Roman arena battles in its conception, it featured a bear staked to a pole while a pack of aggressive dogs—usually mastiffs or grumpy English bulldogs—were sicced on the poor animal. Jeering spectators placed bets on who would win. As in Ancient Rome, the animals fought to the death, but it was a far less dignified experience; the bear wasn't deemed worthy of a human foe. This performance was beloved by both commoners and royals alike. The latter even employed a Master of the Bears to oversee all ursine activity in London, issuing licenses and generating income from entertainers. The most famous bear gardens—a lovely name for a perfectly terrible place—were at the Paris Garden and King Henry VIII's Palace of Whitehall, where royals had constructed special pits surrounded by bleachers. In the sixteenth century, Robert Laneham, a court official, described bearbaiting as "a very pleasant sport . . . to see the bear with his pink eyes leering after his enemies approach, the nimbleness and wait of the dog to take his advantage, and the force and experience of the bear again to avoid the assaults." Queen Elizabeth I was a reputed superfan; when Parliament tried to ban bearbaiting in 1585, she overruled them.

The brown bear likely disappeared from the British Isles at some point in the early medieval period, forcing street entertainers to obtain their bears from elsewhere in Europe. Over time, the popularity of bear performances declined. Still, it wasn't until 1835 that the British Parliament finally banned bearbaiting. Dancing was permitted to continue until 1911.

When Europeans had at last succeeded in purging their own geography of wild beasts, they sailed across the Atlantic and attempted the same feat in North America, arriving on shore with unbridled enthusiasm for extinction. As colonists pushed westward across the continent, they sculpted a new landscape—one no longer meant for wild predators. Fearsome animals were vanquished in the name of protecting livestock and homestead. The settlers' trepidation in the face of such vast wilderness is perhaps best captured by the Latin name of the brown bear: *Ursus arctos horribilis*. Writing in his journal on May 5, 1805, William Clark—of the Lewis and Clark Expedition—described the largest grizzly he had ever seen as "a verry large and a turrible looking animal" and "extreemly hard to kill." But kill he did. His men laid waste to that bear with ten well-placed bullets, as they did to dozens more of its kind. And so did the generations that followed.

Governments issued bounties on the continent's fifty thousand grizzly bears with the aim of eradication. Wherever they were found, bears were trapped, shot, and poisoned. Wilderness was slowly sanitized. Woodlands were cleared for towns; towns grew into cities, then metropolises. Roads sliced through the bears' den sites and foraging grounds. By 1900, the forested area of the United States had fallen from 1.1 billion acres to less than 741 million acres. Herds of vacuous bovines dotted pastures born of denuded forest. Grizzly populations dwindled in concert. State by state, the great bear disappeared: Texas in 1890; New Mexico in 1931; Colorado in 1953. By the mid-twentieth century, grizzly bears had almost been expunged from the continental United States, with fewer than one thousand left. Even black bears, though far less "turrible looking," were pushed to the brink of local extinction in many places: fewer than twelve individuals remained in Mississippi, and the Florida population plummeted from eleven thousand before European settlement to as few as three hundred by the 1970s. Expanses of boreal forest in Canada and Alaska ensured that a wellspring of black and brown bears remained on the continent, even as they vanished from the lower latitudes.

While the temperate forests of North America and Europe were chopped and felled for food, fiber, and fuel, tropical forests fared relatively well until the early twentieth century. Sloth bears roamed from India to Bhutan, Nepal. Asiatic black bears were abundant across wide swaths of the continent. Sun bears, too, were plentiful in Asia, ranging from northeast India to southwestern China. But as human populations grew, so did the pace of deforestation. Forests in Afghanistan, Bangladesh, Bhutan, India, and Nepal were cleared for cropland, leaving resident sloth bears and moon bears exposed. By the time China's population reached 541 million in 1949, forest cover had declined to 10 percent of the country's land area. Many of these losses occurred in the bamboo forests where the giant panda lives. And in Southeast Asia, high-value tropical timber, oil palm, and rubber plantations have come to replace the fragile rain forest ecosystem.

BEARING WITNESS TO THE natural ruin and muted forests that surrounded them, Americans veered from their path of destruction in the twentieth century. The poetic words of writers like John Muir and Aldo Leopold shepherded millions of people into the conservation movement, encouraging them to protect what little wilderness remained. "The last word in ignorance is the man who says of an animal or plant: 'What good is it?'" Leopold lamented. In *Sand County Almanac*, he recounted the story of Old Bigfoot, one of Arizona's last remaining grizzly bears killed on Escudilla Mountain. He wrote that the monolith was defined by the grizzly bear, "the outstanding achievement of the . . . pageant of evolution":

> The government trapper who took the grizzly knew he had made Escudilla safe for the cows. He did not know he had toppled the spire off an edifice a-building since the morning stars sang together. . . . Escudilla still hangs on the horizon, but when you see it you no longer think bears. It's only a mountain now.

Americans came to value an untamed world and all the creatures it contained. US president Theodore Roosevelt established the Forest Service, five national parks, and eighteen national monuments, ultimately placing 230 million acres of public land under protection during his time in office. But his name lives on for another reason.

In 1902, Roosevelt went on a four-day bear hunting trip to the forests of Mississippi. He soon fell behind his hunting guide, who ran off ahead with his hounds and cornered a small female black bear. The distressed bear attacked one of the dogs, crushing its spine, then went at another. The guide jumped into the fray and cracked the bear on the head with the butt of his rifle. Tying the helpless black bear to a willow tree, he called for the president to come and finish the kill.

When poor Teddy finally caught up, he refused to shoot the semi-conscious bear as he believed it was lacking in sportsmanship. Instead, the bedraggled Roosevelt instructed his companions to kill the bear with a knife and put the animal out of its misery. This questionable act of compassion soon made its way into the newspapers as a political cartoon labeled "Drawing the Line in Mississippi," and it featured a small feeble black bear with big round ears. This cartoon would allegedly serve as the inspiration for the first "Teddy" bear. By the end of the decade, nearly a million of the stuffed toys were in production.

At a time when America was still in the throes of a love affair with extermination, the Teddy bear helped turn things around. It boosted the bear's popularity like nothing ever before seen. Parents complained that their children were choosing these fluffy toys over more savory options. "From all quarters of the globe," wrote the *Washington Post*, "comes the demand for Teddy bears, with poor Miss Dolly gazing woefully out of her wide open eyes powerless to prevent the slipping away of her power." Some adults joined the fandom, too. By 1905, it was common for grown women to take Teddy bears with them when they went out to tea.

American urbanites who had once traded forest for concrete streamed out of cities to seek out nature. They peered at black bears through binoculars and, errantly, fed them sandwiches out of automobile windows. Decades later, they even extended an olive branch to the fearsome and vanishing grizzly bear by protecting it under the Endangered Species Act.

Black bears and brown bears are now slowly returning to their old haunts. In 2021, a US Fish and Wildlife Service (USFWS) report found that grizzly bears in the Lower 48 now occupy 6 percent of their historical range—up from 2 percent a few decades ago—and number nearly two thousand between Montana, Idaho, Wyoming, and Washington. Thanks to decades of state and federal protections, black bears are reclaiming the American Southeast. The Louisiana black bear, a subspecies ranging from Texas to Mississippi, was deemed recovered and removed from the Endangered Species list in 2016 after twenty-four years on the list. And black bears are moving into areas where they haven't been seen in centuries; they have been spotted wandering through the DC suburbs and recently into Yonkers, a stone's throw from New York City.

Such success has not been replicated elsewhere in the world. Sloth bear populations are declining, and the bears have disappeared from Bangladesh and likely Bhutan. The tropics, where the tiny sun bear makes its home, are losing roughly 10 million acres of primary forest cover every year. In turn, the sun bear population is thought to have fallen by a third in just the last thirty years. The future of South America's shy spectacled bear is also intertwined with the fate of forests, as climate change robs trees of quenching clouds. Polar bears face a precipitous if not extinguishing descent at the end of this century due to melting sea ice. And in Asia, human interference is even more direct, with thousands of moon bears stolen from the wild and held hostage on bile farms.

Still, not all was lost. Some of these challenges, I reasoned, might be easier to overcome than others. Could people learn to coexist with the bears in their backyards? Would governments unite to ban the cruel practice of bear bile farming in Asia, cut planet-warming greenhouse gas emissions, or scale back deforestation? And might the world's eight bears make changes to their own habits and routines that would allow them to persist, in true wilderness, beyond the end of this century?

So I set out for South America, where this book begins, to meet with scientists studying the continent's last surviving bear species. Then, on to Asia, where I found individuals working to save sloth bears, pandas, moon bears, and sun bears from extinction. In the United States, I learned of some unusual adaptations that resident black bears were making to keep pace with encroaching human populations. I spoke with stakeholders on both sides of the political aisle as brown bears gained ground in the American West, often at a deadly cost. And finally, I journeyed to the tiny subarctic town of Churchill, Manitoba, to see what hope remained, if any, for the bear with the bleakest outlook.

This book is the story of the remaining eight bears. It is a human story, too. Ever since *Homo erectus*, the vanguard of hominid expansion of broad face and unified brow, walked out of Africa's Great Rift Valley and entered Eurasia, people have dictated the bear's fate in this world. We have written their stories and shared their mythologies. We have both waged war against nature and worshiped its kings.

We have sought to conquer the great predators, and we have submitted to their prowess. We have turned bears into spectacle, commodity, and champion. And now, we will determine their future.

PART I

SOUTH AMERICA

The bears will soon be here
to take you away.

—MITO DEL OSO ANTEOJO

CHAPTER ONE

THE CLOUD DWELLERS

Spectacled bear, Ecuador & Peru
Tremarctos ornatus

When Paddington Bear set out for London in 1958, equipped with only a small brown suitcase and a tag around his neck imploring strangers to "Please look after this bear," he claimed his homeland as "darkest Africa." Of course, Africa is filled with all sorts of magnificent beasts, but bears, unfortunately, are not one of them.

Michael Bond, the creator of Paddington, was blithely unaware of this fact when he sent his manuscript to literary agent Harvey Unna, who swiftly responded enthusiastically, but with an important correction:

> I have now read your novel, *A Bear Called Paddington*, and I think it's quite a publishable tale and I like it well. My spies tell me, however, that you have slipped up in that there are no bears in Africa, darkest or otherwise. . . . Children either know this or should know this and I suggest you make suitable amends for which purpose I am returning herewith the script. There are plenty of bears in Asia, Europe, and America, and quite a few on the Stock Exchange.

Unna was right. Africa is decidedly bear-free, though this wasn't always the case. The Atlas bear (*Ursus arctos crowtheri*), a subspecies of brown bear, could be found in North Africa's Atlas Mountains until around the seventeenth century, when hunting—likely following centuries of capture and trade for Rome's arena games—pushed them to extinction in the wild. One source alleges that the king of Morocco still had an Atlas bear living in captivity as late as 1830 and even supplied another bear to the Zoological Garden of Marseille that same year, but those claims have never been substantiated. Certainly, by the time Paddington arrived at the railway station in the twentieth century, the African bear was a beast lost to time.

It was an embarrassing gaffe. To correct it, Bond set out for the Westminster Public Library to investigate other ursine candidates for the starring role in his story. A visit to the London Zoo in Regent's Park followed. He passed through the park's gilded iron gates and wandered down the paved path that took him past the penguin pool with its concrete waddle-ways and the zoo's most famous resident, Guy, the western lowland gorilla. He saw fat grizzlies and Brumas the polar bear, but decided they would not do. They lacked the intrigue and exoticism he sought. After much deliberation, Bond settled on an enigmatic bear he had encountered in the library's zoology collection: the spectacled bear (*Tremarctos ornatus*). Its small population in the jungles of South America seemed just right, and, though it was the only bear species found on the continent, not much was known about the animal. This would lend an air of mystery to his fictional stowaway, Bond thought, and so he returned home where he put pen to paper once more.

"You're a very small bear," said Mrs Brown. "Where are you from?"
The bear looked around carefully before replying.
"Darkest Peru."

ᴋ

THE DISTANCE BETWEEN CUSCO AND the cloud forest wasn't far—no more than 40 miles as the quetzal flies—but the journey in a crowded van from the city center took nearly five hours on a vertiginous dirt road through the Andes. The driver greeted every hairpin turn with speedy enthusiasm before slamming the brakes. Nauseous, I leaned my forehead against the window's cold glass and closed my eyes, blocking out the thousand-foot drop off the crumbling cliffside. Many of the roads here were prone to landslides.

Squeezed into the seat next to me was Russ Van Horn, a biologist who had made this journey dozens of times before. As such, he was largely unfazed by the washed-out patches and serpentine corners. A native of Minnesota, Van Horn admitted he was partial to vast uninterrupted fields and endless sky uncluttered by trees—nothing like the landscape of Peru. But while on the job hunt, he'd come across a posting for a scientist to work on bears—a choice between Southeast Asia's sun bears or South America's spectacled bears. (In South America, spectacled bears are generally referred to as Andean bears.) Little was known about the two species, but the former, Van Horn thought, was too wrapped up in national politics over palm oil production. That wasn't the case with the South American species. "It seemed like science might actually be able to help the Andean bear," he told me. And so he had been traveling these roads for years to access his shy research subjects. Today, he works for San Diego Zoo Global and serves as cochair of the International Union for the Conservation of Nature's Andean Bear Expert Team.

I had met Van Horn the night before on the steps of the Cusco Cathedral in Plaza de Armas. Tucked into a tiny restaurant in the northwest corner of the square, we'd discussed the looming expedition hunched over bowls of steaming quinoa soup and jugs of *chicha morada*, a sweet purple corn drink beloved in the Andes. Van Horn traveled to Peru every year during the dry season to gather baseline information on the bear's behavior. This time around I'd asked to join him. Our goal was to spend three days traversing the vertical gradient of the cloud forest, which began at around 2,000 feet and extended to 12,000 feet, to check a network of camera traps placed at different elevations. This would reveal how the bears were moving through the forest and making use of its resources, from valley bottom to mountain peak.

What Van Horn really wanted to figure out was why the bears in southwestern Peru's cloud forests weren't dropping down into the lower elevations. In three years' worth of camera trap photos at a nearby field site, he'd never detected a bear traveling lower than 4,900 feet. In the cloud forests of other parts of South America, the bears were rarely moving below 2,000 feet into the Amazonian lowlands. It was a line of scientific questioning made all the more pertinent by climate change.

Scientists have found that the warming climate could shrink and dry between 60 and 80 percent of the Western Hemisphere's cloud forests in as little as twenty-five years. As temperatures over land increase, humid air is forced to travel farther up mountain slopes before it cools enough to condense into clouds, ultimately moving the cloud immersion point upslope. The magnificent assemblage of air plants and trees that grow below the shrinking cloud base are inevitably left high and dry. If bears weren't able to use the warmer, drier lowland habitat, where would they go? Scientists had already witnessed dramatic changes in the Monteverde cloud forest of Costa Rica, one of the best-studied cloud forest plots in the world. In 1990, herpetologists deemed the extinct golden toad, once abundant in a minuscule 1.5-square-mile patch of cloud forest in Monteverde, to be the first victim of climate change. When I'd thought of how climate change might impact the world's bears, I'd thought only of melting sea ice and swimming polar bears, but if greenhouse gas emissions remained unchanged, an astounding 90 percent of western cloud forests will be impacted as early as 2060. What would happen to the shy spectacled bear?

Now, we passed by crude clay houses, their outer walls painted with the fading political symbols of a past election—an ear of corn, a mountain, a soccer ball. Ceramic bulls and crosses graced terra-cotta roofs. Hundreds of years ago the Incas drew alpacas to ensure a good harvest. Now, Cusco locals place the bulls at the peak of a house during construction to bring good fortune. When we stopped for lunch, women in colorful, knee-length puffy skirts known as *polleras* doled out sizzling noodles with lamb in a green herb sauce and *papas fritas* at roadside stands. I ate some grape-flavored anti-nausea medicine instead to stave off motion sickness. In the final ascent, white fog stamped out the road. I dozed off—a dramamine-induced strategy to combat the fear of driving blind at nearly 10,000 feet—and later awoke to the driver haphazardly slinging our belongings off the van's metal roof rack onto the wet red soil next to a sign marking the area as Wayqecha Cloud Forest Biological Station.

The station is located along the southern boundary of Peru's world-famous Manu National Park, less than 200 miles from the country's border with Bolivia. Whereas tourists flock to Manu's Amazonian lowlands to see howler monkeys and jaguars, scientists come here to study the rare cloud forest. Nine miles of maintained trails provide unfettered access through the Kosñipata River valley—meaning "the place with the smoke" in the Indigenous Quechua language, in veneration of the hugging fog. Researchers carting heavy scientific equipment into the forest couldn't ask for a better field site.

When we made our way down the main trail the next morning, plant ecologists hurried past us pushing wheelbarrows filled with plastic tubes and syringes to gather water from the clouds, which moved in waves through the forest. One minute we were overlooking a verdant mountain valley with bromeliads, orchids, ferns, and lichens scaffolded onto ficus trees; then, in an instant, the forest vanished. A misty chill descended. We were enveloped in a roiling sea of white. The thick air pulsed with the reverberations of hummingbirds' wings as sparkling violetears and shining sunbeams dived at passionflowers in a nectar-induced frenzy, brandishing their slender bills like miniature swords.

Van Horn plodded ahead down the narrow trail, the sound of squelching rubber boots signaling his tedious path forward. For all its beauty, the vegetation was dense and stubbornly snagging. Two lowlanders, we huffed at more than 9,000 feet of elevation. I reached to pull myself along on a slender tree covered in soft pale green lichen. "Watch out for the serrated tree ferns—they're worse than stinging nettle," the biologist warned me, his voice muffled under a bushy mustache. At 6 foot 3 inches, Van Horn towered over the all-women team of local biologists, grad students, and field techs but moved through the damp forest more slowly, outdone by the lithe Peruvians who deftly sliced through wayward vines with 2-foot-long machetes. The scarcity of oxygen seemed to have no effect on them.

It was difficult to discern the tree ferns from the thousands of other climbing plants in the cloud forest. Tufts of springy wintergreen moss, pink-tipped bromeliads, and the meddlesome ferns seemed to sprout from every square inch of tree bark. These plants, which belong to a group known as epiphytes, don't lay their roots in soil, but dangle freely in the air, growing benignly on top of other plants while they absorb the cloud's moisture through spongy tissue known as velamen.

"It takes just a few minutes of walking in these forests to understand that much of the vegetation here is quite strongly adapted to moist, wet conditions with lots of clouds," one forest ecologist had told me. In flora alone, the ecosystem is more diverse than the Amazonian lowlands, and exceedingly rare—cloud forests make up just 3 percent of the earth's tropical forests.

Down in the rain forest, the trees were tall and thin and stretched toward the heavens in search of sunlight. Here, the trees were stubbier. They tangled themselves into twisted knots in the canopy. Long woody vines, known as lianas, swung from the treetops like Rapunzel's unleashed hair. Lichen looped around branches like tinsel. The fairytale foliage enveloped Van Horn and me as we hiked deeper into the clouds. Only jagged slivers of sunlight reached the thick waxy leaf litter covering the forest floor. Paddington's home was, in fact, very dark.

More than one-third of the 270 native birds, mammals, and frogs that can only be found in Peru live in the country's cloud-shrouded forests, including the rare spectacled bears that scramble up the slick trees to gorge on bromeliads—spiky, scoop-shaped plants—and fruit. (There is no record of a spectacled bear ever eating a marmalade sandwich.) "They'll make this sloppy shelf of sticks, like a nest," Van Horn explained, gazing toward the interlocking canopy. Though it's less common in southwestern Peru, where we were hiking, scientists have documented this bizarre behavior in several sites across South America. The bears often rest on a bed of squashed epiphytic plants, sometimes staying in the canopy for up to two days.

Bears in the Southern Hemisphere don't hibernate. The consistent day length at the equator, mild temperatures, and an abundance of food mean that they're almost always alert and active. I had hoped this synchronous internal clock and the bear's size would make it easy to spot in the forest. Male spectacled bears, weighing around 340 pounds, are among the largest animals in the tropical Andes, second only to the hefty mountain tapir. But that was a naive assumption. Even when the bears aren't hiding up in the canopy, they remain elusive and shy, Van Horn explained. Biologists who spent months in the field rarely saw the bears. If approaching on foot, the spectacled bear never ran toward them like a bluff-charging brown bear—it ran away. "One of the things that's really striking about these bears is that they're not aggressive," he said as we pushed through the choking forest. Branches bounced off Van Horn's khaki Tilley hat, which he'd pulled down tightly around his head. "They don't attack people." (Even the winsome panda occasionally bites tourists.) In addition to the spectacled bear's mystifying nature, which had so beguiled Michael Bond, another element was working against us: there weren't many spectacled bears left.

The bears once roamed from the cloud-quenched forests to the grass paramo in the Andean highlands, to the rain forests to the dry forests, and to the coastal scrub desert. But as human populations boomed in the fertile Andean valleys during the last few centuries, they razed the bear's habitat for cropland and cattle pasture. Bears perceived to attack grazing cows were persecuted by farmers. Surviving bears sought refuge in a few hideouts, primarily in the cloud forest and the highlands that run along the spine of the Andes. Today, scientists estimate that only between thirteen thousand and eighteen thousand spectacled bears remain, found in Venezuela, Bolivia, Ecuador, Colombia, Argentina, and here in Peru, where the largest population—around 3,800 bears—lives.

Our small team shouldered day packs filled with bagged lunches of beans and rice, notebooks, camera batteries, sachets of powdered instant coffee—in Peru, all the good stuff was exported—and a few coca leaf candies to aid with the altitude. The coca plants grew lower down near Manu, Van Horn told me when I inquired about trafficking in the area, but every now and then researchers would find harvested bundles of dry leaves while following wildlife trails. The *cocaleros* used these passages to transport coca from the valley to high Andean villages. He was careful not to place cameras in those locations.

Van Horn spoke infrequently in a flat Midwestern accent, and he brought a similar energy to his Spanish. Often, long pauses punctuated his speech and I was never sure when he had completed a thought. At a bend in the woody trail, our team came across a spiraled pile of feline scat. It was rare to find feces in the cloud forest at all—the wet weather combined with a voracious dung beetle community made short work of mammal droppings. This one had to be fresh. The scat shortage proved especially frustrating to Denisse Mateo Chero, a young Peruvian biologist from Lima who was accompanying us. She was studying how spectacled bears disperse seeds in their poop throughout the cloud forest, aiding in its natural reforestation.

"Puma," she deduced from the excrement.

Jaguars, more svelte than the bear, didn't travel this high up the mountain in southeastern Peru, she explained. Pumas were abundant in the cloud forest; however, those living around the equator were smaller than the mountain lions of North America. I found this tidbit reassuring as I surveyed the dense foliage capable of concealing any number of wild cats.

From there, the trail grew skinnier, forcing us to tread carefully along a steep embankment that led down to the valley floor. Another group of Peruvian biologists had split off from our group to survey cameras placed near the river to see if any bear had made a cameo appearance. Van Horn and I were mercifully spared the steep and treacherous hike, since we hadn't yet fully acclimatized to the altitude. Still, some parts of this trail were so ensconced by trees and drooping lichen that we had to scramble through the muddy tunnels on our hands and knees. Though it was the middle of the dry season, the clouds made everything wet. After several miles, we reached the first of five camouflaged cameras anchored 2 feet off the forest floor. We plopped down our gear, soaked in a mix of sweat and cloud, and Mateo pulled out a yellow waterproof pocket notebook to jot down the elevation—8,858 feet—and coordinates. We were hiking nearer the cloud forest's upper limit that ran along the ragged edge of the Andes.

Karina Vargas Serrano, one of the local biologists and an expert machete wielder, unlocked the camera box. She popped its memory card into a small blue point-and-shoot camera to review the findings. The team had placed the camera trap here five months earlier and it had snapped more than eighteen hundred images during its sylvan residency. I began clicking through the photos. Swaying vines or a scattering of light had triggered most of the captures. Mateo peered over my shoulder. A tawny Andean fox had strolled past in March. A dwarf brocket deer, a tiny threatened ungulate with comically stubby antlers, followed. Finally, a few hundred images in, she exclaimed, "*Ah, aquí!*" We had found what we were looking for.

Paddington may be the world's most famous spectacled bear, but he looks nothing like one. For starters, the spectacled bear isn't golden, but rather black with pale rings of fur encircling tiny black eyes. This gives the animal the appearance of wearing *spectacles*. The bear has a short, muscular neck; a broad muzzle; and strong legs for shimmying up trees. Thin pale lines threaded over the snout and traced the small intelligent eyes of the bear staring at us from the LCD screen. Spectacled bears are the only bear species that can be distinguished by their unique facial markings. Some appear to don thick-framed furry bifocals that make their faces more blonde than black. Others have only a small pale Y shape above their eyes. Scientists who spend enough time in the field can identify individuals solely by these designs, akin to the way big-cat biologists can tell tigers apart by their distinctive stripe patterns.

Van Horn hadn't seen this particular bear before. In the first photo, taken three months earlier, the bear had nonchalantly ambled past the camera. Then, according to the photo series, he did a double take at the snapping shutter, circling back to inspect the foreign apparatus. Blurry black ears popped into the frame at close range—consistent with the two wiry bear hairs Mateo plucked from the camera box. Out of all the animals stored in digital memory, the bear was the only one to display such intelligent curiosity. "The bears here will rub on the cameras, but up in northeastern Peru, they broke a number of them," Van Horn said. "They pull on the cameras until they snap."

Here, at more than 8,000 feet above sea level, it wasn't surprising to find a spectacled bear. We were well within their ecological comfort zone. Spectacled bears also live up in the Andean highlands, known as the paramo, eating giant ground-dwelling bromeliads. As thrilling as it was to find evidence that a bear had passed through this spot months earlier, it wasn't cause for relief. Scientists estimate that cloud forests will be about 5°C (9°F) hotter by the end of this century. To cope with the heat, some plant species have already begun migrating upslope, chasing moisture and cooler temperatures. But because the spectacled bear already inhabits the Andes' upper elevations that the cloud forest is invading, he has nowhere else to go. A lifting cloud base will only mean a loss of habitat if the bears aren't able to exploit the expanding, humid lowlands. With bountiful maracuyá (passion fruit), bacaba, and aguaje fruit, the bears *should* be thriving in the Amazon. But something is holding them back.

"It might seem like kind of an abstract question—'Why don't the bears go lower down?'" Van Horn said when we arrived at the second camera, soon erased by a cloud bank. "But if it's because of heat, and the climate is warming, then maybe that will affect the bears. And if it's because jaguars are keeping them out, and the jaguar's range changes due to climate, that would be a constraint, too."

The latter was already happening in the Bolivian Andes. Ximena Velez Liendo, the cochair of the IUCN's Andean bear expert group along with Van Horn, had told me that conflicts between top predators were spiking in Bolivia due to human activity and warmer temperatures in the lowlands. "We're seeing more stressed animals from the lowlands going up into the highlands. We have capybaras where we shouldn't see capybaras. And the jaguars are following them." She compared it to the stories of a house. "The puma is on the top floor, the bear is in the middle, and the jaguar is on the lower floor. But now we are seeing areas where we have all three of them overlapping. You're talking about three apex predators in one ecosystem. That's not equilibrium."

Any prediction about the future of the spectacled bear seemed to depend on two countervailing scientific facts. Tropical organisms have a very narrow thermal tolerance—a small change in the environment can easily be an extinguishing force. At the same time, bears are some of the most adaptable animals on the planet. If any cloud forest creature could persist during such drastic environmental upheaval, it was the spectacled bear. "If food sources change in one forest patch, the bears are probably going to be okay . . ." Van Horn said. A golden-collared tanager chirped, filling Van Horn's long pause. ". . . And they're not big. If they were the size of a brown bear, they'd be more nutritionally constrained."

THE NEXT MORNING, we set off to check the fourth camera for bears. I walked behind biologist Vargas, giving a wide berth to her machete swings, and four other Peruvian field techs. We were walking single file on a skinny trail tracing the edge of the vegetated slope. Van Horn and Mateo fell behind. Rounding a bend, the sound of rushing water filled my ears. Someone had wedged a worn wooden plank bridge into a deep ravine formed by an old landslide. Water gushed over the crumbling edge. The thick vegetation made it impossible to discern where the water hit the bottom, but it must have been at least 30 feet. We had no choice but to cross the rickety structure. The four field techs went first, one at a time. I estimated I had at least 20 pounds—and a fear of heights—on them. When it was my turn, the bridge bounced and creaked with every step. I moved slowly and steadily with my eyes focused on the opposing slope. When my boots hit solid ground, I let out a sigh of relief. Safely on the other side, we now waited for the others to catch up. But thirty minutes passed and the two biologists had yet to reappear. We shouted their names across the gorge. No answer. I thought of the puma scat.

Vargas decided she would head back to look for the missing scientists. As she again crossed the wooden bridge in her heavy rubber boots, the second-to-last plank gave out with a loud *crack*. She crashed through the splintered platform. It took me a moment to realize that my unstated fears had suddenly become a terrifying reality. Vargas had been able to catch herself by her forearms on the bridge so that her right leg was kicking wildly below her while her hips remained stuck in the hole. As with a skater fallen through the ice, we dared not rush out onto the bridge to help. Cautiously, she hauled herself out—nearly losing her balance in the process—and crawled on her hands and knees back to our group—just as Van Horn and Mateo turned the corner, unharmed, and happily chatting away about bears. The broken bridge carved up our scientific expedition. Van Horn was almost double the weight of Vargas, and she alone had been enough to cause the bridge to fail. We would have to split up. Van Horn and Mateo would retrace their steps back to the field station headquarters, and I would continue on with Vargas and the field techs to check the final cameras.

The fourth and fifth cameras bore no bears, and before long we were all reunited at the Wayqecha canteen, a little worse for wear. The river crew had returned, too, with no news of low-elevation bear sightings. Still, our hike through the cloud forest had laid bare just how important this ecosystem was for the well-being of the planet. Moisture intercepted here trickled down the slopes via rusty orange mountain streams and fed into the Amazon River. The Amazon then flowed for thousands of miles to reach the Atlantic Ocean. Millions of people and animals depended on its waters along the way. Sunnier, hotter days with fewer clouds drifting through the forest would transform not only the fragile forest, but environments far beyond.

The electricity at Wayqecha was only turned on between six and nine in the evening. In the minutes after sunset, we worked in darkness. Van Horn checked the news on his phone. "Did you hear there was a volcanic eruption?" he asked as I sipped hot coca tea. "In southern Peru.... The ash is falling on Bolivia." It was a tectonic reminder of just how interconnected this landscape could be, from the mountains to the water to the bears. The lights flickered on. Giant moths, some the size of sparrows, threw themselves against the panoramic glass windows in desperation.

"I'm cautiously optimistic about the spectacled bear's future," Van Horn reflected. "At least where there are large, connected blocks of habitat." A long pause. Uncertainty clouded his voice when he continued.

"Except...we don't have the information to say what is or isn't quality Andean bear habitat.... That could turn out to be a really naive assessment."

THERE IS AN OLD TEMPLE at Chavín de Huántar. The archaeological site lies halfway between Peru's tropical lowlands and the coast, near the confluence of the Mosna and Huanchesca Rivers, tucked between jagged mountain cordilleras. Inside the temple, a U-shaped flat-topped pyramid, intricate carvings of animals exotic to the highlands cover the stone passageways that form a labyrinth between chambers. Jaguars. Harpy eagles. Caimans. Anacondas. Devotees once came here to consult oracles and perform bloodletting rituals. In the middle of the central cruciform room, illuminated by a beam of sunlight, stands a 15-foot-tall, triangular granite monolith that connects the floor to the ceiling. A figure has been etched into the rock. Googly eyes sit above a broad snout with round nostrils. Curly hair ending in snake heads, like Medusa, frames a snarling face. One hand is raised in the air, palm forward, as if permitting passage to another world. The other lays down at its side. Five curving claws protrude from its feet, where worshippers once laid lavish gifts of food and ceramics. This is El Lanzón.

El Lanzón is the supreme deity of the ancient Chavín civilization, which flourished in this part of Peru between 900 BCE and 200 BCE. Scholars consider Chavín to be not only the mother culture of the Andes, but one of six pristine civilizations in world history deemed to be unique and not derivative of civilizations that came before. El Lanzón, its central figure, is purported to represent a key motif within Chavín art: the jaguar. Some anthropologists believe that the Chavín were even the founders of a jaguar cult and that those who visited the temple revered the ferocious characteristics of the big cat. But when conservation biologist Susanna Paisley looks at El Lanzón, she doesn't see a jaguar. She sees a bear.

Despite England's affinity for the marmalade-spattered Paddington, there's a surprising dearth of spectacled bears in the ancient iconography of South America. The bear is noticeably absent in material artifacts from Incan and Amazonian cultures; there are no carvings, no pottery shards, no basket weavings created in the bear's likeness. It was an absence that frustrated me as I strolled through the halls of the Pre-Columbian Art Museum in Quito—their animal exhibit had just opened—the Museum of Aboriginal Cultures in Cuenca, and the Museum of Pre-Columbian Art in Cusco. There were golden serpents and jaguar pipes and clay jugs shaped like fat monkeys, but not a single bear was to be found in the collections.

When I had bemoaned the bear's absence to Van Horn at Wayqecha, he told me I should get in touch with Paisley, who had spent years in the forests of South America studying bears. She had since returned to the United Kingdom and was now creating stunning textiles drawn from a career spent in wild places. One pattern even featured the spectacled bear reclining in a tree whilst chewing on a bromeliad.

Paisley believes that the scarcity of South American bear iconography is no coincidence. Bears, much like jaguars, inhabited a large expanse of the vertical world in primitive times, she told me. Even now, spectacled bears are sometimes seen wandering among the ruins at Machu Picchu. The people of the Andes, she said, would undoubtedly have noticed the spectacled bear traversing the canopy or raiding their crops. She argues that bears aren't lacking in representation because our ancestors deemed them irrelevant compared with big cats, but because they were *so* important to the early Chavín civilization that a taboo emerged around depicting bears in any tangible form that *wasn't* El Lanzón.

Part of the blame for the bias toward the jaguar narrative, she thinks, lies with the circumpolar bear cult tradition, which holds that veneration of the boreal species of bears is a defining characteristic of cultures in the Northern Hemisphere, from the Sami in Scandinavia to the Inuit in Canada. As anthropologist Lydia T. Black put it, "Since Paleolithic times, most ursids have been a source of potent ritual symbols," often offered as a sacrifice so that humans may communicate with the spirit world. Bears in the tropics, however, have been left wanting for attention. The attitude in South America, Paisley relayed, is along the lines of, "'Bears are what the Gringos have. We have cats.'" She questioned whether this had led to a cultural blind spot. Were archaeologists failing to see the bears right in front of them?

While pondering the invisible bear, Paisley had a eureka moment: "All this time I'd been wondering if there were any early representations of bears, and then I looked down at the book I had on Indigenous South Americans. There was a picture of El Lanzón on the cover. I went 'Holy shit! This is a bear.'" She wasn't alone in such an interpretation. Van Horn had told me that nearly every other bear biologist who had seen a photo of the sculpture agreed with Paisley that it bore much closer resemblance to a bear than a jaguar. But the big-cat enthusiasts had already deemed the case closed.

Paisley eventually traveled to Chavín de Huántar to inspect the central deity. She took note of its erect posture—bears are fairly unique among the large mammals in being able to walk on their hind legs. Cats can only move through the forest on all fours, and most jaguar art reflects this quadrupedalism. Moreover, as Paisley observed, the monolith was reminiscent of the bear totems made by Indigenous tribes in the Northern Hemisphere. One paw up. One paw down. Archaeologists note that this position symbolizes a duality revered by ancient cultures—but it's also oddly similar to the waving bear motif. And yes, the deity *did* have two protruding fangs that might indicate a jaguar. But plenty of circumpolar bear cult art pieces also depict bears with two gleaming canines. When I reviewed photos and drawings of the sculpture, I could see the bear's likeness, too. The gravitas of such interpretation couldn't be ignored. As Paisley wrote in the journal *World Archaeology*, "El Lanzón dwells at the centre of the centre" of Chavín culture. If her hypothesis is correct, the spectacled bear is not a forgotten beast of the tropical forest, but rather the singular most important animal in pre-Columbian Andean culture.

RUSS VAN HORN AND I didn't go to Chavín de Huántar. But we did stop in the small town of Paucartambo in the south of Peru on our way back from Wayqecha. The town, bisected by a rushing river draining the Andes' melting glaciers, appeared unremarkable from the road. Bus drivers traveling away from Cusco often used it as a pit stop for food and fuel. Nonetheless, Van Horn insisted it was worth a visit. Heavy clouds hugged mountain spires and it began to rain as we walked through the town. Children in crisp white school uniforms dashed for cover. We crossed a worn cobblestone bridge to arrive in a plaza fringed by pale stucco buildings with cobalt-blue shutters and doors. In the center stood a large golden figure.

The statue's face was covered in a ski mask. Its eye slits were pointed toward the heavens. Bent legs straddled a decorative pile of rocks and cacti. A shapeless, shaggy tunic cloaked its body. Muscular arms and a vascular neck protruded from the unseemly frock, clutching a smaller figure slung over its back: a young girl with sculpted curls. Her dress was hoisted up to midthigh and her sandaled feet flailed out behind her. Her fist was raised high in the air, as if about to beat down on her emotionless captor: the Ukuku.

The Ukuku is a mythical creature said to be half man, half spectacled bear that falls outside of whatever taboo exists around physical ursine artifacts in South America. These bear-men travel the Andean highlands in Bolivia and Peru as mediators of social life. They link highland with lowland, human with animal, sickness with health, and order with chaos. That's the benign definition, anyway. The Ukuku—the Indigenous Quechua word for bear—is best known for another defining trait: stealing and raping women. In Incan mythology, the bear is "strongly associated with human fertility and sexuality, notoriously running off with shepherd girls," Paisley wrote in *World Archaeology*. Many highland sagas tell of the arrival of a bear-man, or bear disguised as a man, who kidnaps young women and hauls them off to a cave where he rapes them. Other versions feature wanton women offering up their virginity to the bear-man, believing him to be God incarnate. Sometimes this unnatural coupling yields a hybrid offspring of immeasurable strength.

I learned that many young women in the Andes fear the real spectacled bear, conflating the animal with the Ukuku. In childhood, parents tell their daughters terrifying tales of bear abductions and sexual assault. Vargas, the machete-wielding biologist, often worked in Indigenous Q'ero communities in the highlands around Paucartambo, and she told me that some women refused to go into the forest alone because of the legend of the bear. I suspected the creepy sculpture in Paucartambo's plaza probably didn't help matters.

"Yeah . . . it is a rather troubling statue," Van Horn acknowledged as we appraised the Ukuku in all its lecherous glory. Rain pounded down.

"Mhm." I nodded. "It looks like a serial killer."

The Ukuku, despite its proclivity for sexual assault, isn't considered all bad. Every June during Qoyllur Rit'i, the largest native pilgrimage in the Peruvian Andes, tens of thousands of revelers travel to Sinakara Valley, about 30 miles southeast of the Wayqecha field station in the high mountains. Here they celebrate the Snow Star Festival, a colorful mishmash of Catholic, Incan, and Indigenous beliefs, honoring not only the return of the Pleiades star cluster at the start of the harvest, but also Jesus Christ and the *apus*, mountain gods.

At the festival's riotous base camp, a special group of men don tubular fringed robes and pull knitted masks over their faces to become Ukukus. (Previous incarnations saw them drape spectacled bear pelts across their shoulders.) The Ukukus then hike 5 miles up the valley—more than 16,000 feet above sea level—with the other pilgrims to the Qullqip'unqu glacier. At the edge of the ice, only the potent bear-men are allowed to continue on the path, traversing the perilous glacier to hold an all-night vigil where they pray to gods and fight condemned souls. When dawn breaks, the Ukukus chip blocks out of the ice and race down the mountain with the frozen cargo strapped to their backs. Waiting pilgrims greet the ice with untempered joy. They mix it into healing elixirs and pay homage to the ice to ensure a good harvest.

Yet even the mythical bear-man cannot escape the ravages of climate change. Peru's glaciers shrank by nearly a third in the last two decades, forcing the Ukukus to hike much farther to reach the retreating Qullqip'unqu terminus. And where once each Ukuku carried his own block of ice down from the mountain, the government began curtailing the collection in 2000 by permitting only a few of the Ukukus to set foot on the glacier. A few years later, the Ukukus announced they would no longer carry ice down from the glacier, expressing concern about the future of the fragile landscape and wishing to play no part in its demise. After all, they were destined to protect the mountain gods; if the glaciers were ailing, removing ice would only hurt the deities. Now the Ukukus return empty-handed.

TWO PINEAPPLES BOUNCED on the truck seat between Francisco Sánchez Karste and me as we drove toward Ecuador's El Cajas National Park, a small 110-square-mile protected area in the lower reaches of the Western Cordillera where thirty-two spectacled bears lived. "A treat for the bears," Sánchez had said with a mischievous smile when he arrived at my hotel that morning accompanied by the spiky fruit. Pineapples

are also a member of the bromeliad family, though they look little like
their cloud forest cousins. Still, after failing to see any spectacled bears
in Peru, I was going to need to try bait.

We departed from Cuenca, a romantic city of domed cathedrals and
sprawling flower markets, following the muddy Yanucay River toward
its headwaters through a twisting valley where women wore large rubber
boots underneath buoyant skirts and wrapped pink-and-yellow plastic
shopping bags around tall brimmed hats to ward off the rain. Love-sick
Latin melodies blared on the radio. Restaurants advertised *cuy asado*,
roasted guinea pig, with signs of the dancing critters dressed in colorful
ponchos. Their jolly expressions indicated they were oblivious to their
position on the dinner menu.

Admittedly, El Cajas National Park wasn't the best place to search
for spectacled bears. A little under a third of spectacled bear habitat is
under permanent protection in Ecuador, and much of this falls within
the country's eastern highlands and foothills—not the cloud forests
west of Quito where we were headed. This leaves the bear population
here more vulnerable, and the El Cajas bears even more so. Cut off from
the other bears living in the Western Cordillera, decades of isolation
had taken a toll on the El Cajas island population: some bears were
now inbred.

Sánchez had worked as a biologist in the park for more than a decade
and had volunteered to guide me through its cloud forests and wind-
swept paramos. He had a round face with a blonde five-o'clock shadow,
and the hair on the side of his head was buzzed short. He donned a pair
of aviator sunglasses, harkening back to his past life as a military pilot
in Germany. "It was thanks to my father that I became a biologist," he
explained. "He was a chemistry professor at the University of Cuenca,
but he loved the taxonomy and cultivation of orchids."

When he was a boy, his father took him on long expeditions to
search for rare orchids in the blooming forests of Azuay Province, where
El Cajas is located. Azuay boasts the largest concentration of orchids in
all of Ecuador, home to twenty-five hundred species of the four thousand found nationwide. "I thought orchids were boring, but my father

pushed me to learn the names. Over time, I started to love to be inside the forest. To see the flowers and listen to the birds. And I helped my father to paint the orchids." The duo collected small samples of flushed monkey-faced orchids and lavender cattleya. "My father put names to many of these flowers."

Disillusioned with aviation, the younger Sánchez eventually returned to his native Ecuador to train as a biologist. Evidently, he could now talk about orchids for hours, constrained only by his English ("I speak German much better"), and yet his floral tangent wasn't entirely off-track. "Orchid bulbs and leaves are also food for the bears," he added excitedly.

When we came to an overlook near the park, Sánchez pointed to a distant spot across a valley. Beyond, the pale blue of the Pacific Ocean merged with the azure sky at the curve of the earth. "You see the palm trees? And the houses? There are just eight or ten villagers living there, but they have a new road coming from the highlands." The dwellings appeared as mere specks in a landscape so all-consuming I could hardly orient myself within it. Cloud shadows darkened the folded mountain ridges below us, spread out in parallel succession so that they rose like pages of a book from their rocky spine. A vein of silver coursed through the valley floor thousands of feet below. Melting glaciers had sculpted this landscape thousands of years ago, pinching, pushing, and pulling the emerging land into narrow horseshoe-shaped ravines. "And this," Sánchez stabbed another finger through the air toward a rusty scar in a green mountain, "is mining."

A rash of new mining concessions was driving habitat loss across the country, putting the spectacled bears' home under siege. In the past, the industry had little impact on Ecuador's rain forests, paramos, and cloud forests, despite the plethora of gold, silver, copper, zinc, and uranium deposits locked in the Andes. The Ecuadorian National Assembly even voted to radically restrict mining between 2008 and 2009, under leftist former president Rafael Correa. However, beginning in 2016, the country's mining ministry issued new rules allowing for exploratory mining concessions on more than 7 million acres of land, opening up an additional 10 percent of the country to extractive industry. Alarmingly, much of this fell within Indigenous territories and protected areas in the mountains and cloud forests where the spectacled bear makes its home. When Lenin Moreno came to power in 2017, he pushed to further monetize the country's abundant mineral reserves in a bid to combat the national debt and end reliance on uncertain crude exports. Though mining remained off-limits in federally protected areas, private reserves—land purchased decades ago by private organizations for conservation—were suddenly ripe for the taking.

Although mining still wasn't permitted in El Cajas National Park, companies were pushing their luck along its edges. Following the government policy change, Ecuador granted mining licenses covering more than 291,000 acres in the surrounding Cuenca Canton—an administrative region lesser than the province—all within the buffer zone of El Cajas. Taken together, active mining concessions added up to 70 percent of the canton's total land area, Sánchez told me, though only a third were actively being explored or exploited at the time.

Mining is an extraordinary force of environmental destruction in South America. Trees are stripped away from mountainsides and forests cleared to build roads that give entrée to heavy equipment. These roads make remote ecosystems more accessible to outsiders, opening up imperiled wildlife to poaching and trafficking. (Spectacled bear body parts are used in some shamanic rituals in South America, with the animal's penis bone coveted for magical potions.) Moreover, roads fragment forest patches, pushing wildlife to live along disturbed edges and breaking off connectivity, damaging the genetic health of populations. Wastewater and mercury from mining operations poison streams and rivers. And from sunrise to sunset, miners blast rock.

"Mining is getting more dangerous," Sánchez said as we surveyed bald exploration areas on a slope near the mining community of Chaucha. The largest one appeared as an elongated camel with two beige humps arching up the mountainside where topsoil and trees had been scraped away. These mining concessions were relatively small, but not without concern. Environmental assessments had found that nearby water sources would be at high risk if drilling muds were discharged directly into the Chaucha River. And El Cajas National Park had only twenty-two rangers to keep an eye on things, Sánchez said.

Next we drove out toward one of his favorite spots—Las Américas Forest, a 250-acre community reserve inside the Molleturo-Mullopungo Protected Forest where five bears lived adjacent to the national park. Beyond the reach of federal protections, more than 90 percent of the land contained within Molleturo-Mullopungo was now under mining concessions.

Along the way, Sánchez spotted something and pointed to a bush growing on the hillside. I felt a small jolt of adrenaline. Was I finally about to see a spectacled bear in its native habitat? I waited with bated breath for the rustling branches that would indicate a hefty animal was taking refuge behind the leaves. Stillness. Sánchez pulled out a pair of binoculars and aimed them at a large burst of yellow flowers that shocked the dry landscape. He grew even more excited. This was it! Any moment now . . .

"*Oncidium excavatum*," Sánchez announced triumphantly.

Wait. What?

I realized that I'd mistaken his enthusiasm for a bear, when in fact he had spotted a rare orchid growing on the mountain slope. "It's thought to be extinct in many places," he proclaimed. "These yellow orchids are called by the locals '*Flor de Mayo*.' When it was common, they used it to adorn religious paintings of the Virgin Mary during Catholic festivities. The churches and towns were all decorated with these orchids. But today you can hardly find any native plants."

I was disappointed, but not exactly surprised. I'd traveled to South America with admittedly low expectations of turning up a wild bear— especially one with a reputation for being cagey around humans. In the past, I'd had pretty dismal wildlife-spotting luck, narrowly missing out on tigers, wolves, and golden snub-nosed monkeys in various geographies. The bear was yet another casualty in a laundry list of near misses. But in the preceding weeks, I'd been encouraged by all the stories I'd heard of chance encounters with South America's only bear. I'd allowed myself to get my hopes up. Now, I was left to contemplate only the species that had made themselves known—Ecuadorian hillstar hummingbirds, giant moths, alpacas, and *Oncidium excavatum*.

🌿

THE DEFLATED SEARCH FOR BEARS continued an hour later. At Las Américas, we began our hike near a farmhouse, sidestepping dozens of cow pies and yapping work dogs who gave chase as we pushed up the bucolic slope. Sánchez carried the two pineapples in a plastic shopping bag. I stopped to admire a bushy tree blooming with amethyst-colored flowers. "*Tibouchina urvilleana*. This flower is found at the edges of disturbed forests—in ten minutes more, we will be in the natural forest."

Near the perimeter of the cloud forest, we heard a bearlike huff and came to a dead stop. Sánchez made a snuffling sound to call to the bear, as if it were a bird. Nothing. *Vamos.* Forty minutes later, past the pasture's edge, Sánchez stopped underneath a large *aguacatillo*, a tree in the avocado family. Mosquitoes swarmed our idle flesh. "This is a good tree for the Andean bear. Sometimes they sleep here." He bent down and rummaged through the thick leaf litter, pulling up a few long bromeliad leaves. "I am starting to see some marks of the bear—this one has been scratched!" He held up the leaf, which revealed a long claw mark at its base. "It is not easy to find tracks in this forest. Footprints are not possible due to the leaves. But you can tell when a leaf is old and has fallen naturally," he explained. The one with the scratch mark, he said, had been plucked by a bear.

The author Michael Bond had chosen his character well. The shy spectacled bear remained an enigma of the forest during the month I spent hiking through Peru and Ecuador. Sánchez, for the most part, had only witnessed bears through his camera traps. But he did have one memorable encounter with a bear in Las Américas. "She came barreling at me and ran up a tree, huffing and throwing these leaves," he said, tossing the scratched leaf up into the air to re-create the scene. He nicknamed her Americo after her forest home. Later, when going through camera trap images, he recognized the bear again by her fingerprint-like facial markings that covered more than half her face. She was mating with her father.

At one of the camera traps anchored on a thin tree, Sánchez pulled out a long knife. He began to peel one of the pineapples and positioned it in front of the shutter. (A possum, not a bear, would ultimately discover this tasty treat before a bear snuffled along a week later.) "I registered another bear on this camera," he said. Then miners began blasting in the buffer zone. "When the dynamite exploded, the bear ran away. I got another picture of him down near the mine. Shortly after that, another camera picked him up even farther away. He had run far, far away from this place." Sánchez never saw the bear again. Many of the workers in the mining camps carried shotguns, he noted darkly. What would happen to the bears, I wondered, if more mining began in Molleturo-Mullopungo and around the borders of El Cajas?

I pictured Paddington standing in his neat blue duffle coat and floppy red hat on the railway platform. Before his death in 2017, Michael Bond told the *Guardian* that he was inspired to create the bear after seeing evacuated children trudging through Reading Station during World War II as bombs battered Europe. Each carried only a small suitcase of their most treasured possessions. The children had permanently left behind one world and would soon enter another. "I do think that there's no sadder sight than refugees," Bond had said. I thought of the spectacled bear resting on an untidy shelf of sticks up in the cloud forest canopy. I thought of the vanishing clouds. I thought of the mining explosions ricocheting through the bear's home. In Bond's hands, the spectacled bear was a parable for the plight of thousands of human refugees and the cost of war. Now the animal was fulfilling Paddington's fiction. If deforestation continues unabated, the spectacled bear, too, would become a refugee, pushed away from its homeland, never to return.

PART II

ASIA

*I thought the secret of life was
obvious: be here now, love as if
your whole life depended on it,
find your life's work, and try to
get hold of a giant panda.*

—ANNE LAMOTT

CHAPTER TWO

DANCING WITH DEATH

Sloth bear, India
Melursus ursinus

Night was falling on Bandhavgarh National Park. The sun hovered above India's red earth horizon as if tethered to the soil. Tendrils of marigold and saffron unfurled across the sky. In the village of Pataur, 8 miles from the park's gates, Pinky Baiga stood outside the small mud brick house that she shared with nine younger sisters and one brother, the youngest in the family. Her siblings crouched around her sock feet that she'd jammed into plastic flip-flops. Others watched curiously from the tin rooftop.

Harendra Bargali, a middle-aged man with a broad face and thin mustache, approached from the dirt roadway and asked the young woman a few hushed questions in Hindi. Pinky surveyed the well-dressed stranger up and down with dark eyes, trying to decide whether to share her story. A gentle lowing filled the tense silence. Men were herding their muddy cows home from the fields. Nocturnal beasts would soon be stirring. Pinky tugged her fraying red sweater closer around her body, then pulled back the white scarf that covered her head, revealing deep gashes clawed through her shorn black hair.

Pinky had been attacked by a sloth bear. She told Bargali that two months ago she was gathering firewood with her parents a couple miles away from the family dwelling. As the sun sank behind the acacia trees, she piled the load on her head and started on the dusty trail toward home. When she turned a blind corner, she came face to face with a hulking bear. With her hands still wrapped around the wood, she was unable to shield herself from the animal's startled assault. Her desperate parents shouted and frightened it away. But the bear had nearly scalped her.

One of Pinky's sisters eagerly ran inside to fetch the doctor's report and handed Bargali the crumpled white sheet of paper. He skimmed the document. In English, it read: "Diagnosis: Bear Bite. Multiple Stitches."

Pinky had spent ten days in Katni District Hospital as medical staff treated her wounds. A scar hooked under her right eye. She told Bargali she was still on bed rest as she pulled the scarf back up, unsmiling in her self-consciousness. At seventeen, she should be getting married, moving into her husband's home, and starting her own family. Instead, she could barely leave the house.

"I hate the bear," she said.

IF THE SPECTACLED BEAR IS the world's most peaceful bear, the sloth bear is its foil. The sloth bear is responsible for more human fatalities than any of the other seven bear species, and yet few outside of the Indian subcontinent seem to have ever heard of the creature. Though fewer than twenty thousand sloth bears may remain in the Asian wilderness, every year the irascible bears attack more than 100 people. Many will succumb to their gruesome injuries. Brown bears, by comparison, number more than two hundred thousand and span three continents, but kill only about six people on average every year.

The sloth bear's high body count can partially be explained by geography. Brown bears and polar bears—more than twice the size of the 250-pound sloth bear—inhabit vast tracts of wilderness where humans are few and far between. India, by contrast, is home to the world's largest rural population and some of the planet's most diverse ecosystems. Elephants, tigers, leopards, and rhinos make for uneasy neighbors for millions of people, as do brown bears, moon bears, and sun bears. (India contains more of the world's bear species than any other nation.) Still, the sloth bear is uniquely aggressive among this toothsome menagerie. In his 1957 book *Man-Eaters and Jungle Killers*, India-born British hunter Kenneth Anderson wrote: "They [sloth bears] have a reputation for attacking people without apparent reason, provided that person happens to pass too close, either while the bear is asleep or feeding, or just ambling along. So the natives give bears a wide berth; together with the elephant, they command the greatest respect from jungle dwelling folk."

A 2021 study in the *Proceedings of the National Academy of Sciences*

(*PNAS*) confirmed Anderson's anecdotal observation. In a survey of more than five thousand households within the buffer zones around protected areas in the Indian states of Karnataka, Madhya Pradesh, Maharashtra, and Rajasthan, researchers found that although elephants killed the most people during a one-year period, the sloth bear inflicted the highest severity of injury. And while sloth bear encounters were rare, "the probability of human injury when an encounter occurs is much higher than for other species." Today, biologists consider the sloth bear to be "the most dangerous wild animal in India."

It is difficult to overstate the ferocity of the sloth bear. In December 2020, for example, a single sloth bear killed four people and injured three others as they returned home from collecting food in the forest. After witnessing the sloth bear kill his friends, a survivor told the *Hindustan Times*, "I climbed the tree at around 4 p.m. and saw that the bear was roaming around the tree waiting for me to come down. I tied myself with an *angaucha* [a towel] to the trunk of the tree and waited for help. After five hours . . . the rescue team came."

Before arriving in the fume-choked streets of Delhi, I had contacted Bargali, one of only a handful of global experts on sloth bears and deputy director of the Corbett Foundation, a nonprofit dedicated to wildlife conservation in India. Bargali and his team were working in a high-conflict zone known as the Kanha-Pench corridor—6,000 square miles of tropical dry teak forest linking the two namesake tiger reserves in the central state of Madhya Pradesh. There are 442 villages in this corridor, populated by the Gond and Baiga tribes, and every morning people enter the forest to gather life's necessities—food and fuelwood. This subsistence foraging puts them directly in the path of the territorial sloth bear, which often dwells at the fragmented edges of wilderness. Between 2004 and 2016, the Corbett Foundation recorded 255 sloth bear attacks in the corridor.

The sloth bear's name is one of the greatest misnomers in the animal kingdom. The animals aren't slow—they can run faster than most humans—nor are they lazy. Moreover, sloth bears aren't sloths at all. It's said that early European explorers spotted this bizarre creature with messy fur and long, fingerlike claws hanging upside down in the dense forests of Asia and reasoned that the animal must be related to the sloths of South America. In 1791, European zoologist George Shaw bestowed the erroneous name *Bradypus ursinus,* bearlike sloth, on the mysterious animal. The sloth bear may be on the smaller size for a bear, but it still would have been impossibly huge for any of the living sloth species. It wasn't until taxonomists realized the species had no connection to the New World that this misclassification was cleared up, and they amended the creature's common name to "sloth bear." A more accurate name may have been "anteater bear."

Sloth bears are myrmecophagous. This means they feed on termites and ants. Pangolins, armadillos, and echidnas also fall into this category, but no other bear. Sloth bears lack first upper incisors and have loose protruding lips, a mobile snout, and raised elongated palate— the perfect appendage for slurping up bugs. They can even close their nostrils to avoid inhaling dust while eating. Compared with the elusive spectacled bear, which I had failed to uncover in the cloud forests of South America, the sloth bear promised to be easier game; the bear is conspicuously noisy as it vacuums its way through the forest, and its unappetizing feeding sounds can be heard from some distance away.

The sloth bear is very much the ragamuffin of the bear world. A brushy mane of fur surrounds beady eyes the color of burnt chai. Along its body, coarse black hair sticks out in all directions. Often, perhaps because of its floppy lips, the sloth bear foams at the mouth. Lanky limbs and big paws with yellow claws conclude the bear's haphazard look. The sloth bear's most endearing trait, in light of its fondness for violence, is how it cares for its offspring. To protect their cubs from tigers and leopards, mother sloth bears transport them—one to three at a time— nestled in the long fur of their backs. This survival strategy is especially important in a place like Madhya Pradesh, which boasts India's largest tiger population—and more than eighty million people.

Though it's the country's fifth most populous state, Madhya Pradesh is relatively underdeveloped compared with India's large urban centers of Uttar Pradesh, Karnataka, and West Bengal. Wide expanses of rice paddies and farmland border nine national parks and six tiger reserves. Gonds and Baigas routinely travel through the parks' buffer zones—

junctures of civility and wilderness—to gather mushrooms, fuelwood, tendu leaves, and sweet mahua flowers. Accordingly, Madhya Pradesh has come to serve as a contested space between people and wildlife. By the time I arrived at Pinky's home with Bargali one February evening, I had been traveling the state's cattle-clogged roads for days and had encountered nearly a dozen victims. People showed off injuries that ranged from mangled hands to scarred thighs. One man even pulled down his pants to reveal where a bear had nipped him on the behind.

Yet, from the road, Madhya Pradesh was deceivingly peaceful compared with chaotic Delhi. There was little indication that a war between man and beast raged in the hinterlands. The land unfolded in warm terra-cotta hues. Above, clouds proved to be actual clouds, not plumes of ashen smog. Sun-creased women in jewel-colored saris heaved on stubborn water buffalo as they worked the land with wooden ploughs and carried dried cow patties (used for fuel) on their heads. The air was perfumed with a musky blend of dung fires and flowering trees. Passing trucks, their flanks painted with gaudy floral motifs, trumpeted in greeting as we drove toward the shadowy horizon where fields met forest.

At the turn of the twentieth century, the sloth bear ranged across South Asia, from India to Nepal, from Bangladesh to Bhutan to Sri Lanka. During the colonial period, between 1850 and 1920, as much as 81 million acres of forest was cleared in India. Overhunting during British rule further decimated India's wildlife populations, with more than eighty thousand tigers killed between 1875 and 1925. Following India's independence in 1947, deforestation again ticked up. The human population boom has since driven the bear's numbers down, with the International Union for Conservation of Nature listing the sloth bear as "vulnerable" on its Red List of Threatened Species in 1990. The sloth bear's official status remains unchanged today, though the species has since been confirmed extirpated in Bangladesh, and possibly Bhutan. India remains the sloth bear's last bastion; the animal resides in nineteen of the country's thirty-six states and union territories.

In an effort to quell intolerance for imperiled species, Indian state governments provide payouts to the injured victims of wild animal attacks. If a sloth bear kills a person, the government compensates family members of the deceased—although the national average for fatal wild animal attacks amounts to just $3,234 per victim. The *PNAS* study reported that as in the case of sloth bears, "a majority of the victims found state compensation for human casualties inadequate to cover the actual cost of treatment and injuries." And so they seek their own payback.

Retaliatory killings of sloth bears are spiking in the parts of India with recurring conflicts. Local newspapers report instances of villagers stoning, electrocuting, and poisoning sloth bears. In one incident, eight men were walking through the forest in the western state of Maharashtra when they spotted two sloth bear cubs coming toward them. The men panicked and killed the cubs with an axe. Unsurprisingly, this displeased the nearby mother bear, who swiftly dispatched two of the men. Another newspaper story recounted the saga of a fifty-eight-year-old woman who was on her way to the family's betel leaf plantation in Karnataka when a sloth bear and cub burst out of a cluster of maize saplings, ripping off the woman's face. A mob chased the bear away and captured its cub, locking it inside the village temple. They refused to release the crying animal until forest officials "end this wild animal intrusion into villages." And in the eastern state of Odisha, officials reported there were an astounding 716 sloth bear attacks on people between 2014 and 2018. During that same period, they recorded eighty-seven bear deaths. Although Indians tend to be far more forgiving of wildlife than those in the West who kill carnivores to protect pets and cows, "if there is no timely action taken to prevent conflicts, after five years that local community will not tolerate the bears anymore and they will be killed," Bargali had told me when we had departed Pinky's house.

A decade ago, the government released a national welfare and conservation action plan for the four bear species native to India. According to Bargali, little has been done since then, and the sloth bear's status has not improved. In a 2016 assessment of the sloth bear's status, he and colleagues projected that the sloth bear population would decline by more than 30 percent in the next thirty years if habitat loss wasn't swiftly addressed.

India's population is projected to boom for decades to come. The country surpassed China in 2023 to become the world's most populous nation. Land conflicts are rife across the subcontinent, with clashes between government and business; business and rural dwellers; and rural dwellers and animals. With increasing pressure on what scant forest resources remain, it's unlikely that humans will afford the mercy of food, water, or habitat to the loathsome sloth bear. The sloth bear occupies an unfortunate branch of the ursine family tree. It is too shaggy and sloppy to be respected for its physical prowess, like the brown bear and polar bear. And it is excluded from the huggable genre to which the panda and sun bear belong. The sloth bear's short temper poses an almost insurmountable challenge in the ethos of human-wildlife coexistence. If even the spectacled bear, the world's most peaceable bear, is at risk of disappearing, how could the world's deadliest bear possibly persist as human populations multiply alongside denuded forests? The sloth bear would need to count on the intuitive kindness and determination of a few conservation champions if it is going to secure a future in India.

IN 1894, A BLACK PANTHER, wolf mother, and Bengal tiger padded into the world of children's stories and forever changed Western notions of Indian wilderness. Published first in a series of magazines, then later anthologized into *The Jungle Book*, Rudyard Kipling's writings on Mowgli the man-cub and his sylvan pals were an instant sensation; he would become one of the most popular children's writers of the period, receiving the Nobel Prize in Literature in 1907. Alongside Shere Khan, Bagheera, and Raksha, *The Jungle Book* introduced another memorable character: "Baloo, the sleepy brown bear who teaches the wolf cubs the Law of the Jungle; old Baloo—who can come and go where he pleases because he eats only nuts and roots and honey."

The "law" mentioned "forbids every beast to eat Man except when he is killing to show his children how to kill, and then he must hunt outside the hunting-grounds of his pack or tribe. . . . The reason the beasts give among themselves is that Man is the weakest and most defenseless of all living things, and it is unsportsmanlike to touch him." Apparently the sloth bear didn't get the memo.

Kipling, a Bombay-born Brit, spent his own childhood not in the jewel in the crown of the British Empire, but at a boarding house in the United Kingdom. At the age of seventeen, he sailed back to India, where he worked for a short spell as a newspaper editor in Lahore (now part of Pakistan). Upon his return, he smugly wrote, "There were yet three or four days' rail to Lahore, where my people lived. After these, my English years fell away, nor ever, I think, came back in full strength." And yet, in seven years' time, Kipling would leave India, never to return. He wrote his celebrated tales about Mowgli from snowy Vermont.

Kipling never visited many of the locales where *The Jungle Book* was said to take place, not least of which were around the Seoni area of Madhya Pradesh, including the Pench and Kanha tiger reserves. Some theorize that the author drew inspiration from the nursery stories he heard from an Indian nanny for his epic rather than from the jungle itself. Kipling's abysmal description of the sloth bear lends some credence to this theory. He describes Baloo (or *bhalu*, as it is written in northern India) as a brown bear, yet by geographical determination alone, Baloo must be a sloth bear. No other bear species inhabits the forests of Madhya Pradesh. Baloo's behavior is also inconsistent with that of the sloth bear. He would likely have eaten termites and mahua, not nuts and roots. And Baloo would have been more inclined to disembowel Mowgli than to teach him the ways of the jungle.

It was on the border of Kipling's Kanha, by the gentle Jamunia River, that I first met Zeenal Vajrinkar. Fragrant jasmine blossoms fluttered to our feet, turning the soil beneath our feet into a starry sky. Harendra Bargali had some business to attend to in Uttarakhand, and so he had arranged for me to travel the Kanha-Pench corridor with Vajrinkar, a young and enthusiastic biologist from Maharashtra. Like Mowgli, she seemed to belong partially to the jungle, as she worked and lived in the Corbett Foundation's Kanha field office, more forest encampment than workplace, and was intimately acquainted with the region's wildlife.

"I heard a langur calling this morning," she said, rubbing her eyes under her glasses as dawn warmed the sky. Jamun trees shuddered in the cold breeze. We sipped creamy chai in small clay cups to stay warm. "It was the leopard-warning call. *Whoop whoop.*" I realized I'd mistaken the langur's call for a phone notification.

Our plan for the days ahead was to visit the villages in the Balaghat and Seoni area and the now-infamous Kanha-Pench corridor to speak with bear attack victims. To prepare me, she showed me a photo on her phone of a man whose face had been partially removed by a bear. His one ghostly eyeball drooped in a way an eye ought not to droop.

"You see, too, how he has no nose?" Vajrinkar pointed out helpfully. I did.

"What does he breathe out of?" I asked.

"He breathes out of this deep gash alongside his nose. You see?"

Again, I did.

Vajrinkar assured me—in a way that was meant to be comforting—that we would see more injuries like this in the forests around Kanha. As we navigated the edges of the dry forest in an enclosed jeep, she happily pointed out the greater racket-tailed drongos gliding through the sun-dappled sal trees: "This is the nasty mimicry bird! It can even imitate the tourist's camera shutter. But it is very beautiful." The bird's long tail feathers trailed far behind its body, two dainty plumes ending in black commas. The surrounding sal trees were one of the most abundant species in Balaghat because their hard wood was resistant to the wood-boring termites that lived in huge clumping mounds around their thin trunks. Termite hills were easily the most striking feature of the Indian forest, and some rose higher than my waist, like earthen skyscrapers. When fruit isn't in season, nearly all of the sloth bear's sustenance comes from insects—a bear can gobble up as many as ten thousand termites or ants, or about a quart, in a single serving.

"One of the Balaghat forest guards here was badly mauled," Vajrinkar told me. She spoke in a steady stream of attack anecdotes. "Now he wears a helmet whenever he goes into the woods because his head is so sensitive." Graceful mahua and tendu trees grew among the sal stands. Tendu leaves are used to wrap *bidis*, the poor man's cigarette, and Madhya Pradesh is the largest state producer in India, with more than one million people collecting the papery leaves for meager wages. Tribals also harvest the mahua's fleshy yellow-white flowers, similar in size and weight to a grape, which they ferment into a strong alcohol or use as a sweetener.

However, these forest products come at a steep cost. The sugary mahua flowers are also highly prized by the sloth bear, and it is during early morning mahua and tendu leaf collection, when people are stooped over, fixated on the forest floor, that sloth bears attack. In one study of the Kanha-Pench corridor, Bargali and his colleagues found that nearly a third of sloth bear attacks occurred during tendu leaf collection, while a fifth happened during the mahua harvest.

New electricity poles, erected as part of Prime Minister Narendra Modi's "Power for All" campaign, lined the roadway into the village of Beltola. Solitary light bulbs illuminated clay huts. Two lean men hovered over a bubbling cauldron brewing mahua liquor in a field. The flowering had begun. It would last until the end of April. Each quaint house in the village—there were only thirty-five—was built around a small open courtyard and stable known as an *aangan*. The tangled forest grew just beyond. Our first stop was the house of Mahasingh Meravi, a gaunt man in his late forties with protruding cheekbones. He wore a fraying white button-down with threadbare shorts. In place of shoes, a thick layer of gray mud caked the bottoms of his feet. We made our introductions, and I perched on the edge of a broken rope cot in the *aangan*. Mahasingh sat down on a wooden stool less than a foot off the ground, his legs extended in front of him like two toothpicks. Chickens scratched at the dirt. He began to speak.

Six years earlier, at the height of the monsoons, Mahasingh had ventured into the forest to collect mushrooms when he surprised a sleeping mother sloth bear with two cubs. Mahasingh tried to get away, but the bear let out a heart-dropping growl and reared up on her hind legs. She latched on to his upper thigh, biting to the bone. He managed to escape and scrambled up a nearby tree. Warm blood flowed down his battered leg. The bear waited under the tree for hours before she finally gave up. Mahasingh gingerly hobbled home. "My family cried when they saw my wounds," he recalled. "They washed them and put herbs on them. The next day I went to the hospital." For two months, he could barely walk.

Work was impossible. Mahasingh hitched up his shorts to show the light scars that raked along his dark thigh.

Sloth bears aren't man-eaters. Though aggressive, they rarely consume the flesh of those they kill. If the bear that mauled Mahasingh wasn't looking to fill its stomach, then why attack? Wildlife biologists have proposed a handful of theories to explain why the sloth bear has such a low throttle point. Perhaps, they speculate, sloth bears choose fight over flight because their long claws—though ideal for digging up bugs—aren't as useful for climbing trees. Adult sloth bears won't climb trees to avoid threats, although sometimes they'll carry their cubs up trees for safety.

Another popular explanation for the sloth bear's aggression stems from its interactions with predators. Sloth bears must contend with tigers and leopards on the Indian subcontinent. Brown bears and polar bears sit atop their respective food chains. Adult pandas have few predators. And spectacled bears hide in trees. The sloth bear has no choice but to explode in a flurry of fur, stumpy teeth, and claws when threatened. Owing to poor eyesight and hearing, it's possible the bear can't well distinguish a tribal person from a big cat and so unleashes the same desperate ferocity reserved for striped enemies on his human victims.

Tahir Ali Rather, a wildlife biologist at Aligarh Muslim University in Uttar Pradesh, believes such conflicts are exacerbated by Indian conservation priorities. If not for human intervention, he explained, tigers and sloth bears wouldn't choose to live as close neighbors; the big cats harass and occasionally kill sloth bears and their cubs. "Mother bears will not feel safe for their cubs if tigers are present in the same habitat," Bargali confirmed. India's staggering population growth, however, had pushed incompatible species into smaller patches of forest. Tahir had studied tiger and sloth bear relations around Bandhavgarh National Park, and he found that although there were few documented cases of tigers actually killing a sloth bear here, bullying tigers had pushed the Bandhavgarh bears into the fragmented edges of the protected area and the buffer zones close to human settlements. On top of this, Bargali noted that Indian conservation authorities often prioritized the charismatic tiger's habitat needs, paying insufficient attention to the sloth bear's necessities. In short, the tiger thrives in the core of protected zones at the expense of the unfortunate sloth bear, who is pushed out into the poorer-quality forest and, inevitably, into conflict with people.

The next morning we headed into the Kanha-Pench corridor. Vajrinkar carried with her a list of victims' names and rudimentary addresses with her. The population of sloth bears living in the corridor—nobody knows how many there are—bore responsibility for more than 250 attacks, and she hoped we would be able to interview a woman who had been mauled a few years earlier near the village of Polbattur. She looked around warily. The area had recently seen an increase in Naxalite activity, with armed cadres from the Communist Party of India moving over the border from neighboring Chhattisgarh. It remained fraught with political tension. Riots could break out at any time.

On the road, we came across a young man in a dark gray shirt with a scarlet-red head scarf, tied in a similar fashion to the Naxalites. Vajrinkar cautiously leaned out the jeep's open window and asked if he knew of the local bear attack victim.

"Is she home?"

The man screwed up his face toward the scorching midday sun and shook his head.

"The bear attack victim? No. She is not home yet. She is still in Balaghat Hospital."

The woman we were searching for had been attacked years ago. Why would she still be in the hospital? After a moment of confusion and further questioning, we deduced there had been *another* sloth bear attack just two days before. The family lived nearby in the village of Jaitpuri. The young man pointed the way.

At the victim's home, a middle-aged man wrapped in an orange *lungi*, a sarong, marched out of the house. We asked him what had happened. The man collapsed to the ground in distress, leaning his forehead into his hands. A small crowd gathered to watch our exchange. The man told us that five of them had been cutting bamboo in the late afternoon. As they walked back to Jaitpuri, his wife, Javantibai Uikey, took off ahead. Her screams followed. A sloth bear had lunged out of the trees, sinking its teeth into her buttocks. Blood seeped through her red sari. The group ran to her and found the woman still clasped in the bear's jaws. *Reech*, the Hindi word for sloth bear, punctuated her husband's angry recollection as Vajrinkar translated. They chased the animal off, he explained, wrapping her wounds, and carrying her for more than three hours through the dark forest. The next morning a neighbor took her by motorbike to the hospital, where she remained. He hoped she would be discharged in two days' time.

In North America, bear attacks are akin to being struck by lightning. They're stories told around campfires to ward off sleep. But in India, the sloth bear isn't an abstract beast stalking nightmares. Fear of such attacks is a lived reality for millions of people living in rural areas. It was a luxury, I realized, to conceive of these animals as fable protagonists, majestic arbiters of wilderness, and cuddly cartoon characters. In many parts of India, the sloth bear is a force of devastation. People have lost husbands and wives, fathers and mothers, brothers and sisters to the bear. It would be a challenge to convince the people living in communities like Beltola or Jaitpuri that they should support the conservation of sloth bears when they bore the emotional and physical costs of the animal's continued presence on the landscape. Even the cheerful, animal-loving Vajrinkar had once provoked the sloth bear's ire.

That evening, as we stood around a crackling fire outside the Kanha office discussing the day's interviews, she told me that while conducting scat surveys near Tadoba-Andhari Tiger Reserve, a bear had charged her. She stumbled backward and fell to the ground. Two forest guards rushed forward to beat the animal back with sticks. But the bear was close enough for her to get a good, long look at the curve of its sharp claws. When she told me the story of how she was bitten by a bamboo pit viper, Vajrinkar laughed it off. The pain was searing—*her arm turned black and blue!*—but she'd gotten a shot of antivenom just in time. The bear was different.

"I took a week off work after that."

PENDRA ROAD, SOMETIMES CALLED GAURELLA, is a small city in Chhattisgarh named for its railway station. This is the only reason most people have to know Pendra Road at all. There is no Taj Mahal, Agra Fort, or lush backwaters to attract travelers here. As in many Indian cities, stores with metal shutters sell scrap electronics in heaps; men peddle *pani puri*, deep-fried puff pastry balls; and Brahman cattle, burdened by absurd humps, stagger blindly into traffic. But for Harendra Bargali, Pendra Road was hard to forget. He was one of the first biologists to intensively study sloth bears in India and had spent many years in Pendra during the late 1990s, researching the 250-odd bruins that made their dens in gray boulder hillocks around the city. He'd even hand-raised an orphaned sloth bear cub that he named Monica—after Monica Lewinsky.

But this wasn't the first place that Bargali had encountered a sloth bear. He had grown up in the town of Bhimtal in northern India. As a child, his world was confined to the dusty streets, the vendors that sold sugary jalebis and roasted sweet potatoes, and the hollers of the chaiwallahs shouldering silver canteens. He knew little of the wild beings that lived in the forests beyond. But one day, while playing on the rooftops of Bhimtal with his brother, a nine-year-old Bargali spotted a strange man moving through the narrow alleys with a great beast in tow. Bargali crouched low and watched them. When they arrived at the market, the shaggy animal stood up on its haunches and appeared to dance, swaying from paw to paw as its master tugged on a rusty chain. Suddenly, the animal let out a fierce growl. Bargali was terrified. "I ran the 2 kilometers all the way home. My mom told me, 'That was a dancing bear,' and my brother teased me for being afraid." It would be nearly two decades before Bargali would see his first sloth bear in the wild.

When I had first contacted Bargali about his research, he had been eager to find an excuse to return to his old study site. He hadn't been back since the early 2000s—barring one short day trip more than a decade ago—and was anxious to see how the region had changed in his absence, particularly in light of the country's population growth from around 1 billion to nearly 1.4 billion people. "I'm eager to see the quality of the forest," he told me halfway into the five-hour journey from

Bandhavgarh. In his excitement, he'd brought his wife, Suman, and two young daughters along for the road trip. The three of them were squeezed in the van's back seat under a pile of Parle-G biscuits and masala chips. He hoped to show them the rugged and nostalgic beauty of the rocky Maikal Hills and the sloth bears that had helped launch his career. Hesitation lingered in his mind. Would Pendra Road be anything like he remembered?

As we neared the city, the bumpy dirt road gave way to smooth pavement, and we passed a vertical labyrinth of steaming pipes and towers. A huge power plant. Thousands of lights punctured the lavender twilight. Bargali looked dismayed. The forest was gone. Beige apartment complexes rose where the elegant mahua trees once grew. We passed an indigo building identified as Hotel Aman. It looked brand new. "That's a change," Bargali said glumly, taking in the transforming landscape. What had happened to the bears?

The people who lived in this region of central India had long claimed a separate cultural identity from their neighbors in Madhya Pradesh. In 2000, heightened by growing mineral wealth in iron ore, dolomite, coal, and bauxite, they voted to separate and form their own state—Chhattisgarh. It now lagged behind its agricultural neighbor in gross domestic product (GDP), but mining had nonetheless transformed the state's wilderness. Trains loaded with the spoils of plundered earth blocked the road to Pendra. I cringed as young men on motorbikes sped across the tracks in front of oncoming locomotives, tempting fate. In the wake of such growth, Bargali suspected there had been at least a 40 percent decline in the bear population of Pendra. In hindsight, "the government should have made this area a sloth bear sanctuary," he sighed.

To many working in wildlife conservation, population growth is a core issue but difficult and sensitive to address. India's population has nearly doubled since the 1980s, and the average population density is more than one thousand people per square mile. In the world's largest democracy, "we don't have a population policy," Bargali lamented. The nationwide education of women, a proven mitigator of high fertility rates, was evidently the best path forward, but it wouldn't happen in time to save many threatened species. "Even if we try our best, the population will not decline until 2060," said Bargali. "It's going to be a big problem."

The next morning, Bargali, his family, and I headed out to visit the boulder hills. Sloth bears, like spectacled bears and other bears that live around the equator, don't hibernate. They often sleep in cool caves to escape the heat. It was 32°C (90°F) as we walked through dry fields. Rocks, some the size of an elephant, were piled 200 feet high. Farmers had cleared the surrounding forest and turned it into fuelwood plantations or sprawling capsicum pepper patches. In some sections they had rolled the smaller boulders away from the hillocks to use in cobbled paths between field plots. The bear dens were their personal quarry.

"Would you like to climb it?" Bargali asked, gesturing to one of the boulder hills. I wasn't sure whether or not he was joking. Earlier, he'd casually mentioned that leopards also slept in the boulder crevasses during the day. I squinted up at the washed-out hills, mentally triangulating the gnarly injuries I'd seen in the Kanha-Pench corridor, the lack of immediate healthcare facilities, and the grittiness of my hotel room in Pendra.

"How likely is it that we'd come across a bear or a leopard?"

"About fifty-fifty," Bargali estimated in a dismissive way that suggested he considered those to be good odds. His wife shook her head out of his view. Bargali wasn't even positive that the bears still lived here. He cheerfully went on: "In some of these areas the stone slabs are so steep and smooth that if you fall in you can't get out. But I climbed to the top of all of these hillocks when I was a young man!"

After a quick deliberation, I respectfully declined and instead elected to inspect the boulders' perimeter, looking for signs of bear activity. Under a large mahua tree with thick mahogany-colored branches that arrested the sky, I came across a pile of scat. Bargali jogged over to dissect the fecal finding with a twig. The crusty outer layer crumbled away revealing a moist layer of partially digested ziziphus seeds—a sloth bear's favorite treat. He inhaled deeply. It smelled sweet like honey. "This is sloth bear scat!" he announced triumphantly. And less than a day old, at that!

We turned to look back at the looming boulders. The bears were still here.

🖌️

FOG HUNG LOW OVER THE CITY OF AGRA, turning the Taj Mahal into a mere specter. The trains were running late. Wiry men pushed wooden carts laden with cauliflower and eggplant through the congested streets to market. Holy cows exacerbated traffic jams, their pious strength exceeding that of the autorickshaw driver who honked and veered wildly down the rutted road, unable to see through the thick air.

Near the Taj Mahal's souvenir bazaar, I hailed a taxi and followed National Highway 19 out of Agra, keen to escape the unfolding chaos. Out of the city, I pointed to the exit for the Soor Sarovar Bird Sanctuary. Down a treed lane, painted storks balanced in the desaturated marsh, appearing like ghostly sentinels. Fog coiled around banyan trees' muscular roots. The taxi driver dropped me off at a small cinder block guard station next to a school for the blind. It seemed a strange and mysterious location; I imagined a conclave of oracles studying in sacred groves. Two men promptly handed me a stack of paperwork to fill out, a hallmark of Indian bureaucracy, then waved me toward a large iron gate.

For more than 400 years, sloth bears were better known among Indians as "dancing bears."

Kalandars, a nomadic Muslim ethnic group that travels across North India and Pakistan, enslaved the bears as entertainers in the courts of Mughal emperors and Rajput kings between the sixteenth and nineteenth centuries. The great shaggy bear, tethered to a coarse rope or chain, would rear up on its hind legs, swaying from side to side with each tug of the rope and bobbing its head, appearing to dance. The captivating spectacle spilled beyond palace walls as the Kalandars busked from town to town, attracting jeering street crowds who tossed silver coins into baskets as the bears writhed in a pain-filled trance. One description of an encounter with a dancing bear along the Delhi-Agra Highway in the 1990s goes: "A Kalandar was forcing her to perform in front of a tourist vehicle and she was jumping up and down in pain as her owner pulled at her rope and beat her with a stick. The hot tarmac below her delicate feet was only adding to her pain."

To obtain the bears, tribal poachers accompanied Kalandar troupes in their travels. When a mother bear was out foraging for food, they would break into her cave with torches and steal her helpless weeks-old cubs. If mom returned too soon, she was often killed. Still, the risk was well worth the reward; a young sloth bear commanded as much as 1,200 rupees, or 22 US dollars, and their buyer received a good return on such investment; a single bear could support an entire Kalandar family—ten to twelve people—bringing in around 1,500 rupees every month from rural audiences. International tourists paid twice that. The lowest castes would even trade vegetables and grains to watch the bear perform.

For centuries, the capture and trade of cubs served as one of the greatest threats to the species, with thousands of sloth bears snatched from the wild. In 1972, when Indira Gandhi introduced the landmark Indian Wildlife Protection Act, the Kalandars were bringing more than one hundred sloth bear cubs into their communes every year. Gandhi's act outlawed the hunting of protected wild animals, even extending its mercy to the scruffy sloth bear, but it would take thirty more years before the first of India's twelve hundred dancing bears would be freed.

The Wildlife SOS Agra Bear Rescue Facility was founded in 1999 to house the battered and broken dancing bears relinquished by Kalandar communities. Today, it occupies roughly 165 acres of former military land in Uttar Pradesh, helping to fulfill the goal of the Indian Wildlife Protection Act.

"In 2002, we rescued the first dancing bear—Rani. He is still here," Rishik Dutta Gupta, a young man from Kolkata with curly black hair and kind caramel eyes, told me as we entered the compound. Wildlife SOS operates four sloth bear rescue centers across the country and has rescued more than six hundred dancing bears in all. The center in Agra is by far the largest. "We have 179 bears right now," Gupta said, "but we've had up to 260 at one time. Now they are dying from old age." Nearly all of the retired dancing bears in Agra had been there for more than a decade. Too broken, too tame, and too traumatized, they could never be returned to the wild. Wildlife SOS's aim was simply for the bears to live out their remaining days away from taunting crowds. Mimusops trees overhung the dirt walkway that wound through the sanctuary. There were enclosures on either side where rubber balls floated in pools and logs filled with honey dangled from wooden platforms. I peered through the wire fencing for any sign of a sloth bear. I'd yet to see one in person and was a little nervous about running into one in the wild. The forested enclosures were big enough for bears to disappear entirely from the human gaze, affording them some well-deserved privacy after years in the spotlight.

Suddenly, three bears appeared to my right. Their shaggy heads were bowed as they snorted along the fence line, breathing deeply. Frothy saliva pooled around the corners of their mouths. They had picked up our scent. Roshan, Arun, and Varun—all in their mid-teens—had been surrendered to Wildlife SOS more than a decade ago. The usually solitary bears had since formed a close companionship to process their collective trauma. I examined the three curious faces now looking over at us. Like the poor tribal people I had met in Madhya Pradesh, the bears were deeply scarred. Delicate S-shaped lines marred white snouts.

A sloth bear's bipedalism is typically reserved for reaching fruit or fighting tigers; a bear does not *dance*. To break a bear's wild spirit, the Kalandars punctured its nose often with a hot metal poker and looped a rope or chain through the oozing wound. Then they removed the young bear's claws and bashed out its teeth, sometimes locking the animal's snout in a muzzle full of nails. The Kalandars trained the cub by striking each of its hind paws with a stick, forcing the animal to raise that appendage off the ground. Following a brutal regime of starvation and beatings, the bear would inevitably grow submissive to its trainer, and eventually the master would need only hit the ground with the stick for the bear to lift its feet on tempo. This dance of fear and desperation created the illusion of merriment.

"In the south of India, they used a metal ring instead of a rope," Gupta said when he caught me eyeing the bears' disfigured faces. "The operations to remove them were particularly tricky. The muzzles were in bad shape. We have one bear here—Kasthuri—and her muzzle is literally hanging off."

The bears of Agra had suffered tremendously for human entertainment. In addition to lacking upper incisors due to evolution, the rescued dancing bears were missing their canines. Arthritis plagued their joints and immobilized their bodies—a woeful testament to years spent dancing on their hind legs. Stumped limbs could be traced back to cubhood, when the bears had stepped into a Kalandar trap. Still, if there were only twelve hundred known dancing bears in India out of a wild population of around twenty thousand two decades ago, I wondered how much of an impact the Kalandars could actually have had on wild bear populations. When I voiced this question to Gupta, he explained that "it wasn't just twelve hundred dancing bears. To get the twelve hundred dancing bears, Kalanders killed the mothers. And as much as 40 percent of the dancing bears died in their first twelve months with the Kalandars. They could not survive one year's torture—the piercing of their muzzle and the ripping out of their teeth."

A 1997 analysis of the dancing bear industry found that "the cubs have a high mortality rate at the market itself; approximately two cubs out of ten succumb to the shock of separation from the mother and simply 'fade' away." Ultimately, "in view of the fact a sloth bear produces her litter of two cubs (on average) only once in 2 or 2.5 years and very often human intrusion can cause her to kill her own cubs, the sloth bear numbers are reducing quite fast. This slow reproductive rate of the sloth bear has important consequences in view of the uncontrolled poaching currently taking place." Animal entertainers therefore exacted a far greater toll on the wild sloth bear population than what one could have gleaned from the streets of India in the 1990s.

"Why were sloth bears chosen as dancing bears instead of any of the other bear species?" I asked.

"They're the most easily available—Asiatic black bears and brown bears are only found in the high-altitude areas," Gupta explained. "And sun bears live only in the northeast."

Roshan, Arun, and Varun had grown tired of our presence, surmising that we hadn't brought them any snacks. Disgruntled, they pawed at the ground in search of insects. Though staff fed them a heaping portion of mushy porridge twice a day, they were unable to suppress their natural instincts. We said goodbye to the three bears and continued on through the complex, which was cleaved by the Yamuna River, the second-largest tributary of the Ganges. A punt boat ferried us across. We saw a bear named Rose, a young amputee who had lost her front paw to a snare trap. Gupta pointed out an exceptionally small bear, Gail, who came to Agra in 2008 from a Kalandar settlement in West Bengal. Malnourishment had stunted her growth. And there was Elvis, a shaggy, good-natured bear who had been rescued in 2015 at just three months old from poachers who planned to smuggle him out of India.

A bear named Raju is touted as the last dancing bear rescued in India. Wildlife SOS liberated him in 2009. Unofficially, many dancing bears have been rescued since then. An investigation by the World Society for the Protection of Animals revealed that the exploitation of dancing bears continued in India into the 2010s, with twenty-eight captives documented in a single year. And every now and then, a new dancing bear is spotted trundling down a red earth road behind its master.

Wildlife SOS's founders convinced many Kalandars to hand over their bears by offering them 50,000 rupees—about 1,000 US dollars—to start a new business venture, or giving them a job at one of the rescue centers. Today, more than half of Wildlife SOS staff at some rescue centers are Kalandars. The men work as food cutters in the facility's kitchen, dicing up watermelon and mangoes, and women make souvenirs for sale in the gift shop. "Some of them grew very close to the bears even though they had been very brutal toward them," said Gupta. He told me they often watched their old dancing bears from afar. "They like to see the bears happy." Still, some Kalandars didn't wish to adopt this new way of life. Instead, they fled north toward India's border with Nepal—bears in tow.

Gupta led me up a low cement ramp to a long tan building with a green metal door. The paint was peeling off. I stepped into a rubber bin filled with pink disinfectant. A small paper sign above the door read: ISOLATION AND QUARANTINE WARD. Inside, we found Rangila, a nineteen-year-old male sloth bear. He had been eavesdropping on our arrival and had pushed his bushy body expectantly against the bars of his cage—one of more than a dozen pens along a tiled walkway reminiscent of a city pound. A decade ago, these cages would have been full. But now Rangila was the only bear here. In 2017, he had been rescued from bear dancers in southeastern Nepal, along with a seventeen-year-old female dancing bear named Sridevi, who later died while in the custody of the Kathmandu Zoo. Rangila was eventually transported more than 600 miles to Agra.

Wildlife SOS veterinarians required all rescued bears to undergo a ninety-day quarantine while they screened them for diseases and treated their wounds. Later, they'd move the bears to an outdoor enclosure where they could socialize with others of their kind. But Rangila had been here for six months. With his companion gone, the male bear was struggling to adjust to his surroundings. Unlike the three teenaged bears we'd seen outside, Rangila didn't even make eye contact with us. He kept his head low to the ground, swaying his neck back and forth in a monotonous fashion. In the wild, sloth bears rarely live past the age of thirty. The majority of Agra's bears had been rescued before the age of ten. Rangila had spent nearly his entire life with the Kalandars.

"Nineteen years is a very long time to be a dancing bear," Gupta sighed.

It would take another eight months for Rangila to grow brave enough to venture out into the world. That September, more than a year after he arrived in Agra, Rangila finally left his concrete cell. For the first time in his life, the sloth bear explored the world without a rope. He dug up mud pits and napped in the cool earth until his black coat turned brown. He batted the honey-laced logs. He tore apart hammocks, much to the chagrin of his keepers who noted, "The hammocks in Rangila's enclosure are replaced more times than any other bear because of his creative streak." He sucked on watermelon and gobbled down soft honey porridge and mushy bananas. He still wasn't fond of human company, but waited patiently for his keepers to visit him each day. He gained weight. His muzzle healed. Scars faded. He saw other bears. Rangila was now tethered not to man, but to earth, as all bears should be.

I WAS ENCOURAGED BY THE TIME I HAD SPENT in Agra among the freed dancing bears, but I knew that saving impotent animal entertainers from a life of cruel exploitation wouldn't prevent the species' extinction in the wild. It was far easier for people to champion the protection of a pathetic captive than it was to advocate for the conservation of a rampaging killer. If the sloth bear—claws, canines, and all—was going to persist on the Indian subcontinent, new solutions were urgently needed. So, five weeks after arriving in India, I headed west.

Gujarat, wedged between Pakistan and the Arabian Sea, is the antithesis of Madhya Pradesh and its six tiger reserves. In the cat's absence, the state forest department has invested in other threatened species, creating nearly two dozen wildlife sanctuaries. Leopards, flamingos, and blue bulls were all deemed worthy of government protection. More importantly, the state managed two sanctuaries with the sloth bear's needs in mind.

Nishith Dharaiya, a wildlife biologist who cochairs the IUCN's sloth bear specialist group with Bargali, is a proud and passionate man from Gujarat. When I met him at his office at Hemchandracharya North Gujarat University, the walls were decorated with conservation awards and badges from the various bear conferences he'd attended around the world. It didn't take much prodding for him to list his accomplishments in Indian conservation. At forty-four, the graying stubble on his chin gave him the air of authority, and he nonchalantly smoked cigarettes that he lit with matches while discussing his career.

We had made plans to hike through the dry scrub of Jessore Sloth Bear Sanctuary, a two-hour drive north from the university campus in Patan. The 70-square-mile reserve in India's Aravalli Hills and adjoining Balaram Ambaji Wildlife Sanctuary were home to about 350 sloth bears, as well as leopards, striped hyenas, porcupines, honey badgers, and jungle cats. This was where he conducted much of his fieldwork. Unfortunately, in an abstract sense, Dharaiya had also recently fallen victim to the sloth bear.

A couple months before I arrived in Ahmedabad, he emailed me with bad news: while working with a small team to set up camera traps in a part of northeastern India where sloth bears, sun bears, and moon bears were thought to coexist, he fell down a steep cliff and into a rushing river, catching his leg between two boulders. The result was a torn anterior cruciate ligament. Now he was on bed rest—doctor's orders. It was in such hobbled form that I first encountered Dharaiya in Gujarat. His leg was wrapped in a tight brace, and he leaned on a makeshift cane between cigarette drags. He complained that he hadn't been back in the forest since his accident and was beginning to feel like a cooped-up rooster. Nonetheless, he insisted that he was well enough to go to Jessore—his solution being to bring along Arzoo Malik, a doctoral student also working on mitigating sloth bear conflict, who would lead me on hikes through the forest while he showed me the sights by car.

A large painting of a sloth bear greeted visitors to Jessore. The sanctuary was created in 1978 to protect the robust bear and leopard populations that lived within the terminal range of the Aravalli. Located a short drive from the front gate were two quaint forest cabins where we would stay for the next few nights. Their tiny windows overlooked Jessore Hill—Gujarat's second-highest peak—and a shallow brown lake where men led their buffalo to cool off. A cotillion of women in fuchsia and tangerine saris were watering plastic-wrapped saplings in a neighboring nursery when we arrived. They smiled and shouted greetings in Gujarati. *Tame kemp cho.*

"They are growing food for the bears," Dharaiya explained. "*Ziziphus, Cassia fistula,* and *Ficus.*" Ten nurseries like this were scattered throughout the sanctuary, growing different trees that would be planted in the wild. At his behest, the Forest Department had begun planting the sloth bear's favorite tree species, and an army of workers had constructed artificial bear dens and dirt mounds in the forest, translocating termites around the sanctuary.

Gujarat records far fewer sloth bear attacks than the states of Madhya Pradesh and Chhattisgarh. In part, that's because fewer people live near protected areas. Only a handful of tribal villages border Jessore. The sloth bear also generally refrains from venturing out of protected areas unless it is hungry or thirsty. If the bears' needs are being met inside the sanctuary, Dharaiya told me, there is no reason for them to roam farther. The Forest Department's strategy of safeguarding sloth bear food had seemingly had the intended effect. But water, or lack thereof, was emerging as a pressing concern. Gujarat was fast moving toward a drought.

Droughts are known to exacerbate human-wildlife conflict; during a bad one in the late 1980s, there were more than one hundred wild animal attacks in Gujarat. Twenty people were killed. Dharaiya had recently combed through years of sloth bear attack data. In North Gujarat, he found that recorded attacks increased from an average of just under one attack per year between 1960 and 1999 to about nine attacks per year since 2009. Water was now the major factor driving sloth bears into human-occupied areas, with attacks mostly occurring in the hot dry summer.

In one of the villages near Jessore, we stopped to chat with a group of local men from the Garasia tribe. In the last four years, they said, sloth bears were moving closer to their village during the summer, when the river dried up. One man's brother had been badly mauled by three bears while he was working in a nearby field. "I would kill the bear if I had an axe," he said angrily. His brother had spent more than two weeks in the hospital and needed eighty stitches to close his wounds. "And if another bear comes into the village, I will kill it!" The others nodded their heads in agreement. They said they wanted more fencing around the village—and more water for the bears. "Tolerance is very low," Dharaiya concluded as he limped back to the car. "There was not enough rain in the monsoon last year."

Before dawn the next morning, I headed into the dry Aravalli Hills, the eroded stub of ancient mountains, with Arzoo Malik. Dharaiya had reluctantly stayed behind at the cabin, attending to his injured leg. Malik had studied botany in Delhi and had initially come to Gujarat to examine the impact of pesticide use on the state's wetlands. She was a strongheaded woman who didn't shy away from speaking her mind and was determined to prove herself in the field alongside male colleagues. "No one knows the water needs of wild sloth bears," she told me as we headed away from the cabin, across a dry river channel. Malik hoped to change that.

For more than two hours, we saw neither drop nor trickle in the dessicated stream channels that cut through the hills. Spiky invasive mesquite trees (*Prosopis chilenis*) grew where water should run. The Forest Department had built a number of artificial water sources—concrete wells and pools fed by tanker trunks or, when possible, rainwater funneled through drainage channels—throughout the forest. They had been strategically located in areas that sloth bears were known to frequent. But with drought worsening, more needed to be done to prevent bear-human conflict. The year before my visit, there had been a 76 percent deficit in the average rainfall during the southwest monsoon. So Dharaiya and Malik were surveying natural springs throughout Jessore in hopes of finding a way to improve water retention during times of drought.

A few miles in, Malik came to a stop by a shallow brown pool of water shaded by towering fig trees. I could feel the temperature drop on my skin. She had identified just five water points in the forest with global information system (GIS), and at each of these she recorded bear pug marks, scat, and signs of digging to determine how often the bears were visiting. "Once we establish that baseline of the bear's water needs, we want to try to engineer the landscape to naturally retain water," she said. This would be critical if they were going to stop bears from wandering out of the sanctuary and alighting on villages. "By summer, there will be no water left inside these hills."

THAT NIGHT, MALIK AND I RECLINED on our cots in the cabin, lethargic from the heat of the day. We'd left the door wide open, hoping for a breeze that never came. The air was hot and stagnant. Lizards skittered across the walls. Dharaiya stood outside looking up at the stars, relishing the feeling of being back in nature for the first time in months. The glow of his cigarette penetrated the darkness. As I scribbled down my notes from the day, I heard a hushed "Come! Come!" I peered outside and saw nothing. Dharaiya began snapping his fingers to get our attention, endeavoring to make as little noise as possible. This time my ears picked up a cacophony of crunching, snuffling, snorting, and slobbering. The sloth bears had arrived.

Malik and I grabbed a flashlight and stealthily tiptoed out of the cabin. "There is a mother and two cubs by the edge of the nursery," Dharaiya urgently whispered. We cast the light toward the saplings. The bears were munching on the long seed pods of the cassia trees. Sloth bears aren't nocturnal, but when humans are around, they tend to be more active after dusk. The flashlight picked up only the bears' eyeshine at first. Six little glowing dots. My mind filled in the blanks with the physical details from the rescued dancing bears. They were maybe 30 feet away, preoccupied with eating the fallen pods. The flashlight's beam of light was too narrow to keep tabs on all three bears at once. Dharaiya motioned for us to follow him to the van parked in front of the cabins. As quietly as possible, he pulled open the driver's side door and we huddled behind it like a shield. Turning the key one notch in the ignition, the headlights clicked on, bathing the cassia tree in light. The bears were gorging on this midnight buffet, appearing as shaggy blobs. While I had reconciled the two incarnations of the sloth bear—vicious killer and tragic performer, this was the animal's third and final act: a wild sloth bear unbothered by people or chains, teaching her cubs the law of the jungle.

CHAPTER THREE

SOFT POWER

Panda bear, China
Ailuropoda melanoleuca

On a spring day I stood in a quaint pavilion smacking a long shoot of bamboo against the ground until it splintered. Fibrous shards rained down on the flagstone. I was already on my fifteenth shoot of the morning, and the sun had just barely crested the looming thirty-six peaks of Mount Qingcheng. This wasn't the kind of work I had expected when I signed up to be a panda keeper for the day. And I wasn't sure why the captive pandas couldn't do the job themselves—or why so many foreigners had volunteered to break the bamboo into fragments on the bears' behalf. I could only guess that our pledged labor prevented the pandas from exerting too much energy and keeling over into extinction.

I had reported for duty at the Dujiangyan Panda Base and Center for Disease Control in Sichuan Province at eight o'clock that morning. The gray-brick headquarters and forty panda enclosures were built along Qingcheng's ambling roots. The mountain is considered the birthplace of Taoism and remains one of the most important Taoist centers in modern China, though today the pandas seemed a bigger draw. About thirty paying volunteers had shown up that morning to look after the resident pandas. Outside the gates I'd encountered dozens of vendors hawking all sorts of grayscale gear that they shoved in my face in a dizzying flourish of capitalism—ball caps with panda faces, panda headbands with tiny ears, stuffed pandas, Panda-brand cigarettes, tea fertilized with panda dung. (I bought some of the tea.) Once inside, Dujiangyan staff took our temperatures—sick people couldn't be near the pandas—and split the healthy volunteers into groups to be dispatched by green shuttles around the 126-acre park. My group was sent to the lower reaches of Dujiangyan, where four fat pandas lived in the Pan Pan Garden enclosure, named for the famously fertile male bear. Pan Pan, who passed away in 2016 at the age of thirty-one, is estimated to have at least 130 descendants. His studly genes live on in roughly a fifth of the world's captive-bred panda population.

In the workyard of the Pan Pan enclosure, I futilely threw my next shoot against the ground like an abysmal javelin thrower, flinching with every snapback. Our supervisor was a young woman who wore her dark hair in two tightly plaited braids tucked under a bucket hat. She barked orders. *Faster! Thinner! Better!* Five of us shuffled around the chain-link enclosure, grabbing shoots off a flatbed truck weighted with roped bundles of bamboo. We each wore an oversized indigo jumpsuit that gave us the appearance of an imprisoned Smurf. A green embroidered badge on the chest pocket bore the words "Panda Husbandry Learner." A retired couple from Santa Barbara stood next to me, wearily smacking their twelfth shoot. We shared a grimace.

Pandas are notoriously picky eaters. Ninety-nine percent of the bear's diet consists of bamboo shoots, leaves, and stems. And though nearly five hundred species of bamboo grow in China, the bears only eat around sixty of them. Three are their favorite. The problem is that bamboo, while high in protein, isn't *that* nutritious. Scientists believe the bears only eat it because it's abundant—and because nobody else wants it. The panda, known for being one of the animal kingdom's laziest members, can't be bothered to fight other species for calories. Accordingly, the panda needs to consume as much as 40 pounds of bamboo every day to survive. This restrictive diet has proved a hindrance to the vulnerable population as bamboo forests have disappeared across western China, coinciding with agricultural expansion.

Wild pandas could once be found in seventeen provinces, but now they live in just three: Gansu, Shaanxi, and Sichuan. The latter is the animal's stronghold. Sichuan, in the southwest, has more forest cover than almost any other province in China. It also contains the last great expanse of secular Han Chinese culture before jade hills confront the ocher slabs of the Tibetan plateau and pandas cede power to all things yak. Lhasa lies some 1,200 miles from here—a journey made along winding roads ribboned with tattered and faded prayer flags. In Sichuan, sacred mountains thrust toward the heavens, gateways for celestial deities, with ornate temples balanced on crumbling precipices.

The Yangtze River coils around rice terraces like a muddied serpent and cuts through valleys where men and women carry baskets brimming with fiery Sichuan peppers, a potent elixir halfway between spice and numbing novocaine.

That China has any pandas left in the wild at all is a small wonder. Half a century ago, three thousand Chinese scientists combed nearly every inch of the panda's known range to count the animal and estimated there were little more than one thousand bears remaining in just six mountain ranges. In response to the disappointing census, China swiftly launched a conservation scheme to pull the bear back from the brink of extinction. By 1983, the central government had established a dozen protected panda reserves, which held a little more than half of the species' population. Still, the panda continued to struggle until the early 2000s. Today, Chinese officials declare—with suspicious precision—that there are 1,864 pandas thriving in the wild.

Many others exist in captivity. The government has been breeding pandas for almost four decades, and more than six hundred pandas now reside in zoos and research centers around the world. The Dujiangyan panda base, where I was volunteering, contained about forty of them. It's one of five government-funded captive centers within China's borders and partially serves as a retirement center for geriatric bears after decades-long stints in international zoos. Tai Shan, the first panda to be born (and survive) at the National Zoo in Washington, DC, was returned to China in 2010. Now in his teens, Tai Shan spent his days lolling around Dujiangyan, and every morning volunteers in the Panda Keeper Program carted wheelbarrows of splintered bamboo into his enclosure.

Dujiangyan was full of old bears with interesting histories. Ying Ying, a stiff twenty-seven-year-old female, had been the first panda to greet me in the Pan Pan enclosure. She was taken from the wilds of Wolong County in Sichuan decades ago and later brought here. Pandas live to around thirty years in captivity, though the oldest captive bear on record made it to thirty-eight. Fu Bao, a tubby five-year-old male born in the Vienna Zoo, lived in the Pan Pan enclosure, too. The other Pan-Panites had been born at the captive panda base in Wolong Nature Reserve. Twenty-three-year-old Fei Fei and her nine-month-old cub, simply dubbed "Fei Fei's Baby," had never set foot in the wild. Many of Dujiangyan's resident bears had been transferred here following the devastating 2008 Sichuan earthquake, which killed nearly seventy thousand people. The 8.0-magnitude quake also demolished the original Wolong panda center, and one bear was found crushed to death under the rubble of her enclosure. (The base has since been rebuilt.) The Dujiangyan center was constructed shortly after the disaster to house the displaced bears and help the region recover; the quake's epicenter lay just 50 miles from here.

When our group had finished breaking bamboo, the staff gave us another exciting job—scooping up the pandas' excrement. Volunteers aren't allowed to enter the forested panda enclosures while the bears are present. Though generally hospitable, pandas have been known to attack tourists who get too close. In 2006, a drunk man jumped into the panda enclosure at the Beijing Zoo in hopes of hugging a bear. Resident panda Gu Gu jumped him instead and tore into the man's legs. The drunk man later told the press that he had bit the panda on its back in an attempt to stop the vicious assault, "but its fur was too thick." A year later, a teenaged boy jumped into Gu Gu's enclosure and the bear mauled his legs, too.

Our supervisor lured the gullible pandas out of the enclosure with carrot sticks, leaving only Fei Fei's Baby dozing in the crook of a tree. We slipped in quietly with our shovels and metal buckets. The supervisor pointed at the ground. "Sweep up old bamboo." We swept. "Pick up panda feces." We scuttled scat into the buckets. The enclosure was overflowing with day-old poop. Fortunately, the panda's poor digestive system means that their excrement closely resembles the bear's latest meal; each pile was little more than a starchy, yellow briquet of mushy bamboo. In fact, bamboo is often left so intact after passing through the panda's colon that scientists can estimate the size of wild panda populations by analyzing the bears' unique bite sizes on pooped-out bamboo fragments.

Finally, at eleven, staff permitted us to take a break from hard labor. The day's schedule labeled this event as the "Regardful Panda Feeding." One of the friendlier staff members ushered me into a little cement panda house that backed onto the green outdoor enclosure. There sat Fei Fei. Upon seeing me—or, rather, the snacks in my hand—the bear scooted her bum along the floor and waited by the bars like a paunchy, meditating buddha. I sat cross-legged on the cold concrete across from her. In my jumpsuit, it felt like a prison visitation. Raising a furry black arm over her head to clasp the gray iron cross bar on her cage door, Fei Fei shoved her snout against the wire fencing that separated us. I deposited an apple slice in her open mouth. It was difficult to make out the bear's slate-colored eyes within the large black patches. Fei Fei smacked her lips. I gave her a carrot. After just a few minutes of this exchange, I was out of treats. Fei Fei lost interest and abandoned me. "Regardful," indeed. The supervisor then came into the panda house and told me that it was possible to take a photo hugging another panda. I need only pay an additional $160. I passed.

A lunch of pig feet and stewed mushrooms marinated in chili oil awaited us at the canteen. Volunteers were embracing and sobbing, having lived out their dream of hugging a panda. A young German woman buried her face in her boyfriend's chest and cried, overwhelmed by emotion. The pandas clearly had a powerful effect on people.

I departed Dujiangyan that afternoon with the distinct impression that the panda was unlikely to go extinct any time soon—no matter how small the wild population. The panda marked a radical shift from the bears I'd encountered in the Andes and India. It didn't exist in the periphery of the mind, like the spectacled bear, and it wasn't feared like the sloth bear. The panda was universally beloved. Whole economies were invested in the animal's continued existence—the panda's "global cultural value" is estimated to generate $709 million every year. I myself was a good deal poorer than when I had arrived at the panda base that morning, even without splurging on a bear hug. I'd shelled out 700 renminbi (RMB), or $120, just to cater to the pandas' every need. Even beyond the monetary manifestations of the panda's power, its continued survival serves as a beacon of hope for all other species threatened with extinction.

THE PANDA HAS UNDENIABLY REACHED a cultural zenith, both within China's borders and around the world. In a recent Beijing Institute of Culture Innovation and Communication survey of cultural icons—which included Confucius, kung fu, and green tea—the panda was found to be the most widely regarded symbol of Chinese culture outside the country. The World Wildlife Fund (WWF) adopted the animal as its symbol in 1961, with Sir Peter Scott, a prominent conservationist who drew the first iconic panda logo, noting, "We wanted an animal that is beautiful, endangered, and loved by many people in the world for its appealing qualities." And far more money and time has been spent on sparing the giant panda from extinction than on any other animal.

Yet for all the panda's modern prominence, the black-and-white animal was largely an afterthought among China's citizenry until the twentieth century. "Traditionally, the panda is kind of a useless animal," Wang Dajun, a panda expert at Peking University, told me. "Lots of people didn't even realize the panda existed in some areas." In the Qinling Mountains, he said, the panda wasn't discovered until the 1960s. "People knew there were pandas in Sichuan, but they didn't know there were pandas in nearby Shaanxi." Wang, who grew up in southern China, recalled that when he traveled around the province in the 1990s and asked locals about their experiences with pandas, they told him he had come to the wrong place. " 'Go to Sichuan. We don't have pandas here,' they would say. People didn't care about the panda because the panda was no harm to them." The bear's docile nature made it forgettable.

China may have invented paper, but there were few renderings of the panda in antiquity. When the Chinese zodiac was created more than two thousand years ago, the panda was embarrassingly excluded—even a rat and imaginary dragon made the list. However, the panda does show up elsewhere. Empress Dowager Bo, an imperial concubine who died in 155 BCE, was found to have been buried with a panda skull when her tomb was exhumed more than two thousand years later. And the *Shan Hai Jing*, a classical text dating back to the third century BCE, explores the mythical geography and fantastical beasts of pre-Qin China, describing over 550 mountains. It also mentions a creature living in the Qionglai Mountains with striking similarities to the modern panda. Others called this animal "Mo" and claimed it ate copper and iron. In ancient times, rural villagers told horrifying stories of metal-eating monsters descending from the mountains to scavenge utensils, iron, and copper. Sichuan tribes believed that drinking the panda's pungent urine would dissolve a swallowed needle. Still, according to Wang, people rarely targeted the panda for traditional medicine, although hunters did sometimes kill the animal for its pelt—sleeping on the animal's coarse fur was rumored to ward off evil spirits and foretell the future. It was also through hunting that the West came to know the panda.

In March 1869, Père Armand David, a French Lazarist missionary, was traveling through Baoxing County in central Sichuan when a local landowner invited him over for tea and sweets on his way to church. In the quaint abode of Mr. Li, Père David noticed a woolly black-and-white skin. Mr. Li told him he would see the animal very soon, as hunters were heading out to kill another one again tomorrow. Twelve days later, Père David wrote in his journal that he had received a young, freshly killed panda. At the start of April, the hunters returned with a supine adult. "Must be a new species of *Ursus*, very remarkable not only because of its color, but also for its paws which are hairy underneath, and for other characters," Père David wrote. He proposed the name *Ursus melanoleucus*, meaning black-and-white bear.

European scientific institutions had already received word of the seven other bear species by the time they heard about the panda. The sloth bear entered the books in 1791, and the moon bear, sun bear, and spectacled bear were all described by 1825. Père David's account completed the bear family tree as we know it. Yet the panda remained an obscure animal for the next sixty years, far from the international celebrity of today. After Père David's visit to Mr. Li's home, decades passed without Westerners spotting another specimen. "[The panda] came to be considered a fabulous animal like the unicorn or the Chinese dragon," the *New York Times* reported in 1936.

That same year, a New York City dress designer and socialite named Ruth Harkness arrived in Shanghai, determined to fulfill her late husband's dying wish—to be the first person to capture a live giant panda.

Financed by her husband's dwindling wealth, Harkness formed an expedition team in hopes of getting her hands on one of the world's rarest animals. She hired Quentin Young, a handsome Chinese youth who spoke fluent English. As Vicki Constantine Croke wrote in *The Lady and the Panda*, chronicling Harkness's adventure: "She had, of course, her sex going against her, and a lack of experience. Young was not so green, but he was Chinese, and barely past his teens. They were both so far outside the elite inner circle of wealthy, well-known adventurers that their 'much hooted-at expedition' in the words of *The New York Times*, wasn't even worthy of the kind of interest these gentlemen took in one another's business."

Harkness was not deterred by such perceived shortcomings. From Shanghai, she and Young—whom she later took as a lover—traveled to Sichuan and hiked into the fog-hugged mountains in search of the giant panda. Her account of how, exactly, she came to possess a panda cub is obscure. Perhaps deliberately so. On November 9, Harkness and Young were accompanied by four other men on an early-morning hike in the forest. They had hoped to check a wire noose snare they'd tied to a sapling. "The visibility was poor—less than three feet," wrote Croke of the journey through a bamboo thicket. "There was a shout from ahead, then the sound of a musket firing. Confusion. Young was yelling in Chinese when Harkness found her way to him. She gasped, 'What is it?' 'Beishung,' Young replied."

Harkness and Young would become surrogate parents to this baby panda. The debonair heiress named the two-month-old male bear "Su Lin," meaning "a little bit of something very cute," and loaded the whimpering cub into a wicker basket for transport around China. She fed Su Lin prune juice, milk, cod liver oil, Gerber's vegetable soup, and oatmeal with nary a splintered bamboo shoot in sight.

Harkness was beaming when she returned to Shanghai by plane. *The China Press* announced:

> The futile search conducted during the past half century by
> scientists, and explorers, for a live giant panda, exported to be
> the rarest, most elusive and high-priced animal of the world,

was being crowned with success in Shanghai this morning when a five-week old specimen, carrying the distinction of being the first of its kind ever to be held in captivity, left here for the United States on board the *Empress of Russia*.

Getting the panda cub out of China would prove a more formidable matter than getting the bear out of the wild. Harkness had neglected to obtain scientific permits for her expedition, nor had she applied for an export permit. On the day she was supposed to embark for America on the *Empress of Russia*, Chinese custom officials detained Harkness and Su Lin. Hushed negotiations occurred in private rooms. Money likely changed hands. A few days later, Harkness—against all odds—was authorized to return to the United States with the bear. She boarded a steamship with the panda tucked into a basket and a voucher that read: "One dog, $20.00."

Su Lin was an instant sensation when he arrived in America. No one had ever seen anything like the adorable animal. Harkness, draped in luxurious otter furs, touted the mewling cub around New York and Chicago, posing in front of flashing camera bulbs and gabbing to the press about her good fortune, the bravery of Young, and her next expedition to catch more pandas. On April 20, 1937, Su Lin debuted at Chicago's Brookfield Zoo. Within the first three months, more than three hundred thousand people visited his exhibit. Even Shirley Temple, Eleanor Roosevelt, and Helen Keller stopped by to greet Su Lin.

The nation was in the grips of a black-and-white fervor that could not be sated by just one bear. It didn't take long for a panda rivalry to develop between zoos. Scientific directors commissioned more expeditions to obtain more bears. In the decade that followed Su Lin's debut, fourteen pandas were taken out of China for private exhibition. Many more were killed by American trophy hunters. By 1946, China was fed up; the government banned the lawless exploitation of its beloved bear by foreigners, signaling a new era of panda relations with the outside world.

Su Lin died of pneumonia in 1938—less than two years after he'd been stolen from the bamboo forests of Sichuan. Today, his body resides in a glass display case in Chicago's Field Museum of Natural History, where he still draws curious onlookers. But his legacy extends far beyond that of a zoo animal: his story lives on in every viral panda video, panda plushie, and captive-bred panda. As the first of his species to travel across the world, Su Lin became something much larger than an ursine trophy: he sparked a cultural revolution.

ʞ

PANDAS REACHED THE UPPER ECHELON of Chinese society in the latter half of the century. Party officials were forced to reckon with the fact that the animal was one of the few things the country had going for it when it came to trading in cultural power. The United States had convertibles cruising down the palm-lined Hollywood Boulevard, the NBA, and pepperoni pizza. China had a noticeable dearth of sparrows. When foreign delegates arrived in Beijing, it wasn't the Great Wall they longed to see. It was the panda. But without government succor, the bear—and its associated cultural clout—were doomed to disappear.

Despite China's ban on foreign hunters and the export of live pandas in the 1940s, deforestation had continued to drive the panda's numbers down. So, in the 1960s, Mao Zedong's party created four wild panda reserves and banned all Chinese hunting of the bear. Anyone caught poaching a panda faced jail time or, under grave circumstances, the death penalty. In 1993, two men were handed death sentences in a South China court for trafficking three panda pelts. A few years later, a farmer in Southwest China was sentenced to twenty years in prison for killing giant pandas and selling their pelts. (In 2017, China changed the maximum penalty for panda poaching and smuggling to "not less than 10 years or life imprisonment and a forfeiture of property.")

Mao's early efforts did little to stem the population's decline. Wildlife biologists criticized the reserves as little more than paper parks— outlined in official documents but receiving little protection and enforcement on the ground. And hunting had never been the key threat to pandas.

In the decades that followed, the central government approved new wildlife laws to safeguard the bear and ramped up efforts in the field, using ironfisted yet sometimes ham-handed tactics to save the species. A restrictive diet of bamboo is considered risky because the plant dies shortly after it flowers. Most bamboo species will only flower once in their life cycle—as long as sixty years—but when they do, some bears will starve to death. During the 1970s and 1980s, there were *two* mass flowering events in western China. Vast acreages of arrow bamboo withered. Scientists found the bodies of 138 pandas in Sichuan's Min Mountains, and another 141 pandas died in the Qionglai Mountains. Pandas should have been able to survive the bamboo die-offs by moving to more productive habitat. But with millions of humans then living in the lower elevations, the bears had nowhere to go. It's believed up to 80 percent of pandas were lost in the worst-affected areas during this period. In response, government officers headed into the mountains to rescue starving pandas. Every bear they found was taken into captivity. When they had recovered, some of the bears were returned to the wild. Others, deemed too old or too weak, were kept at the captive base in Wolong. Among those "rescued" were more than thirty lone cubs taken under the mistaken belief that the bears' mothers had abandoned them or died. Wildlife biologists didn't then know that it was typical panda mom behavior to leave young cubs behind in trees for four to eight hours while they foraged elsewhere. (The longest separation ever documented was fifty-two hours.) The government's well-intentioned rescue mission was, in effect, a mass kidnapping.

Indeed, authorities knew very little about the panda in general. Biologists weren't even certain that it was a bear. Père David's astute observation that the animal seemed to belong to *Ursus* didn't carry much weight within the cautious scientific community. They remained perplexed by the panda's odd behavior. The animal didn't hibernate. And it bleated rather than roared. In consideration of the panda's smudged eye patches, they proposed that the animal *might* belong to the raccoon family. The Chinese were similarly confused. In Mandarin, *xiong mao*—the word for panda—translates to "bear cat." It wasn't until the 1980s, following robust molecular testing, that scientists finally reached a consensus: the giant panda was very much a bear.

One of the greatest advancements in our understanding of panda biology and the species' conservation arguably came about when China acquiesced to a visit from George Schaller, a scientific emissary with WWF. Schaller would be the first Western scientist to conduct field-work in the country. In 1978, China had announced its Four Modern-izations program, focused on agriculture, industry, defense, and science. "Pragmatism had won out over the country's desire for seclusion," wrote Schaller of the decision. "Wrapped in a pride based on centuries of glory, the Chinese had long avoided what they saw as the crude cultures surrounding them; but now they needed technology." On May 15, 1980, Schaller hiked into a forest inhabited by pandas for the first time. It would not be his last.

Schaller's research forms the basis of what the West knows about the giant panda today. The biologist would go on to spend nearly five years in China, primarily at the Wolong Nature Reserve and Tangji-ahe Nature Reserve in Sichuan. He studied the ecological conditions needed for pandas to thrive. He made notes on what part of the bamboo the pandas ate and how it changed with the passing of each season. He analyzed the nutritional content of bamboo in the lab. And he marveled at the great bear lumbering through the fir and birch forests, along ridge lines that curled like a dragon's tail. In *The Last Panda*, he wrote:

> Having transcended its mountain home to become a citizen of the world, the panda is a symbolic creature that represents our efforts to protect the environment. Though dumpy and bearlike, it has been patterned with such creative flourish, such artistic perfection, that it almost seems to have evolved for this higher purpose. . . . And it is rare. Survivors are some-how more poignant than casualties. Together, these and other traits have created a species in which legend and reality merge, a mythic creature in the act of life.

Schaller left the panda project in 1985. Four years after his depar-ture, surveys by WWF and China's Ministry of Forestry revealed that the size of panda habitat in Sichuan had fallen by nearly half since 1974. The grave statistic barely registered in international media. For around that time, thousands of troops from the People's Liberation Army were descending on Tiananmen Square.

*

SICHUAN'S WILD PANDAS MAY HAVE BEEN few and far between, but the urban panda was evidently thriving. Pandas were ubiquitous as I strolled through the capital city of Chengdu. Delightfully cartoonish black-and-white faces, with big eyes and jittery grins, plastered the sides of buses. Pixelated bears waved from LED billboards. Statues pirouetted in faunal whimsy. And a 26,000-pound, 49-foot-tall panda sculpture dangled, like King Kong, off the edge of a building in Chengdu's International Finance Square. In the shops of Kuanzhai Alley, a series of wide and narrow streets modeled after the traditional towns of the Qing dynasty, vendors sold stuffed panda toys and panda stationery. Among the tongue-numbing peppercorns and everything-on-a-stick delicacies, food carts peddled bao buns with frosted panda faces, their ursine features slowly melting under the Sichuan sun.

Surveillance cameras dangled off street lights as I later rode in a taxi through the labyrinth of overpasses and underpasses toward the Chengdu Research Base of Giant Panda Breeding, located about thirty minutes by cab from the city's core. Nearly every car on the road seemed to be no more than ten years old. At each intersection, a highly organized fleet of men and women scuttled leaves into dustbins with bamboo brooms. A month earlier the National People's Congress had abolished the presidential term limit, effectively instating President Xi Jinping in power for life. The Chinese barely blinked. As long as the money kept flowing, it seemed unlikely that Xi would lose support. Plus, criticism of the Chinese Communist Party was largely censored. For example, after Xi Jinping was photographed looking a little pudgy next to a lean Barack Obama in 2013, Internet memes drew snide comparisons between Xi and Winnie-the-Pooh. In response, government censors blocked all Pooh memes and the government banned the release of the *Christopher Robin* movie in China. (Suffice to say, China's panda love does not extend to fictional bears.) Officials labeled such jabs as a "serious effort to undermine the dignity of the presidential office and Xi himself." Oh, bother.

Although China banned the foreign exploitation of pandas long ago, the Su Lin hysteria never fully waned and pandas remained a coveted species both within and beyond the country's borders well into the latter half of the twentieth century. With few bears remaining in the wild, the central government turned to scientific innovation to capitalize on the panda's political power. In 1987, they established the Chengdu panda base with just six pandas—three males and three females.

More than 190 bears lived there when I visited. Despite its scientific-sounding name, the government-funded research base appeared more like a theme park than a laboratory on first approach. A large cement pavilion led up to turnstile gates and a ticket office ensconced in a huge, arching panda sculpture built out of white metal and bamboo poles. Baby panda videos looped on a large monitor. A crowd of domestic tourists watched in awe.

It's nearly impossible for Western journalists to speak with Chinese government scientists, especially on the topic of panda breeding, and so it took the better half of a year for me to orchestrate an interview with the man who has led China's panda breeding efforts for almost four decades. Zhang Hemin is the director of the China Conservation and Research Center for Giant Pandas (CCRCGP), which oversees the Wolong, Dujiangyan, and Bifengxia panda bases. In China, he's known simply as Papa Panda.

Zhang graduated from Sichuan University with a degree in wildlife biology in 1983—the same year as the second arrow bamboo die-off—and was immediately hired by the CCRCGP to work at Wolong, where he would later collaborate with George Schaller and a handful of other Chinese scientists to study the small panda population that lived in the reserve. The government was keen to learn more about basic panda biology following the starvation deaths in the Min and Qionglai Mountains (Zhang was also one of the rescuers). They also hoped to determine if artificial reproduction might be feasible to conserve the imperiled species. So, Zhang and his colleagues began some of the first research on the captive breeding of pandas, aspiring to revolutionize panda copulation in China.

In the beginning, Zhang said, the scientists working at Wolong knew very little about panda reproduction. When did the female bears enter estrus, the period when animals are sexually receptive? Why did a female choose to mate with one male and not another? And how did panda moms keep their pathetically minuscule cubs alive? Early captive breeding efforts were a profound disappointment. Between 1983 and 1990, "there was almost no success," Zhang said. The bears at Wolong didn't show much of an interest in anything other than eating and sleeping. Anxiety plagued Zhang. What if these bears—all rescued from the wild—didn't even know *how* to fornicate in captivity? Out in nature, roaming pandas cue into the scent marking and mating calls of their peers. They build dynamic social relationships, perhaps even flirtations, before doing the deed. There was none of that here. The research base was overwhelmingly sterile and its pandas chaste. It would be up to Zhang and his colleagues to teach the bears about the birds and the bees.

The scientists began by setting up a series of panda meet-cutes. Pandas were transferred from solitary dens into an enclosure with the opposite sex in hopes they would grow accustomed to one another's heady pheromones. When this strategy failed, they screened panda pornography and administered herbal remedies to bolster the bears' libido. "We used Chinese Lion Pills and even Viagra," Zhang explained. Still, nothing. Zhang, trying everything he could think of, eventually patronized an adult toy shop in Chengdu to purchase a female genital stimulator for the pandas. Despite his noble efforts, the pandas remained stubbornly abstinent. The females were barren. No fuzzy, tumbling cubs brought cheer to the center's empty enclosures.

To crack the code on captive breeding, there were three problems that Zhang and his team needed to address. The first was to figure out when and why a female goes into estrus. Only a quarter of their captive pandas at Wolong were going into heat. Second, only a quarter of those pandas would actually become pregnant. And slightly less than a third of the pandas born in captivity survived. "It took us fifteen years to completely solve these problems," Zhang said. Their research later revealed that a female panda's fertility window is incredibly narrow, lasting a maximum of seventy-two hours once per year. A male panda therefore needs to mount a female with striking precision to achieve reproductive success.

The scientists decided that as a female neared spring estrus, a dedicated team of panda doulas would monitor the bear's urine samples to confirm when she had reached optimal hormone levels for insemination. Then the team would spring into action. If the female panda showed attraction toward a genetically distant male, they would let the pandas get down to business naturally. But if she was lusting after a male who was too similar genetically, the team would intervene. The female would be sedated and taken to see a fertility specialist who would plunge a syringe full of harvested panda semen into the female. Artificial insemination is critical for ensuring a high level of genetic diversity in captive populations. These tactics solved the second problem of conception.

Once the female was successfully impregnated (hard to confirm because fetal pandas are almost microscopic on ultrasounds), it was up to Zhang to finish the job. Until 2002, Zhang was present for every single birth at Wolong. Like clockwork, the panda's water would break, Zhang would rush to the laboring bear's side, and within two hours she would give birth to one or two little cubs. But later, after he was promoted to director and the pandas had become more fecund, it was impossible for him to be present at every birth. "One time when I was on a business trip far away and I heard that the panda's water broke, I immediately started to head back because I still wanted to assist with a twin birth." But the panda wasn't progressing. Staff were worried she would die. He finally arrived sixteen hours later, and "as soon as I entered the delivery room, the infant pandas were born." This, he noted, continued to happen with surprising frequency. Pregnant pandas would wait hours until Zhang showed up, at which point they gave one big push and out popped the cub. "People thought this was strange and they started to say, 'Are you the panda's father?'" This was how he earned the nickname "Papa Panda."

Today, the Chengdu panda base—full of roly-poly cubs—is one of China's most popular tourist attractions. Around nine million visitors—half that of Disneyland—pass through its gates every year. When I visited it was almost China's *Láodòng jié*, Labor Day, and the base was packed with panda-festooned vacationers. Inside, open-air shuttles—

panda themed with black circles painted around the headlights—moved the tourists through bamboo tunnels between three adult and subadult giant panda enclosures. I chose to walk instead, eagerly pushing through blue ponchos as rain pounded the pavement.

The panda base featured a museum, a cinema, two lesser panda enclosures, a nursery, a research center, a panda hospital, and a restaurant. After grabbing coffee at the restaurant, where a large portrait of Steve Jobs with a panda eating an apple hung next to the espresso machine, I headed to the Moon Nursery. A group of pandas is called an "embarrassment" and for good reason. Inside the large exhibit, nine cubs were somersaulting off bamboo platforms and tripping over their own feet, barely able to move on their own without some sort of misfortune befalling them. The panda paparazzi, the legions of tourists double-fisting iPhones and Nikons, clamored for a closer look behind the glass. One cub waddled by and instantly collapsed on his dozing friend in yet another charming display of ineptitude. A chorus of "aww" floated up from the crowd—universal in any language. Shutters snapped.

Why are humans predisposed to find pandas so cute? In 1987, the *New York Times* posed this question to Edgar E. Coons, a behavioral neuroscientist at New York University. He theorized that the allure of pandas is driven by "hedonic mechanisms." We're delighted by the big black patches that make the panda's small eyes appear ten times larger. (The patches are actually part of the bear's defensive camouflage meant to trick predators, not lure in cooing primates.) This combination of big eyes, a snub nose, large head on a tiny body, and clumsy gait, he said, reminds us of a human toddler.

So . . . evolution is the answer. We're besotted with pandas because we're programmed to be besotted with children to ensure the survival of our species—an overlap in the brain's wiring. (Panda love is merely an unintentional consequence of our own self-absorption.) Lucky for the panda, this means that we're almost as invested in the future of its species as we are in our own.

The skies had cleared by the time I exited the nursery and headed to the Sunshine Delivery House, where the newborns lived. This was the base's most popular attraction, and a long line snaked around the building. Spring is typically the panda mating—and inseminating—season, with babies born during the late summer and early fall. But the delivery house nurses did have one young panda in their care in the maternity ward. Here, behind the plexiglass, a baby—maybe two months old—had fallen asleep against the window ledge instead of in his crib. The nameless panda's eyes were firmly shut, and it had only a thin layer of peach fuzz over its pink skin. As newborns, the bears are hairless and the size of a pear. If fed a steady diet of bamboo, they'll grow nine hundred times larger. Pandas, I learned, are actually born at a developmental stage considered premature in all other mammal species. Pushed out at around 135 days, the bears are effectively exiting the womb in the equivalent of the third trimester. This leaves newborns especially vulnerable in the hours after their birth and constitutes the third problem of Zhang Hemin's initial quagmire: keeping the cubs alive.

Half of all panda cubs are twins. But the mother can usually only manage to keep one alive. In the wild, she leaves the weaker one to die. "The greatest thing about the panda mother is that, within the first twenty-four hours, she will do everything possible to keep the cubs alive, but after that she is exhausted," Zhang explained, "so she decides to take only one and abandon the other." At Wolong, scientists were horrified to discover that so many cubs were being left to fend for themselves at just a day old. It took Zhang and his colleagues "a lot of energy" to figure out how to solve this problem. Eventually, they found that by bolstering the baby's immune system and learning how to raise the cubs themselves, they could keep both bears alive. Now, captive cubs are secretly swapped out during a set rotation and cared for by human staff before they're returned to the mother, who is none the wiser.

Panda breeding has come a long way since the fumbling attempts of the 1980s. Since it opened, more than two hundred bears have been born at the Chengdu base. In Wolong, the captive panda population has increased from just eight bears to 330—the largest embarrassment of pandas in the world. China's breeding program, once regarded as a moonshot, is now lauded as a clear success, with pandas considered one of the most genetically diverse endangered species in captivity. Yet few captive-born pandas have ever set paw outside the manufactured world. As of 2021, just twelve captive-bred bears have been released to the wild. Twelve bears amount to a mere 2 percent of the captive population. Where, I wondered, had all the other bears gone?

ON A BLUSTERY APRIL DAY, Queen Margrethe of Denmark arrived at the Copenhagen Zoo. She was smartly dressed in a white ankle-length wool coat with black heeled loafers and black leather gloves. For good measure, she'd added a pair of black-and-white earrings. A red velvet rope separated her from the jostling crowd of onlookers dressed in panda onesies. A few dissenters waved Tibetan flags in protest declaring that "China fails human rights." They hardly distracted anyone from such a momentous occasion. Tossing aside the rope with an awkward flourish, Queen Margrethe made her announcement: "Congratulations to all of us. We now have two pandas in a fabulous enclosure that we can look at for many, many years." Preceding the day's celebration, the Danish Parliament had—*by sheer coincidence*—passed a memorandum recognizing China's sovereignty over Tibet.

Xing Er and Mao Sun, shipped from the Chengdu Research Base of Giant Panda Breeding, would soon make their much-anticipated debut. Their round grassy enclosure, shaped like the yin and yang symbol, cost the Danish government a cool $24 million. The panda rental would add another $1 million per year to the bill. (Giant pandas are the world's most expensive animal to keep in captivity due, in part, to their specialized diet.) Danish critics lambasted the cost of the swirling panda pen and rental fee. In response, Bengt Holst, the zoo's scientific director, justified the price tag to the *New York Times*, stating, "For such an iconic animal, we need an iconic setting. You wouldn't put the Mona Lisa in an ugly frame."

Confronting an increasing accumulation of cubs in captivity and a desire to propagate soft power, China routinely dispatches panda delegates around the world. To date, the Middle Kingdom has shipped bears to more than two dozen zoos in twenty-three countries. In the last decade, Finland received two bears, ostensibly to mark the one-hundredth anniversary of its independence, though the panda loan coincided with a state visit by Xi Jinping, during which Finland signed a stack of investment agreements. Ahead of the G20 Summit, Berlin's Tierpark Zoo received two adult pandas. Scotland accepted a pair of pandas seemingly in return for trading offshore drilling technology and salmon with China. And Australia, France, and Canada all received loaner pandas after agreeing to sell uranium to China.

Among experts who study Sino relations, such ursine bribery is known as "panda diplomacy." China prefers the term "friendship envoys." The country has long struggled to amass soft power, the capacity to attract and co-opt allies through cultural influence rather than coerce them with brute force. Unlike the panda, China isn't viewed as warm and cuddly. A string of controversies on the world stage—from Uyghur camps to Hong Kong—have tarred the country's social reputation in the West. The panda, accordingly, is China's greatest tool in its quest for cultural domination, with more than seventy bears dispatched from mainland China.

The origins of panda diplomacy can be traced back to 685 CE, when Empress Wu Zetian of the Tang dynasty presented a panda duo as a gift to Japan. Centuries later, in 1941, the wife of Chinese general Chiang Kai-shek bestowed two black-and-white bears upon the Bronx Zoo— one of the key rivals at the Su Lin auction—in thanks for America's wartime aid in fighting the Japanese.

When Mao came to power, he kick-started a new era of panda diplomacy, using the bears to broker strategic relationships, first with Soviet Union president Nikita Khrushchev in 1965, then with Kim Il-sung of North Korea. Chairman Mao soon set his sights beyond communist nations. Following US president Richard Nixon's state visit to Beijing, Mao sent two pandas to the National Zoo in Washington, DC. Nixon returned the favor by shipping two musk oxen to China. (It's the thought that counts.)

From 1957 to 1983, China dispatched two dozen pandas to nine nations—free of charge. But when Deng Xiaoping took over the Chinese Communist Party in 1978, he embraced the capitalist ideologies Mao had rebuffed. Deng did away with panda freebies. If foreign powers wanted pandas, they could pay for them. Gifts, henceforth, became loans; friendly countries were offered panda rentals for six-figure sums, plus a cut of panda merchandise sales. A series of lucrative deals were shored up with Western zoos. Growth in the panda sector, however, was hindered by the fact that China still had relatively few bears to give out. Captive breeding changed that.

Not everyone was happy about the panda—a living creature—being used as a political bargaining chip. Facing pushback from conservation scientists and new guidelines under the Convention on International Trade in Endangered Species (CITES), USFWS banned the short-term import of pandas for commercial purposes in the early 1990s. American zoos could only obtain pandas through special loan permits under the guise of research purposes. The WWF later sued USFWS for its lax panda oversight, and in 1998, the service announced a new policy requiring China to put more than half of panda rental fees toward the conservation of wild pandas if the bears were to travel to America. (After the Sichuan earthquake, China used some of the panda loan money to help repair the damaged Wolong panda base.)

Scholars believe that China has since entered a third stage of panda diplomacy, as the Asian nation now boasts the world's second-largest economy and second-largest defense budget. Kathleen Buckingham and Paul Jepson, under the auspices of a University of Oxford study, argue that in Xi Jinping's version of panda diplomacy, China grants panda loans to nations that supply it with valuable resources and technology to build *guanxi*, or "deep trade relationships characterized by trust, reciprocity, loyalty, and longevity."

Pandas are also used to reprimand countries when they behave badly. China giveth the panda, China taketh away the panda. In 2010, days after China warned President Obama against meeting with the Dalai Lama, the pandas at the Zoo Atlanta and Tai Shan at the National Zoo were repatriated to China. Every panda loan agreement stipulates that all the biological material from a panda—fur, semen, blood, and cubs—remain the property of China. The Middle Kingdom can call the bears home whenever it wants.

In part, because of its diplomatic ties, breeding pandas remains a contentious topic among scientists. "I'm not a big fan of captive breeding," Wang Dajun at Peking University had told me. "I don't think that's key for panda conservation. We must protect habitat and the forest for the pandas. Then they will do well." George Schaller, too, has been a vocal critic of keeping pandas in captivity ever since his days at Wolong, where he often butted heads with a young Zhang Hemin. As he wrote in his book, Schaller believed that the research center could become nothing more than a "home for the living dead," and he felt he "had been unable to develop among my Chinese colleagues a feeling for the major goal of our joint venture: the panda must be assured its freedom and survival in the wild."

Now retired, Schaller's views haven't changed much. In a 2013 interview with *National Geographic*, he lambasted China's panda mills, saying China "doesn't need three hundred pandas in captivity—it needs to restock the forests [with pandas] and protect them."

IT WAS SNOWING HEAVILY in the bamboo forests of Longxi-Hongkou National Nature Reserve on a winter's day when two young pandas named Qinxin and Xiao Hetao walked into the wild for the first time. Born at Wolong in 2016, the two-year-old females had been training their entire lives for this moment. Spectators cheered as the radio-collared duo, released from their crates, ran off into the wet snow, eventually disappearing into the white forest.

Under the tutelage of their keepers at the Hetaoping Wilderness Training Base in Wolong, Qinxin—"Heart of Qin"—and Xiao Hetao—"Little Walnut"—had mastered the basic skills of walking, climbing, finding shelter, gathering food, and avoiding danger in a semi-wild environment. Following a health check, the bears were deemed to be in good condition for release into the nature reserve, less than 20 miles from the Dujiangyan panda base. The medical report observed that Qinxin was "naughty, active, and lively" while Xiao Hetao was "gentle, graceful, and pretty." The young bears were only the tenth and eleventh captive-bred pandas to be released into China's wilderness. In 2003, Zhang Hemin began training captive-bred pandas at Wolong to survive in the wild. Since then, the program has expanded rapidly. "Our ultimate goal with captive breeding is to protect wild pandas," Zhang told me, countering the panda diplomacy narrative and perhaps Schaller's criticisms. "It's not to keep pandas in captivity." Pandas live in thirty-three populations across western China, but the majority of them only contain about two dozen individuals each. As such, the bears are badly in need of new genes. "If we do not help these small populations, they may become extinct within thirty years."

Similar to Zhang's early struggles to breed bears, training naive captive-born bears to survive in the wild was an almost insurmountable feat. Xiang Xiang, the first bear Zhang released in 2006, fell off a cliff and died less than a year after he'd been set free. The scientists had raised the young pandas according to human habits. "After this, we began to learn from mother pandas," Zhang explained. The cubs at Hetaoping were now kept with the mother, and while in her care, staff slowly pushed the captive-born cubs toward wild behaviors. Once a year had passed, mom and cub were moved to a large fenced habitat up the mountain slope where the panda mom continued to teach her offspring how to survive in the forest. The pandas learned how to establish their own territory, avoid predators, and find the best bamboo to eat. It was also important that the young pandas didn't get used to human presence if they were going to survive in the wild. "We designed a panda outfit that we wore to look like pandas," Zhang noted. (These black-and-white costumes, scented with panda urine, are veritable nightmare fuel.) Of the eleven captive-bred pandas that have been released since Xiang Xiang, two more have died. One succumbed to a bacterial infection after being attacked by another animal, and another died just forty days after she was set free. Wolong staff believed that she succumbed to the trauma of being caged for several days before release.

Not all pandas passed the test to be released—some never managed to learn the ropes—but Zhang deemed the wild reintroduction program a success. "We have already solved the problem with genetic diversity in a population in the Xiaoxiangling Mountains, and now we are bringing this success to the Min Mountains and releasing pandas at Hongkou. We need to quickly expand this work," he said.

The giant panda reached a milestone in 2016. For the first time since being listed as endangered more than a quarter century ago, the International Union for the Conservation of Nature downgraded the panda's population status from "endangered" to "vulnerable," citing an increase of 17 percent. (The IUCN defines endangered species as those facing a *very* high risk of extinction in the wild. Vulnerable species face a high risk of extinction in the wild.) With nearly two thousand wild individuals, the panda was defying everyone's expectations.

"The recovery of the panda shows that when science, political will and engagement of local communities come together, we can save wildlife and also improve biodiversity," WWF International director general Marco Lambertini said in a press release celebrating the announcement. At a meeting in Beijing, deputy forestry minister Chen Fengxue explained that the population figures had been gleaned from thousands of scientists traversing 10.7 million acres of forest. He attributed the panda boom to successful conservation policies and forest protection. The census found a marked increase over the previous 1998–2002 survey, which recorded just 1,596 individuals. But rarely are statistics originating in China quite so forthright. Some experts questioned the validity of how the government obtained these numbers: Census takers had combed an area almost 72 percent larger than the previous panda count, they said, making it impossible to accurately determine whether the population had grown.

Still, the panda has undoubtedly prospered since Schaller published *The Last Panda* in 1991. Extinction, at that time, was a very real concern. With people like Zhang Hemin, Wang Dajun, and George Schaller on its side, the panda is unlikely to vanish within our lifetime. Even if its numbers have only modestly increased, the panda has managed to persist through a century of tremendous upheaval. The species survived the world's most astounding human population explosion—from 400 million Chinese in 1900 to 1.4 billion people today. Now, human population growth has slowed. People are moving out of the rural areas where the panda lives and into cities.

In 2019, a team of Chinese scientists warned that another large-scale bamboo flowering could occur in the Min Mountains between 2020 and 2030, noting that because more giant pandas now live in small habitats without areas to disperse, "bamboo flowering could be a disaster for them." However, the scientists acknowledged several actions the government could take to head off any population decline. For example, they could expand habitat corridors between protected areas or physically move pandas between nature reserves with healthy bamboo plots. China has established sixty-seven reserves to safeguard panda populations since the 1960s, and nearly all of the panda's habitat will be protected within the next decade. The government is currently creating Giant Panda National Park, which will be ten times the size of Yellowstone when completed. The scientists also highlighted that the government could stage another intervention to rescue starving pandas, either by dropping off food for them or bringing them into "temporary captivity until the bamboo recovers." Even if the bamboo supply is impacted, it's hard to imagine a future where China allows its wild pandas to starve.

Though the panda may be the world's least populous bear by a large margin, I left China with a feeling of hope. The cultural connection between people and pandas seemed to transcend not only our relationship with the other seven bear species, but perhaps with any other wild animal. Indeed, the panda may be the only creature in the animal kingdom that has been spared the worst of human nature. Beloved beasts like tigers, elephants, and rhinos are relentlessly exploited for their skins, tusks, or horns. Not pandas. Nor are they exploited for traditional medicine. And despite their cute and cuddly appearance, they've yet to be abducted into the exotic pet trade. In a largely agnostic society, the panda, it seems, has ascended to be China's greatest cultural deity. And while the bear may not rank among the pig, snake, goat, and monkey in marking the passage of time, in China, every year is the year of the panda.

CHAPTER FOUR

LIQUID GOLD

Moon bear, Vietnam
Ursus thibetanus

The small glass vial was cold to the touch. Its sunny liquid had frozen into sharp crystals, like fossilized amber, and remained motionless when I turned the illicit vessel over in my hands. "If you're tired, then you can mix the bile with alcohol. Then add honey," the woman with long bushy black hair told me. She looked to be in her late fifties. Dark patches of freckles sat under her eyes like heavy bags. A single strand of opulent pearls encircled her squat neck. She looked nothing like how I'd imagined a bear farmer.

"It's good to treat body pain. Bone pain. Good for health in general," the woman continued. I returned the vial—1 cubic centimeter—to the upturned silver lid from a biscuit tin that she was using as a platter. The vial had come in a bundle of ten held together by a rubber band. Each one was individually wrapped in black duct tape bearing a gold foil label in Vietnamese. Fresh Bear Bile. Purity 100 percent. A little black bear logo was stamped above the text. The woman sensed another sales opportunity. "Do you know honey? Do you want to buy honey, too?" she implored. I demurred. My translator, whom I'll call Anh Tran, interjected. "Can we see the bears?"

I had met Tran in one of Hanoi's newer neighborhoods, on the outskirts of the vibrant Vietnamese city. Locals knew it as Koreatown for its large population of migrants packed into skyscrapers between fried chicken restaurants. Tran grew up in Vietnam, but she'd lived in Ohio as a Fulbright Scholar studying international relations, and her English, as a result, was impeccable. A colleague had worked with Tran and a Vietnamese investigative journalist, tracking the movement of rhino horn and elephant ivory in the country, as well as bear bile. Tran, she assured me, would be able to connect me with the bear farmers. The Vietnamese journalist reported under a different name now, Tran had told me that morning as we climbed into a large beige sedan with leather seats. "He was attacked and his writing hands were badly beaten. Everyone knows who he is and no one trusts him now." Instead, we would be working with a man who had already arranged a meeting with a farmer in a district north of Hanoi. But he, too, was scared. He met with us just long enough for me to slip him 2.3 million Vietnamese dong, equivalent to 100 US dollars, through the rolled-down car window before Tran and I departed for the community of Son Loc in the district of Phuc Tho.

In the back seat, Tran applied dark brown eyeliner and red lipstick to her bare face. She wore a skin-tight scarlet dress and knee-high black boots with a stiletto heel. A matching red headband held her shoulder-length hair in place. I'd strategically worn a Tibetan shawl over my shirt to conceal the bulge of a recorder hidden underneath. Tran had insisted I pose as a foreign investor interested in the bear bile market. It was too risky to travel outwardly as a journalist. Plus, no one would speak to us. "Don't expect it to be like before," she told me sharply. "Things have changed. It's less open now."

It was cold and damp outside Hanoi. Promises of rain moored gray clouds. We passed dozens of nurseries growing ornamental shrubs, phở bo stands, and vendors selling sữa, a sweetened condensed milk. The villages in Vietnam were often known by their most prominent wares. There was Tho Ha, the village where spindly rice noodles hung from balconies to bask in the sun. Women gnarled their once-nimble fingers against weaves in Phu Vinh, crafting elaborate rattan and bamboo bags. And hundreds of gardeners tended to blooming roses in the flower village of Sa Dec. However, the villages of Phuc Tho District, about 20 miles northwest of Hanoi, were best known for the bile secretions of their imprisoned Asiatic black bears.

Our first stop was a farm in Son Loc that Tran had been to a few years before. The small plot of land in the center of town contained no fields or stables, but rather a skinny two-story building painted yellow and blue. Because the government had once taxed residents based on the width of their homes, many of the houses in Vietnam were tall and narrow. Locals called them "tube houses." A sun-faded sign featuring a large grazing grizzly bear hung above the building's gold-framed glass doors. A phone number and the Vietnamese word for bear, *Gấu*, were scrawled below. Tran chuckled darkly. She translated the rest of the text on the sign: "For the Conservation of the Bear."

The dusty red-tiled sidewalk continued into the entryway of the house, where we were coolly greeted by the bushy-haired woman. She surveyed us through cautious eyes, no doubt wondering why a foreigner was so interested in bear bile. Still, she sat us at a round wooden table in the front room and fetched a green plastic jug of hot tea. The room was sparsely decorated. A patchy mounted deer head hung over the doorway. There was also a large photo of elephants with a smaller snapshot tucked into the edge of the frame—a military friend of the woman's husband shaking hands with Bill and Hillary Clinton during their 2000 visit to Vietnam.

Tran fiddled nervously with the clasp on her leather purse as we sipped our tea. She asked about the sign out front. "The sign shows that we keep bears, not that we are selling bear's bile," the woman replied smartly. She had likely uttered this line a dozen times before. "Keeping bears is totally okay." Only, she continued, the bears were not here as they had been when Tran last visited the woman's husband. They were now kept at her in-laws' house in the next village over, where hired help attended to the animals. "I'm old and weak. I can't raise much more bears."

I whispered my questions in English to Tran, who translated them for the farmer. "How many bears do you have now?"

"Six bears."

"All of them in one place?"

"Yes."

"How long have you had them for?"

"Quite a while," the woman replied imperviously.

Tran was frustrated with her vague answers. She pressed on, shooting questions in rapid-fire succession, hoping for a slipup.

"How many years has it been?"

"A few years."

"Ten years?"

"Yes. Ten years."

"Where do you buy these bears from?"

"Here and there."

Tran repeated the question. The woman doubled down. I doubted whether this method of interrogation would endear us to the farmer. Yet when Tran inquired about bile prices, the woman swiftly abandoned her cover story, trundling off to a back room. She returned with the silver tray of frozen bear bile. Each vial sold for between 25,000 and 50,000 dong, between $1 and $2, depending on purity. "It was expensive before, around 70,000 dong. Sometimes even 150,000. It was very competitive," she said morosely. Demand was decreasing. Only locals were buying from her. "We are poor now."

Tran asked about all the business signs she had seen promoting bear bile on her last trip here. "Where are they?"

"Gone. And Phuc Tho's people hide the bears away now."

The bear farmer wasn't going to divulge much more. We stood up to leave and the woman suddenly rushed at me, clutching my sides firmly. I shot an anxious glance at Tran. The world of wildlife trafficking was a dangerous place. But rather than drag me into some sketchy enclave, the bear farmer guided me over toward a full-length mirror where she launched into open-mouthed laughter at our reflection.

"She thinks you're very tall," said Tran with a tight smile. The stout woman's head didn't even crest my shoulder. I smiled too, hoping this could be a crack in the old woman's armor. Tran took the same cue. She asked once more to see the animals.

"I can't show you the bears."

BEAR BILE HAS BEEN USED in traditional medicine for thousands of years. First described in a Chinese pharmacopeia in 659 CE, the honey-eyed substance slowly trickled across Asia, finding keen buyers in Korea and Japan. Healers prescribed bear bile for a wide range of ailments—colds, cancer, even hangovers. Some people rubbed it into their leathery skin to soothe stiff knee joints and aching backs. Others ingested it, like the farmer had told me, mixed with a small amount of rice wine.

Bear bile is no snake oil cure. Unlike rhino horn, tiger penis, and pangolin scales, which have no proven benefits to human health, medical scientists have found that ursodeoxycholic acid—the active molecule found in bile—*can* reduce inflammation and lower cholesterol. (Snake oil, for that matter, is no snake oil either. The oil collected from the Chinese water snake is rich in omega-3 acids—a legitimate treatment for arthritis.) The US Food and Drug Administration has even approved ursodeoxycholic acid for the treatment of certain liver diseases, and in preclinical trials, the molecule was found to slow the progress of neurodegenerative diseases, including Parkinson's, Huntington's, and Alzheimer's, and holds promise for other conditions, such as Lou Gehrig's disease. "It protects the brain cells, kidney cells, heart cells, lung cells, and the list goes on," said Clifford Steer, director of the molecular gastroenterology program at the University of Minnesota Medical School.

It's not just bears that produce ursodeoxycholic acid, despite the Latin root *urso*. However, bears are the only animals that produce useful quantities of it. In humans, ursodeoxycholic acid is between just 1 and 5 percent of the bile supply. Our bodies utilize bile—produced by the liver and stored in the gallbladder—to aid in digestion and break down fats. In bears, ursodeoxycholic acid staves off programmed cell death—a process known as apoptosis—during long periods of inactivity, such as hibernation. In some bear species, ursodeoxycholic acid makes up nearly 40 percent of the bile pool. "If you or I hibernated for six months, there wouldn't be much left of our bodies," Steer, who specializes in the substance, explained. Our muscles would waste away. And we'd likely have brain damage when we came out of it. But when bears enter hibernation, their ursodeoxycholic acid levels surge by over 10 percent. The molecule is clearly protecting the animals from cell death. And it could protect us, too.

Steer didn't mince words, referring to ursodeoxycholic acid as "a remarkable drug" and "nature's gift to mankind." He and his team were the first to map the molecule's unique abilities in animal models in the late 1990s, finding that it could reduce brain injury and heart injury by as much as half. But could any other drug do the same? Steer told me that although other anti-apoptotic drugs exist, none are as robust or as protective against mitochondrial damage as the "Bear Molecule." The good news is that the acid doesn't *need* to come from bears. To carry out his research, Steer didn't rely on real bear bile. Instead he obtained semisynthetic ursodeoxycholic acid, extracted from cow gallbladders and heavily processed. The topic remained a bit of a sore spot for the distinguished researcher.

"When our first research was published it hit front-page news and they said we were using bear bile," Steer sighed. "I started getting a lot of hate mail. But we were getting it from commercial vendors who got it from slaughterhouses." If the drug were ever manufactured on a larger scale, it would also be a semisynthetic. So far that hasn't happened, he said, because ursodeoxycholic acid is a generic compound; it's not patentable and therefore Big Pharma has no financial incentive to invest. It's also unlikely a synthetic alternative would hold water among those trolling Asia's medicine markets. Most people aren't attempting to treat their Parkinson's disease or Alzheimer's with bear bile. They're using the bile for run-of-the-mill ailments: a sore back from planting crops, chronic inflammation, headaches. There are more than fifty herbal alternatives for such things. Or Advil, in a pinch. Bears don't need to be farmed for the common cold.

Steer is a friendly and passionate man who spent more than a decade at the National Institutes of Health. He's also a bear advocate and has even advised the Chinese government about synthetic alternatives. But at the onset of the coronavirus pandemic, China promoted the use of traditional medicines, including *Tan Re Qing*, or bear bile, as treatment for COVID-19. Steer, too, had coauthored a paper arguing that ursodeoxycholic acid merited consideration for a clinical trial as a remedy for the hyperinflammatory immune response caused by the virus. Did he worry that his research could bolster the bear bile trade? If people were willing to consume tiger penis in the absence of any evidence, wouldn't medical scientists calling ursodeoxycholic acid "a remarkable drug" boost demand? Steer didn't see it that way. He wasn't convinced that the average consumer cared much about the science behind the drug. Ergo, his research shouldn't have an impact. "In traditional Chinese medicine, they think of bile as magical. And so they're going to keep farming these animals."

Sun bear
Helarctos malayanus

IN VIETNAM, IT WASN'T UNCOMMON TO HEAR the farmed bear referred to only by its perverse cause for exploitation, as if *Ursus bilis* was a species unto itself: "This bile bear is my most beloved pet—like a family member!" or "Stop taking photos of my bile bear!" Taxonomy fell to the wayside. Though the caged bear may have little in common with its wild counterpart, the bile bear does not constitute a scientific class unto itself. The wretched animals living on Asia's farms belong to two species: the Asiatic black bear (*Ursus thibetanus*)—known colloquially as the moon bear—and the sun bear (*Helarctos malaynus*).

Moon bears are some of the world's widest-ranging bears, found as far west as Afghanistan and the arid Zagros Mountains of Iran, throughout the Himalayas, on the islands of Taiwan, Honshu, and Shikoku in Japan, and roaming up into Siberia. Sun bears, in contrast, are one of the world's rarest bears. They live in the hot equatorial lowland forests of Asia, foraging on fruit, honey, beetles, figs, and scorpions. Both bears are black with golden crescent chest markings, and their ranges overlap in the muggy forests of Southeast Asia, particularly in Cambodia, Myanmar, and Laos where the majority of farmed bears originate. But their similarities stop there.

Sir Thomas Stamford Bingley Raffles, a former lieutenant governor of Bencoolen in modern-day Indonesia, was the first to describe the sun bear in scientific literature. In the early nineteenth century, a friend gifted the commander a pet sun bear cub he'd ostensibly bought off a villager. Raffles, a man who might claim the description of debonair if not for a decidedly weak chin and heavy-lidded eyes, was positively chuffed with the bear. Rather than chain the animal up, he raised the cub in a "nursery with the children; and, when admitted to my table, as was frequently the case, gave a proof of his taste by refusing to eat any fruit but mangosteens, or to drink any wine but Champaign," Raffles wrote. "The only time I knew him to be out of humour was on occasion when no Champaign was forth-coming." Oh, to have been a bear in Raffles's time.

The lieutenant general went on to found modern Singapore, and later established the Zoological Society of London before succumbing to a stroke on his forty-fourth birthday in 1826. The imbibing bear had passed away six years earlier, to which Raffles wrote: "The only loss in our family has been in the death of my favourite bear, whose demise I shall not fail to notice with due honour when treating on natural history." True to his word, the benevolent Raffles coined the Latin name *Ursus malaynus*, Malayan bear, that same year. Later, an American naturalist would propose that the bear actually belonged to a new *Helarctos* genus, coming from the Greek word for sun, *helios*.

Despite a nickname meant to draw the animals into genealogical comparison, the sun bear and moon bear aren't close cousins on the bear family tree. The sun bear is thought to have evolved from another small bear, named *Ursus minimus*. Moon bears, or Asiatic black bears, are most closely related to the American black bear—both species diverged from Europe's Etruscan bear more than two million years ago. When American black bears eventually arrived in North America around the Holstein interglacial period, they looked almost identical to the Asiatic black bear. Today, the two bears remain fairly similar in size and shape.

This explains the sun and moon bears' disparate appearances. Large, dish-shaped ears pop up from the top of the moon bear's head like a cartoon bear, while sun bears have small ears that lie flat against their skulls. A moon bear weighs as much as 440 pounds; the sun bear is the smallest of all eight bear species—and smaller than many dogs. And whereas the moon bear has long, luxurious black fur, the sun bear has a stubbly, sleek coat to avoid overheating, reminiscent of a moon bear with a close shave.

Much is known about the moon bear. Although generally solitary, the bruins may live in family groups of two adults and two litters of cubs. Asiatic black bears are also some of the most talkative bears, producing a cacophony of bizarre vocalizations. They grunt. They whine. They roar. Often they make popping sounds when anxious or alarmed, and they'll snap their tongue against the roof of their mouth to make a tut-tut noise when approaching other bears.

The sun bear remains the world's least studied bear—even less is known about the species than about the elusive spectacled bear. The bear's nature is partially to blame for this knowledge gap. Like spectacled bears, sun bears are partial to trees, and they spend their days hiding behind palm fronds and nesting in hollow logs and trunks. Tropical terrain, though ideal for the bears, also complicates things for researchers. Scientists can't use helicopters to dart bears because the vegetation is too dense, and the bear's stubbly fur is too short to be snagged in hair traps for DNA sequencing. And where the sun bear's range overlaps with the moon bear, biologists can't survey locals about possible sun bear sightings because they mix up the two black-and-gold species.

Much of what we do know about sun bear behavior comes from Gabriella Fredriksson. She serves as cochair of the IUCN's sun bear expert team and helped to establish a sun bear education center in East Kalimantan on Borneo, where she spends most of her time. Not long after beginning the first field studies on sun bears in the 1990s, the Indonesian wildlife department started sending her sun bear cubs confiscated from wildlife traffickers. The government had no idea what to do with them, and Fredriksson's research camp in the middle of the rain forest seemed as good a place as any. (Officials had previously tried to house one of the bears with a confiscated gibbon, but it was a disagreeable roommate and killed the ape.) The first cub to arrive was Ganja—"like Ganja weed"—followed by Ucil, then Schitzo. Every day Fredriksson and the three bears would go on long walks through the forest. An assistant would plumb the forest for wild bears while Fredriksson observed the three cubs' unique behaviors. "Their instincts were still there," she told me. "The moment we let them out of the cage, they would go straight into foraging. They were just machines—never a dull moment and not like other bears. They dug up stuff then one minute later they'd break into a rotten log, then run up a fruit tree. They were just constantly doing stuff."

Sun bears have also been observed to use facial mimicry—a key component of human interactions, but rare in the animal kingdom. At the Bornean Sun Bear Conservation Centre, twenty-one studied sun bears were found to mirror their playmate's open-mouth facial expressions, "suggesting a degree of social sensitivity." This was the first time researchers documented such a behavior in a bear species. Sun bears, though solitary in nature, exhibited complex communication techniques reserved for highly social species, like the great apes.

Of course, none of these impressive natural behaviors are of interest to the bear farmers. They couldn't care less about the moon bear's unique noises or the sun bear's expressive faces. What they care about is bile. And Asiatic black bears produce more ursodeoxycholic acid than any other bear species found in Asia. Moon bears don't hibernate at the southern extent of their range in Southeast Asia—Vietnam, Laos, Cambodia, Thailand, Myanmar. But in northern mountainous areas—China, Russia, Japan, Nepal, India—they're voracious sleepers. The bears enter their dens around October and emerge again between April and May. For more than six months the bears' slumbering bodies are manufacturing copious amounts of the special acid to stave off deterioration. The tiny sun bear, on the other hand, has been dragged into the sordid bear farming business largely by association. Because they live in hot equatorial forests rife with food, they don't hibernate. When scientists analyzed the composition of the different bear species' bile, they found that only about 8 percent of the sun bear bile pool was made up of ursodeoxycholic acid.

THE VILLAGE OF PHUNG THUONG HAS tube houses and banana trees and soggy rice fields and motorbikes that beep in unending cacophony. It has uniformed schoolchildren who commute by foot down dusty roads and old women with mirthful laughs and blackened teeth. It has hot phở and cold coffee poured over sweet milk. In May, the southwest monsoon arrives and lingers until October. Indeed, Phung Thuong would be very much like any other village in northern Vietnam, if not for the bears—164 of them.

Phung Thuong is one of the last holdouts of bear farming in Vietnam, with more bears than anywhere else in the country. About a quarter of the country's remaining captive bile bears can be found in the houses and yards scattered across this fertile 2-square-mile radius of the Red River delta. As farmers have relinquished their bears to the authorities (or worse), bear farming hot spots have collapsed, one by one, over the last decade. Yet no one in Phung Thuong had ever surrendered a single bear when I visited. To do so would be to break ranks with friends and neighbors in a town where everybody knows everybody. When rescue workers came knocking in hopes of convincing farmers to hand over their animals, the villagers presented a united front: No bear was leaving Phung Thuong.

Today, around twenty thousand bears are believed to be kept on bile farms in Asia. The majority of them are held captive in China, where demand is greatest and farming is legal. Others are imprisoned in South Korea, Myanmar, Laos, and Vietnam. (Cambodia is one of the few places in Southeast Asia where bear farming never managed to gain a foothold.)

Up until four decades ago, almost all bear bile came from wild bears. Skilled hunters shot and killed the animals, carefully carving out the bile-filled gallbladders to sell at wildlife markets. Unabated poaching soon depleted bear populations and stymied the flow of bile. Hoping to appease the frustrated supply chain, China thoughtfully proposed the idea of commercial bear farming. It had worked well with other animals—civet cats, bamboo rats, and snakes. So why not bears? In 1984, around the same time that Zhang Hemin was starting the Wolong breeding program to save pandas, other Chinese officials were teaming up with North Korean scientists to refine bear bile farming techniques. And yes, that sentence is every bit as horrifying as it sounds. The North Koreans had already developed a tortuous method for extracting bile from the gallbladders of living bears. It went something like this: Farmers would cut into the bruin's abdomen, inserting a stainless-steel needle through the incision to create a permanent canal leading directly into the gallbladder. They named this the "free-dripping fistula technique." Gravity was all that was required to drain the bile. Animal welfare advocates who have witnessed this farming method say the bears "moan and quiver" throughout the process. China saw it as a win-win. Using this ingenious method, more bile could be obtained for far less effort while purportedly mitigating the impact on wild bears; a single caged bear generated the bile equivalent of forty or fifty poached wild bears annually. The resulting flood of bear bile products—capsules, ointments, plasters, pills, eye drops—spiked consumer interest and legitimized the practice of bear farming. The number of bears on farms exploded. Once destitute villagers grew rich from "liquid gold."

When the bile market was at its peak in Vietnam, busloads of Korean tourists traveled from Hanoi to Phuc Tho District, where Phung Thuong is located, to buy bile directly from the source. Even when the customers didn't come to Phung Thuong, farmers could quickly get their product out to market; China's southern border lies less than 250 miles from the Vietnamese village. From there it's only 100 miles to the city of Nanning, one of China's centers of bear bile farming. (The legal Chinese bear bile industry is primarily located in Yunnan and Sichuan and valued at $1 billion.) During the bile bonanza years of the early 2000s, it was easy to tell who farmed bears in Phung Thuong. They lived in the biggest houses and drove the fanciest cars. But with the industry on the decline, bear farming had moved behind closed doors.

Outside a lime green tube house, Tran was speaking impatiently into her phone. We'd been scheduled to meet a man and his wife who owned a single bile bear. Now that we'd arrived, the man had called to say he wasn't feeling well and could no longer show us his bear.

"He is not sick," Tran hissed as she hung up. "He is worried."

Next to the man's house, nearly within view of the farmer's window, I noticed a large billboard towering over a green field. In Vietnamese, it read: "Transfer bears to the state for a better life." There was a phone number to call. And a photo of two bear friends happily living out their remaining days in a sanctuary. How many times, I wondered, had the farmer passed by this sign?

In the grand scheme of global agriculture, a bear farm is most similar to a factory farm. In China, the animals are kept in what animal rights activists disturbingly call "coffin" or "crush" cages. These narrow enclosures—too small for a bear to stand up or turn around—sandwich a bear between iron bars. The bear will stay this way for years, maybe decades, as farmers extract bile. Some animals are put in cages as cubs and never removed. The owners feed the bears cheap grain mash to keep them alive and secreting bile. With no way to burn off the calories, the animals grow fatter by the day, squeezed between the unrelenting bars of their cage.

Bile extraction methods, I learned, differ from country to country. Vietnam's bears live a slightly less miserable existence than those on Chinese farms. They're kept in barred cages—bigger than a coffin but smaller than a Toyota Prius—stacked on a cement floor. Still, some will only survive a few years in a cage, succumbing to infection from surgical wounds, bone deformities, liver cancer, and hernias. Animal rights activists report instances of old bears who fail to produce bile being left to starve to death in their cages. The farmers of Phuc Tho District prefer to knock the bears out with ketamine, an illegal anaesthetic in Vietnam, and extract the bile with a temporary catheter and syringe. It can take a dozen jabs before they find the right spot, and the ketamine often leaves the bear semiconscious. This is done about once every two weeks, with farmers extracting between 80 and 100 milliliters of bile each time. Or so I'd been told. Tran and I had yet to turn up a single bear in the country's foremost bear bile hot spot. The lime green tube house was a bust.

BEAR FARMING IS NO LONGER LEGAL in Vietnam. The government outlawed the practice in 2005 following aggressive lobbying by animal welfare groups—a rare success story in the dark world of wildlife trafficking. Between the late 1990s and mid-2000s, bear farming had exploded within the country's borders, jumping from an estimated four hundred bears to about forty-three hundred at the industry's peak. Hundreds of fat, sad bears could be seen sitting in sidewalk cages throughout Vietnam's terraced countryside. Animal welfare groups were justifiably unhappy about such astronomical growth. Farming hadn't curtailed the impact on wild bears as promised. It had done the opposite. Activists from Vietnam and farther afield pushed the government to ban the cruel practice and crack down on illegal cross-border trade; Vietnam had previously signed onto CITES, which prohibits international trade in endangered bear parts, including bear bile. Even so, many vials were finding their way to China and Korea. Facing growing international stigma, the Vietnamese government finally capitulated to activists' demands and barred farmers from extracting and selling bear bile. In their haste, however, officials failed to address what should be done with the thousands of bears already trapped on farms across Vietnam.

The government's shortsighted solution was to declare that *keeping* existing bears was still perfectly fine, as the bushy-haired woman in Son Loc had attested to, provided farmers didn't extract their bile. Bear owners were required to register their animals with the government and get them microchipped for tracking. This would ensure that no new bears were illegally added to allegedly defunct farms. Following such logic, the four hundred or so caged bears left in Vietnam today should all be at least fifteen years old. Though moon bears live as long as thirty years in the wild, most live nowhere near as long on farms.

Despite Tran's grandstanding about the difficulties of tracking down bile bears, when she and I drove back through Phung Thuong, we happened upon one of the largest bear farms in Phuc Tho District. The buttery yellow compound stretched across nearly an entire city block, with four large openings adjacent to the sidewalk. Metal shutters were splayed open, and a wire fence stretched across each one. Inside the dark enclosure several miserable-looking moon bears were locked up in individual cages. Someone had strung a pennant banner of rainbow flags between the ursine prison and a fig tree, creating a disquietingly cheerful mood.

An older man wearing green army fatigues and a camouflaged pageboy cap greeted us as we approached. Tran began chatting him up, buying me time to move in for a better look. The bear in the center cage closest to the sidewalk was severely obese. She sat on her behind with her back rolls braced against the bars of her cage. Two chapped paws poked out from under her heft, and her round pop-up ears seemed to wilt on her head. The floor consisted of rust-colored bars, raised a foot off the ground, so urine, feces, and food scraps could fall through. Her cage wasn't furnished with so much as a water dish—just a small slat where workers could dispense food. The bear stared blankly out onto the street, watching the noisy motorbikes pass. Her golden crescent had all but faded away, and her rotund belly bore the scars of bile extractions. When the bear took notice of me, her dull eyes fixed on my own. The spark of curiosity that I had witnessed in the captive pandas was absent. Even Rangila, the rescued dancing bear in India, had seen better days than this moon bear.

At first, I had perceived only a handful of bears in the enclosure. Now, as I peered into the dim light of the compound, I realized there was row upon row of cages containing furtive black shapes anxiously popping their jaws. There were at least fifteen bears, and next to the plaintive bear resided a moon bear with cracked and bleeding paws protruding between the bars' gaps. These two bears were better off than the rest—at least they could see the sun and passersby. A sign in front of the bears warned pedestrians of "Dangerous Animals." Its words may well have applied to the bears' owners.

Fewer than five hundred of the forty-three hundred bears that were alive in the mid-2000s, when Vietnam's bile ban came into effect, have found their way to the rescue centers run by animal welfare nonprofits. Most of them died. Those that didn't perish from maltreatment were chopped up for their parts as farmers attempted to recoup the money they'd spent on the animals. Even farmers willing to abide by the ban often failed to surrender their animals to sanctuaries; instead they sold their bears to farms in China, where bile extraction remained legal.

Still, not everyone was keen to close up shop. The ban's loophole on "keeping" bears had effectively formed a noose. Authorities rarely checked on bear owners to ensure that bile wasn't being extracted, and those that did were easily bought off. Moreover, the ban had succeeded in lowering bile demand by as much as 60 percent in Vietnam, but as profits plummeted, the quality of bear care declined even further. Bears were fed less nutritious food when they were fed at all. A 2018 study found that Vietnamese bear farmers spent less than $4 a month on food for the animals in their care.

Tran cleared her throat. The man, she said, had invited us inside the house that lay beyond this torture chamber. I followed the two of them through a courtyard, where a tan dog with pointy ears was locked in a small wire cage. Tran assured me he was simply a guard dog. She endeavored to put a positive spin on the experience, ingratiating us with the bears' owner. She complimented the beautiful yellow flowering tree in the courtyard.

The man's house was easily the grandest one I'd entered in Vietnam. It was much wider than the cost-cutting tube houses, and ornate wood furniture decorated the teal-painted living room. Large cabinets boasted a vast collection of corked spirits. On the wall, next to a wedding portrait of a young couple, hung an enormous oil painting of two tigers. The young man and woman from the photo, presumably the older man's son and his wife, joined us. Large pharmaceutical corporations run most of the farms in China, but in Vietnam bear farming is still a family business. This was one of the reasons I'd come here instead; it was feasible to report on pandas in China, but not bile farming.

As the smiling woman poured tea from a silver pot, Tran began to work her charm.

"I was just at Mr. Ho's. He is famous in Son Loc! He has six bears. I'm working in a travel agency so I buy from him every time I get here," she blathered. "The last time I was here he fed the bears every Saturday at 8:30 in the morning and he allowed everyone to come and buy."

The three bear farmers were less standoffish than Mr. Ho's wife. Then again, they weren't exactly discreet about their operation.

"How many bears do you guys have? Around thirty?" Tran asked innocuously.

"No, only twenty," the younger man replied, his words translated by Tran. In any other context it would be an absurd statement. *Only twenty bears.*

"How long have you had them for?"

"A long time. Since 2002. All the bears have chips and numbers," the wife replied carefully. How lucky that all twenty bile bears had lived for nearly two decades! Her husband cut in, "It means they're managed by the government."

"It's legal to have bears." The woman repeated the same party line we'd heard in Son Loc. "But it's illegal to harvest the bear bile," added the husband. They finished each other's sentences, as if performing a rehearsed skit. The wife insisted that government officials paid him a visit every month to make sure everything was on the up and up.

It wasn't. Without hesitation, the couple asked if we would like to buy some bile.

"The people you bought from—[Mr. Ho]—they also bought from us," the woman proclaimed. She was proud of their product. "We only do wholesale. Retail price is 50,000 Vietnamese dong [$2] for 1 cubic centimeter," the man again chimed in. His wife explained they sold mostly to Chinese and Korean customers.

The older man got up and left the room, returning with five clear glass vials. We examined the bile. It was unfrozen and dark brown in color. Tran hemmed and hawed over its quality as the couple pushed the sale. How fresh was it? They told us they normally harvested the bile every month, sometimes every two months. They sold hundreds of vials at a time.

Tran put on a good show of pretending the bile was too expensive. She would just buy one vial as a sample. But maybe she could take his phone number? She promised to put him in touch with some of her fabricated high-end clientele back in Hanoi. This seemed to appease the bear farmers. We politely thanked them for their time and returned to the courtyard. The tan dog yipped at us. It was then that I noticed a barred metal door that led to the back of the bear compound. Through the cracks I saw a woman hosing down the bear cages with water. A pressure cooker boiled dozens of brown eggs. It was almost feeding time. I inched closer to the door. An enormous moon bear was violently thrashing his head against the walls of his cage. The farmer shouted at me to get away.

Out on the public-facing sidewalk, the depressed bear I'd been looking at before was now standing on all fours. My stomach dropped at the sight of her. All of the shaggy fur on the bear's backside was gone. Many bile bears, I later learned, suffer from chronic skin infections that lead to hair loss. Tran chucked the bear bile vial in a garbage bin.

I was hard pressed to come up with another animal that lived a life of greater misery than the bile bear. Tigers and rhinos are poached and pulverized for tonics, art, and wine, but death often comes quickly. Factory-farmed animals—chickens, pigs, cows—seemed a close contender, yet most are killed within a few years if not months. Highly intelligent animals like dolphins and elephants live distinctly terrible lives at amusement parks and aquariums, but they aren't subjected to daily surgical torture. And this was only weighing the bile bear's life against other mistreated animals. Never mind the species who are adored for arbitrary reasons. Had the moon bear been born black and white instead of black and gold, he would have been worshipped. Instead, the bile bear knows only pain.

On our way out of town, Tran and I passed the same banana trees and phở shops and soggy rice fields and elders perched on squat stools. We also passed two obese and bald bile bears caged in a sidewalk prison. They didn't raise their heads. A woman brandishing a broom shouted at us to move along. We sped onward to Hanoi, leaving Phung Thuong and its bears behind us.

❦

ANYONE WHO STEPS FOOT INSIDE A BILE FARM will understand why animal welfare advocates have fought so hard to shut them down. The sights, smells, and sounds aren't easy to forget. There is, however, another reason wildlife crusaders are concerned about the persistence of bile farming in Asia. Nearly every farmed bear was once a wild bear. And the continued snaring and trapping of sun and moon bears to stock farms pose an urgent threat to the future of the two species.

Brian Crudge oversees the research program of Free the Bears, a global organization dedicated to ending bear bile farming, and he's spent years studying the impact of bile farming on wild bear populations in Southeast Asia. In Laos, protesters' megaphone chants, chirping birds, and motorbike horns drowned out his lilting Irish accent when I phoned him one morning to chat about how farms had contributed to the decline of wild bears.

Bear farming, Crudge said, "definitely didn't help and may have hurt wild bear populations. It created a demand for having bears and a market for live bear cubs." When Crudge surveyed Vietnamese bear farmers in 2016, only eight respondents said they had ever attempted to breed their bears. Of those, only four farms reported any success—and at all but one the litters died after one week. Almost two-thirds of farmers readily admitted to getting their bears from the wild. Even in the absence of such confessions, wild-sourced bears are easily distinguishable. Around a third of Asia's captive bears are missing paws—evidence they once fell victim to a steel leghold trap.

TRAFFIC, an agency that monitors the illegal wildlife trade, determined that there is still an active flow of live bears entering Vietnam from Cambodia, Laos, and Thailand. Between 2000 and 2011, regional authorities intercepted 152 smuggled live bruins in Vietnam. Though it's likely that traffickers were moving the bulk of these bears to China, inevitably some were intended to fulfill orders from Vietnamese farmers. It seems "highly likely that many bear farms in [Vietnam] are still active participants in the trade in live bears, despite the overall decline of bears in farms," a TRAFFIC report concluded.

When Asian governments gave bear farming the stamp of approval, it spiked demand for the real thing. Such an outcome was inevitable. It happens nearly every time a farmed alternative emerges on the market. It happened with salmon. It happened with ginseng. And now it was happening with bears. Practitioners of traditional Chinese medicine frequently push the belief that wild-sourced products are more potent. In turn, bile imbibers only want *wild* bear bile, and they're willing to pay a premium. "People were just not satisfied with farmed bear bile," Crudge told me. Vietnamese bile buyers opine that products from farmed animals are "lower quality." And at market, shopkeepers quote the highest prices for bile and gallbladders they claim are sourced from wild bears. As TRAFFIC puts it, "If consumers are willing to pay more for wild-origin products, then incentive to acquire and trade in wild bears will persist, regardless of how many farms there are."

The hunting of wild bears to stock farms, and for their parts, has taken a heavy toll on bear numbers. Sun bears and moon bears are both classified as vulnerable to extinction. The moon bear population is estimated at between fifty and sixty thousand individuals, but has declined by as much as half in the past three decades. Biologists believe the sun bear population has plummeted by more than a third during the same time period—or in merely three generations of bears. The conversion of more than 3.5 million hectares of pristine rain forest to oil palm plantation in Malaysia, Indonesia, and Papua New Guinea over the last thirty years has robbed sun bears of space, shade, camouflage, and food. Bears living along the edges of these plantations that inadvertently venture too close to the plantations are caught and maimed in snares set for bearded pigs and wild boars. What forest hasn't been converted to oil palm has largely been logged for the valuable hardwood of dipterocarp trees— where the sun bears make their home. Though "reliable estimates of sun bear populations are lacking," it's generally accepted that today the sun bear is one of the world's most imperiled bear species, just behind the famously endangered panda.

Historically, sun bears occurred throughout Vietnam, except in the northeast above the Red River delta. Asiatic black bears were abundant in mountainous areas. When Crudge and his colleagues wanted to figure out how bile farming had affected the country's wild bears, they interviewed more than fourteen hundred people living in villages adjacent to twenty-two protected areas. Had the villagers ever seen a bear? Did they think bears were numerous? Had they noticed any sort of decline in the population? Overwhelmingly, 98 percent of the villagers reported that they thought bear numbers had fallen—with the dip beginning around 1990 and continuing on into 2005. There was a clear parallel. "Bear populations declined dramatically during this period which coincided with the time that bear farms were being established and expanding rapidly in Vietnam," Crudge told me. In fact, their study failed to turn up a single site without evidence of a population decline. Bear farming, he and his colleagues concluded, had dramatically increased hunting pressure in a "poaching free-for-all fueled by heightened demand, access to markets, poor law enforcement, and the allure of financial profits."

SOME OF THE TALLEST MOUNTAINS in northern Vietnam bubble up from the tropical evergreen and lowland bamboo forests of Tam Dao National Park. Moon bears once lived in this jungle, but they've been gone for decades. "I've never seen a wild bear in my life," admitted Tuan Bendixsen, who was to be my guide through Animals Asia's Tam Dao Bear Rescue Center.

Since its inception in 1993, this animal welfare nonprofit has rescued more than 630 bears from across Asia, and 178 of them were housed at Tam Dao on the day of my visit. "Many of the children from Phuc Tho District have visited this place," Bendixsen told me as we entered the jungle-hemmed complex through an iron gate. Tam Dao was about 20 miles north of Phung Thuong, but it couldn't have been more different. The forested oasis gave me whiplash from the conditions I'd witnessed in the infamous bear village. "I would love to bring their parents here, too. But they won't come." Instead, on Saturday mornings, Bendixsen, the Vietnam director of Animals Asia, traveled to Phuc Tho District to oversee the organization's mobile medical clinic. Set up in a small one-story building, traditional healers would listen to residents' complaints and prescribe them cocktails of free herbs, hoping to wean them off bear bile.

In the early 2000s, Animals Asia initiated a concerted lobbying effort to ban bear farming in Vietnam. When animal welfare groups succeeded in 2005, the forest department agreed to cordon off a verdant strip of land running through the valley of Tam Dao National Park for Animals Asia to use as a rescue center for surrendered bears. (Animals Asia also operates another bear sanctuary in Chengdu, ironically not far from the panda base.) Moon and sun bears freed from the cruelties of the bile industry were now able to live out their final days in comfort.

Bendixsen was a soft-spoken but iron-willed man with frameless oval spectacles and short, dark hair that he parted down the middle. Born in Saigon, modern-day Ho Chi Minh, he grew up in Australia after his parents moved the family there in the early 1970s. At university, he studied animal husbandry and later worked with the Australian government to improve the welfare of farm animals before returning to Vietnam in 2000, where he ran a small veterinary clinic in Hanoi, treating cats and dogs. A German veterinarian friend was the first person to mention bear farming to Bendixsen. He grew determined to join the fight and began volunteering with Animals Asia. Since then, he'd become one of the most recognizable faces of the movement to end bear farming. He had made frequent visits to the villagers in Phung Thuong to try to convince them to hand over their bears. Still, none had relented.

"They all tell me they're not extracting the bile," he said as we crossed a small footbridge over a creek toward the bear enclosures. The Tam Dao rescue center spanned 27 acres of semi-forested habitat in a mountain valley. "But it's obvious they are. Why else would you keep them? If you're a business person, you cut your losses quickly."

"No one has ever been sent to jail for bile extraction in Vietnam," he bemoaned. Under the law, a person caught extracting bile from a bear could be sentenced to a maximum of five years in jail (or fifteen years for more than six bears). But they needed to be apprehended in the middle of the act by a government official or a police officer. In the absence of clear-cut guilt, fines and the occasional confiscation of a bear were the worst punishments handed out, leading most farmers to operate with a sense of impunity.

The sanctuary sun bears, eleven at the time I visited, all lived together in a large house closest to the center's entrance, and I was immediately charmed by the comical sight of them. The small bears were waddling around the grass on their hind legs, causing the extra skin folds that normally gathered around their faces in expressive wrinkles to pool around their hind quarters like a soggy diaper. The sun bears looked nothing like the other bear species I'd seen. They had wide-set eyes, and their golden markings were far thicker than the moon bear's Batman-like crescent. Plus, their hooked claws were exceptionally thick and long. One bear was using them like fingers to strip protective bamboo off a tree trunk. The slippery poles had been placed there to prevent the bears from climbing up and escaping over the tall fence.

"The cubs are very active," Bendixsen observed as we looked

through the fence. "They'll put on a show for you. But the older bears rescued from bile farms often struggle to walk." We had timed our visit to coincide with the bears' enrichment period, when workers hid strawberries, pineapples, and carrots throughout the enclosure for the bears to discover. Such playtime was critical for the bears: not only did it stimulate the bears' starved minds; it helped them build up muscles that had wasted away during their years spent in a cage. New arrivals were often too weak to even climb up the ladders and wooden platforms installed around the yard.

A sun bear named Layla approached us with a juicy strawberry poking out of her mouth. She bore a distinctive black birthmark on the right side of her golden crescent that made it easy to tell her apart from the others. Poachers had killed Layla's mother when she was a cub. Authorities had intercepted them trafficking her through Vietnam five years earlier and brought her here. Layla loudly slurped back the berry in her mouth, then crinkled her snout into a big yawn. Her impossibly long tongue lolled out of her mouth like a Fruit Roll-Up. At nearly 10 inches, the sun bear's tongue is the longest of any bear species—the perfect tool for getting honey and bugs out of nooks and crannies.

Tam Dao's sun bears had made their way to the sanctuary for a variety of reasons. Three cubs, including Layla, were rescued from traffickers. One had been kept as a pet. Sun bears, with their small stature and cute wrinkles, are a popular species in the exotic pet trade. Malaysian pop star Zarith Sofia Mohd Yasin made headlines in 2019 when a sun bear was photographed curiously peeking its head out of her apartment window in Kuala Lumpur. The singer claimed she "found" the bear at the side of the road and thought it was a dog. Yasin was forced to pay a nearly $9,000 fine, though she maintained she did not mistreat the bear. "If Bruno [the bear] could talk, it would surely say the food I gave him was delicious," she told the Malaysian media, pleading her case by noting she'd fed Bruno chocolates.

Five of the center's sun bears had been rescued from bile farms across Southeast Asia. "In Cambodia, sun bear bile is twice as expensive as moon bear bile," Bendixsen told me. Though bear farming declined in Vietnam after the 2005 ban, the illicit activity had moved across the border. "Laos is getting big," Bendixsen said as we followed a dirt path toward the moon bear houses, where dozens of the animals were plodding around a grassy enclosure, appearing like shaggy cows in a pasture. "It's like a leaking bucket. You plug one hole and it begins to leak from somewhere else." Myanmar could be the next hot spot. It remains Asia's wellspring of wild bears.

Hundreds of bears are still in need of rescue in Vietnam. But Tam Dao only had space for a few more bruins. "We can't expand any more because we are blocked by the mountains," explained Bendixsen when our tour concluded back at the rescue center's veterinary offices. It was critical that they found more room, and soon, he said. In 2017, the Vietnamese Administration of Forestry had signed an agreement with bear welfare groups operating in the country: Every captive bear in Vietnam would be moved into a sanctuary within the next five years. The agreement closed the loophole created by the 2005 ban. Bear farming was finally coming to an end in Vietnam.

TWO WEEKS AFTER I LEFT VIETNAM, I received an email from Animals Asia. A farmer in Phung Thuong had surrendered his female bile bear to the Tam Dao sanctuary. What would be considered a routine rescue anywhere else in Vietnam was an astonishing achievement in Phuc Tho District. A farmer had finally broken ranks with his peers, disregarding the community's pact to never give up a single bear. A crack had formed in their resolve.

"The first bear is the hardest bear," Bendixsen told me two years after my visit to Vietnam. "We're starting to see a shift in attitudes. When we visit farmers in Phung Thuong about their bears, it's no longer a firm 'No.' It's a 'Maybe.'" Recently, he said, an old man had come into the mobile medicine clinic in Phuc Tho. He had a sore back. Bendixsen began chatting with him and realized he owned one of the biggest bear farms in Phung Thuong. Bendixsen asked the man why he had visited the clinic rather than use bile for his aches and pains. "He said, 'I just need something that will work.' And then he agreed for us to come visit him at his farm to have a conversation."

Slowly but surely, progress is being made across Asia. Five thousand residents of Phuc Tho District signed a petition in 2019 calling for an end to bear farming in the region. In 2015, the Vietnamese Traditional Medicine Association agreed to stop all prescriptions for bear bile. Wild sun bears are turning up in places where they haven't been seen in decades. And dozens of moon bears are arriving at sanctuaries. Maybe the furless bear in Phung Thuong would make it to a rescue center, too. And while moon bears and sun bears are still a long way away from achieving panda status, public sentiment in China is turning against bear bile farming. Many Chinese citizens now consider bile extraction to be a cruel practice. In 2018, a representative from Hebei Province at the National People's Congress submitted a proposal to end bear farming by 2035. In China's major cities, protesters have frequently gathered to speak out against the cruelty of bile farms. Everywhere I look, there are glimmers of hope, rising over the horizon like the sun and moon and casting their light into the darkest places.

PART III

NORTH AMERICA

Lonely? I don't know. They tell me this is cold. I don't know what cold is, because I don't freeze. So I don't know what lonely means either. Bears are made to be solitary.

—IOREK BYRNISON, IN *THE GOLDEN COMPASS* (PHILLIP PULLMAN)

CHAPTER FIVE

OUT OF THE WILD

American black bear, United States
Ursus americanus

The modern plight of the American black bear starts out much like a joke. Have you heard the one about the bear who walks into the grocery store and grabs a bag of Tostitos? Or, how about the bear who breaks into a gas station and snarfs down a few chocolate bars? Or the bear who binge-eats 24 pounds of pure butter in a confectionary's kitchen? If you live near Lake Tahoe, you've no doubt heard them all—and then some—on the local news.

Lake Tahoe is the cerulean gem shared between California and Nevada. It's a popular vacation spot for millions, evoking an American nostalgia for the nuclear family getaway when city dwellers would roll up, en masse, with tents and camp stoves to spend five glorious days in the Sierra Nevada. But today, the Lake Tahoe Basin—a textbook example of the wildland-urban interface—is known not just for its azure waters, but as ground zero for black bear–human conflict in the United States. Motels, mini golf courses, barbecue joints, and blackjack casinos ring the 200-square-mile alpine lake, which serves as a critical water source for the region's wildlife in times of drought. Once humans began developing its shoreline, resident black bears were given two options—they could either move along or move in. Most chose the latter.

The American black bear is the world's most bountiful bear and arguably the species that people are most familiar with in their daily lives. If I asked you to picture a bear, you'd probably conjure up images of short black fur, pale snout, a lean build, humpless back, and round ears. Aided by national rewilding efforts over the past century, the black bear has been restored to roughly half of its historical range in the United States. It can be found in the hickory forests of Appalachia; the swamps of Louisiana; the pinyon juniper woodlands of the Southwest; and the palm-fronded Florida Keys. But black bears can also be found rifling through dumpsters like oversized raccoons and denning under homes in places like Yonkers, New York; Raleigh, North Carolina; and Boston, Massachusetts. Only the Hudson River separates Manhattan from New Jersey's booming bear population. This sharp increase in black bear numbers combined with rampant human encroachment has given rise to a new breed of bear in America: the urban bear.

AT A SUMMER HOME IN INCLINE VILLAGE, on the Nevada side of Lake Tahoe, Carl Lackey was crawling on his hands and knees through a prickly bed of rust-orange pine needles, appearing much like a bear himself. He shone a flashlight into the dark recesses of the crawl space that ran along the house's foundation. A large male black bear had taken up residence in the owners' absence and ripped out the fiberglass insulation, dragging in a cache of pine nuts for late-night snacking. Fortunately—or unfortunately for me—the bear wasn't home at the moment. "There are tons of sites like this throughout Incline Village," Lackey said in a gruff tone cultured by the West. He stood up and brushed the clinging needles off his faded blue jeans. "We get a lot of bears here denning underneath homes. Every garbage night they're out roaming the neighborhoods looking for food."

Lackey, a biologist with the Nevada Department of Wildlife, was a compact man with a bald head, ginger goatee, and the weathered complexion of a fair-skinned person who had spent a lot of time in the sun. When I'd met him on that drizzly morning in Incline Village, he was driving a truck with two spunky black-and-white Karelian bear dogs named Rooster and Dazzle in the back cab. Karelians—appearing like a cross between a husky and a border collie—originate in northern Europe, where they were used by hunters to chase brown bears. The fearless dogs have since been popularized by wildlife managers as a tool to scare black bears and grizzlies away from communities in the Mountain West. Lackey was a big proponent of the canine companions, and he'd gotten his first dog, Stryker, from a breeder back in 2001 to respond to the increase in bear incidents around Tahoe. Rooster, the speckled offspring of Stryker, and Dazzle now accompanied him on most of his calls. They'd already chased hundreds of bears away from Nevada's lakeside towns.

Lackey understood the daily rituals of cosmopolitan bears better than almost anyone else in the American West. He'd been dealing with Tahoe's urban bears for more than two decades and was one of the first people in America to wise up to the ursine rebellion at the nation's doorstep. The Lake Tahoe Basin is home to the second-highest density of black bears on the continent, with several bruins roaming nearly every square mile. So, when American black bears began reclaiming towns and cities, locales near Lake Tahoe experienced some of the largest influxes of migrants. Beginning around 1990, bears that had once spent their entire lives in the wilderness areas surrounding the lake started showing up in Tahoe's tourist traps, crossing the highway to soak in the lake's cool waters and tearing into trash cans.

At first, Lackey wasn't sure what to make of this sudden influx of bears. California and Nevada weren't in a drought, and the backwoods were full of food. Running through the ecology of American black bears, he and his colleagues concluded that odiferous garbage left unsecured by clueless tourists must be drawing bears out of the wild. Incline Village, on the north shore, was the epicenter.

At the time of my visit in March, the height of the tourist off-season, Tahoe's bears should still have been hibernating. Black bears typically don't emerge from their dens until April, timing their reappearance to match the growth of spring forage. But the urban environment had altered their natural behavior. "Yeah, they're not really hibernating anymore," Lackey said nonchalantly as we left the summer house and headed toward the commercial area of Incline Village, skirting the lake and dodging the huge Jeffrey pine cones rolling across the highway. "Instead they're finding a daybed and coming out once or twice a week."

Lackey's throwaway statement took me aback. *Bears were no longer hibernating?* That seemed like a pretty big deal. Birds fly. Fish swim. And bears hibernate. Under normal circumstances, cold temperatures and reduced natural food availability in early winter send a signal to bears that it's time to den down. But with a plethora of human food scraps now available year-round, bears had become insomniacs rummaging through the fridge at midnight. In a 2003 study, researchers tracked thirty-eight urban bears around Lake Tahoe and found that while back-country bears in the nearby Carson Range were entering dens in early December and hibernating as usual, Tahoe's urban bears were staying up until January. Five of the thirty-eight tracked bears never entered a den at all.

Climate change has compounded this behavioral shift. Warmer winters, later falls, and earlier springs have reset bears' biological clocks across North America. Some bears no longer hibernate while others are entering the den later or waking up too early. A few winters ago, the National Park Service (NPS) warned visitors at Yellowstone National Park to prepare for possible grizzly bear encounters after above-average February temperatures had grizzlies abandoning their dens weeks ahead of schedule. A similar pattern was found in black bears by Heather John-son, a wildlife biologist with the US Geological Survey. She determined that for every 1°C (1.8°F) increase in the minimum winter temperature, black bears living in western Colorado were hibernating for six fewer days. By midcentury, black bears could be awake for an additional two to six weeks.

Johnson told me that although hibernation seems to slow the cellu-lar aging process—apoptosis—in bears, reduced hibernation isn't neces-sarily detrimental to bears at a physiological level. After all, many bear species don't hibernate in the parts of their range where it's too warm or where food is available year-round. But, she stressed, if North Amer-ica's bears are hibernating less, they have more time to get into trouble. "When bears are awake for more of the year, they're more susceptible to getting killed," she told me. "Bears don't die in hibernation." In a paper published in the journal *Ecosphere*, Johnson found that urban areas had become "population sinks and ecological traps" for bears—sucking them out of the backwoods and sending them to an early grave.

THAT SEEMED TO BE WHAT WAS HAPPENING around Lake Tahoe. In Incline Village, Lackey and I met up with his longtime research partner

Jon Beckmann, a biologist then with the Wildlife Conservation Society, at the I.V. Coffee Lab, where saline bags filled with coffee beans dangled from metal poles. The three of us grabbed an empty spot near the front window as a thunderstorm rolled in.

Beckmann lived in Kansas, but was in town on bear business. He was tall with dark features, heavy-lidded eyes, and a five-o'-clock shadow—Lackey's physical opposite in almost every way. In the early 2000s—the backyard bear boom times—Beckmann had led a landmark study to figure out what was going on with the bears living at the juncture of the Sierra Nevada and Great Basin Desert. American black bears are known to be fairly transient, and an adult male might stake out an area of 60 square miles or even larger as his home range. Beckmann's study found that bears in this area had drastically contracted their ranges in the preceding decade, moving around between 70 and 90 percent less. And yet, they were still fat. *Too fat.*

Bears typically lose between 15 and 30 percent of their body weight during hibernation. (This is why it's so important that bears accrue enough calories before heading into the den.) Beckmann's unprecedented findings suggested that Tahoe's townie bears were continuing to pack on the pounds all winter; their collective weight was a third more than the bears who stayed in the backcountry. Disconcertingly, he discovered there had been a tenfold decrease in the density of bears living in the woods. The bears were overwhelmingly trading their forested digs for city living.

It didn't take long for conflicts with people to spike. Between the 1990s and 2000s, the number of interactions involving bears and humans skyrocketed by 1,000 percent. Yet the actual number of bears in the Lake Tahoe Basin hadn't increased. In a single year, the city of South Lake Tahoe and El Dorado County, in California, recorded more than 450 instances of an animal getting into trash. Nevada wildlife managers ultimately euthanized 132 bears in the Lake Tahoe Basin and western Great Basin Desert between 1997 and 2013. And far more bears were struck and killed by cars while attempting to cross the highway during times of drought to access water and food.

Black bears continued to empty out of the backwoods at an alarming rate. Where once it was mostly adult males hanging around urban areas, Beckmann told me they were now seeing more females with cubs around town. The urban death toll combined with this demographic shift meant that black bears were no longer repopulating the backcountry. In a 2008 study, Lackey and Beckmann were unable to turn up a single wild black bear in the 50-mile-long Carson Range except for one small pocket. "Bears are used to eating grasses, forbs, nuts, and berries," Beckmann said. "Then they come down to urban areas and you have a year-round food source of garbage, fruit trees, bird feeders, and koi ponds. The bears see it as a buffet and it's hard to get rid of them."

This was especially true in times of drought. In the last decade, eastern California suffered a particularly intense one that killed millions of trees and plants. Town dumpsters remained the only reliable source of food for bears in the late summer and autumn—a time when bears enter a food-frenzied stage called hyperphagia to prepare for hibernation and, in the case of females, giving birth.

All bear species except sun bears experience a phenomenon known as delayed implantation during the reproductive cycle. In wild black bears, a male bear's sperm will fertilize the female's egg during the summer, but the early-stage embryo, known as a blastocyst, won't implant on her uterine wall until late autumn. If the female doesn't gain enough weight before she heads into the den—if she's below 20 percent body fat—she'll reabsorb the blastocyst for energy instead of giving birth. This mechanism is nature's way of performing crowd control in bad food years. And it worked pretty well until humans showed up. Bears soon realized that, independent of berry and nut production, delicious food could still be found in backyards, trash bins, cars, and even grocery stores. So, instead of forgoing pregnancy altogether during the California drought, Lake Tahoe's black bears were still pushing out new cubs every year, even in times of drought. With no food to be found in the woods, young bears learned from mom to hit up lakeside communities.

Though the average alleyway bear shares more in common with a dumpster-diving raccoon than a grizzly, one thing does trigger aggressive behavior: food. Of the sixty-three people killed by American black bears between 1900 and 2009, nearly half of all incidents involved a person standing between a bear and its perceived meal. Moreover, according to a 2011 study by renowned bear biologist Stephen Herrero, 86 percent of fatal black bear attacks on humans have occurred since 1960. The strongest correlation: more people living, playing, and working in the wildland-urban interface.

No one has been killed by a trash-mucking American black bear around Lake Tahoe. At least not yet. But more than a handful of people have been mauled, swiped, or charged at by bears near homes and businesses on the California side of the lake. In one memorable instance, a man came face to face with a black bear that had broken into his friend's cabin. "I blast the [blow] horn and the bear goes up on its hind legs . . . the bear lunges at me and I did a jump kick and hit him square in the sternum and knocked the bear backwards," he recounted to local media.

"Right now, we're taking those bears out before they hurt someone," Lackey explained. "If a bear kills somebody, our politicians are going to force us to start taking more drastic actions. You're going to see an increase in the number of public safety kills. Guaranteed." He pointed to an incident over the Arizona border. In the summer of 1996, a 300-pound male black bear attacked teenager Anna Knochel camping in the Santa Catalina Mountains, less than 50 miles from Tucson. The bear severely mauled her head, neck, face, and leg. After spending three weeks in the ICU, undergoing surgery to reattach her scalp, Knochel's parents sued the US Forest Service and Arizona Game and Fish Commission. The bear that had attacked Knochel bore a yellow tag, marked #166, indicating it had a past run-in with the law. It was later revealed that Mount Lemmon, where Knochel was attacked, served as a state relocation site for "problem bears." Mere days before the incident, the US Forest Service had received another complaint about the bear's habituated behavior. Wildlife officials blamed drought conditions for drying up the bear's natural food supplies. The state ultimately settled out of court with the girl's family for $2.5 million.

Before leaving, I asked the duo why the Lake Tahoe Basin was considered the worst locale for bear-human conflict in the country. Lackey disagreed with my assessment. Tahoe wasn't worse, he asserted, just better known due to decades of study. "When you look at New Jersey, they might get seven hundred complaints in just one month. But they haven't been doing the research we have, so you don't hear about that."

If anything, Beckmann chimed in, Nevada was a success story. In 2018, he and Lackey had joined forces once more to write an authoritative study chronicling twenty years of lessons learned from black bears in Tahoe's wildland-urban interface. They noted that conservation measures had led to a recolonization of the Great Basin Desert by bears from the Lake Tahoe Basin and Sierra Nevada Range and that bruins were now moving into parts of Nevada where the species had been absent for more than eighty years. "There were almost no bears in Nevada back in the 1920s," Beckmann underlined. But now, Nevada's bears were a winning bet.

⟨

BEARS ARE INCREDIBLY SMART. Too smart for their own good in a place like Lake Tahoe. Aided by a large brain relative to their body size and a super-sniffer nose—bears can smell about two thousand times better than any human and seven times better than a slobbering bloodhound—bears are capable not only of locating human food, but of figuring out how to gain access to it, even if that requires breaking into an RV, cabin, or bear-*resistant* trash bin. When I'd used the term "bear-*proof* bin" in my early days of reporting on garbage management, wildlife managers had swiftly corrected me: almost nothing in this world is bear-proof when confronted with a determined bruin.

The majority of ursine cognition research has been carried out on captive American black bears. However, some field studies on other species hint at the bear's cognitive capabilities. In China's Qinling Mountains, where temperatures regularly reach −5°C (23°F), scientists have found that pandas ingeniously smear themselves with horse manure to bolster their cold tolerance. Over the span of two years, they recorded thirty-eight "horse manure rolling behaviors." (The manure contains chemical compounds that interact with the pandas' thermosensitive receptor pathways, preventing the bear from feeling cold.) Wild brown bears have been found to create complex mental inventories of their surroundings—they can remember where their favorite berries grow and where other bears live long after a first encounter. If relocated, they know how to return home—like a spawning salmon swimming back to its streambed. And for more than three hundred years, Inuit have reported observations of polar bears using tools—pieces of stone or ice—to bludgeon walrus over the head. (Less than 1 percent of animals have been documented using tools.) Still, American black bears remain the most popular subjects of clinical research.

Jennifer Vonk, a comparative psychologist at Oakland University in Michigan, has published what is among the most authoritative bodies of research on how bears understand the world around them. Yet Vonk didn't set out to study the minds of bears. Like many animal psychologists, she was primarily interested in primate cognition and the lives of social animals. Bears, though they live in close-knit family groups as cubs, are considered solitary beings. Shortly after Hurricane Katrina battered the US Southeast, Vonk began working with a lonely chimpanzee named Joe at the Mobile Zoo, a small roadside attraction in Wilmer, Alabama. Joe had been surrendered by a Hollywood trainer and was kept in a barn with a family of four American black bears—Elsie, the mother, and her three adult children, Brutus, Dusty, and Bella. As her experiments with the chimpanzee wore on, Vonk began to wonder whether the forgotten bears might also benefit from some mental stimulation.

Vonk devised an experiment to test the bears' simple discrimination between objects. She began by teaching the bears how to use a touch-screen device. Then she instructed them to indicate the difference between an image of a bear and an image of a human. If the bear touched the black bear image, it received a food reward. If it touched the image of the human, it heard a buzzer. She would cycle through about twenty different sets of randomly paired pictures in different conceptual categories, and once the bears reached 80 percent accuracy, she would swap out the set of photos to see if the bears could maintain the same precision. This would indicate that they had generalized the information. Could they tell the difference between a primate and a nonprimate, such as a horse? Between an herbivore and a carnivore? Between an animal and a landscape? They could. "They were the most rapid learners," she told me. "They were super motivated. Over time, they became my favorite subjects."

Brutus, born in captivity, was Vonk's first superstar performer. "He quickly learned he was getting treats when he responded correctly to the touch-screen and he wouldn't let the other bears near the screen." For more than a year, Vonk only worked with Brutus. She discovered he could distinguish and understand numbers—a key barometer of animal smarts. When Brutus was shown images with different arrays of dots, he could tell the difference between larger and smaller assortments, even when the dots moved around on the screen. "The pattern of performance was similar to that found previously with monkeys, and suggests that bears may also show other forms of sophisticated quantitative abilities," she wrote in her peer-reviewed study in the scientific journal *Animal Behaviour*. Later, when the bear siblings were moved to a new enclosure that allowed for some degree of separation, Brutus was no longer able to hog the device, and so Dusty began to shine. In the image discrimination experiments, "[Dusty] was ninety percent correct on the animal versus non-animal photos in his very first session," she told me. "There was pretty compelling evidence he understood he was supposed to be choosing those images."

In another of Vonk's cranial explorations, she gauged black bears on their ability to make the mental connection between the two-dimensional image of an object and its real-life manifestation. In others, she expanded on this concept to see if the bears could understand numbers and 2D or 3D objects at the same time. For example, if she showed a bear an image of three almonds, would it understand that this meant it would receive three almonds? When Vonk showed an American black bear at the Detroit Zoo a unique set of objects and their corresponding images, the bear was capable of transferring their meaning from one to the other. This is something that gorillas have never mastered, said Vonk.

"I don't like to talk about intelligence—it's a bit anthropocentric— but in terms of quickness to acquire discrimination and the markers of some of the things we would call 'intelligence,' bears have outperformed the great apes I've worked with on many tasks."

For those who live in close proximity to bears, this may come as no surprise. "We know they're super clever just in terms of getting into food at campsites," Vonk confirmed. She told me that some of the grad students at Oakland University had been working on another experiment that gave puzzle boxes filled with food to different species. To break into the box, the study bears displayed evidence of hypothesis testing and causal reasoning—much the way a bear might figure out how to get into a sealed garbage can. "It seems like the bears persist longer than cats. Cats will give up, even if they know there's meat inside. Bears keep working at it, testing different solutions."

As fascinating as it was to learn of such cognitive feats, it pained me to think that the moon bears on bile farms in Asia were acutely and intelligently aware of their surroundings. The whole ordeal would be much more tolerable if, say, they had the brains of goldfish. Vonk's findings certainly didn't improve my peace of mind. But there was another critical argument for why it was important to appreciate bear intelligence: understanding the behavior of bears is essential for minimizing conflict with their species and ensuring their long-term survival in our complicated world.

FOR NEARLY A CENTURY, some of the smartest bears could be found in Yosemite National Park. California has more black bears than anywhere else in America (outside of Alaska), and nearly half of the Golden State's thirty thousand black bears reside in the Sierra Nevada. The mountain range swells from the deserts of the Great Basin and slowly unfurls westward, splitting the landscape into jagged fragments that rise and fall, from alpine meadows to granite cathedrals to sequoia groves. General Sherman, the world's largest tree, holds residence here. So does Mount Whitney, the highest point in the contiguous United States, and the Yosemite monoliths—Half Dome and El Capitan. Though the national park is only about a four-hour drive from the Lake Tahoe Basin, when it comes to black bear management, it's a world apart.

It was dusk when I pulled up to the Hodgdon Meadow Campground on a September evening. Twenty-five miles northwest of Yosemite Valley, Hodgdon Meadow was one of the less desirable campgrounds in the park but had been the only one left with vacancies when I'd booked on short notice. The ranger booth was unmanned, and I found my campsite number on a whiteboard, scribbling down my license plate in the log book. A stack of bear safety brochures sat on the booth's window ledge. I followed the looping road along the perimeter, crawling at 5 miles per hour. Douglas squirrels nattered from tree branches. Families were roasting hot dogs over roaring campfire flames, the parents nursing sore knees and feet. I parked by a pile of sawed logs at #45, a site on the outer edge that backed onto wilderness instead of the restrooms—a decision I came to regret in the middle of the night. Smoke, with subtle notes of grease and meat, wafted through the thin pines. I hurried to set up my tent before darkness fell.

Site #45 contained a fire pit, a picnic table with past campers' initials carved into its surface, and a food storage locker—a brown metal box large enough to fit two coolers and a few bags of food. A sign stuck to the front read:

ALL FOOD MUST BE KEPT IN THIS LOCKER. LEAVE NO FOOD OUT. LEAVE NO FOOD IN YOUR VEHICLE. VIOLATORS WILL BE CITED (CFR 2.10). PROTECT YOSEMITE'S BEARS. REDUCE PROPERTY DAMAGE.

Another sticker informed me that I could be fined up to $5,000 if I didn't obey the rules. I carefully put my own green Colemans inside. Then I struggled for longer than I'm proud to admit to secure the locker in the dwindling light. Evidently, a long pin attached to a chain needed to be inserted through two small holes, locking the doors. The process required problem-solving and ample dexterity. It was hard to imagine Yosemite's bears would be able to figure out how to open this complicated contraption, let alone maneuver their furry paws into its mechanisms. Yet, they had.

Hodgdon Meadow's 109 campsites were the last in the park to still use this outdated locker model. Through years of trial and error, the bears had successfully cracked the code. These lockers, I later learned, were scheduled to be replaced over the coming winter. It wasn't uncommon for Yosemite staff to retrofit old lockers or come up with new designs altogether. It was this resilience and relentless innovation that had made the park so successful at keeping the bears at bay. Hundreds of campers were crammed into Hodgdon Meadow that chilly evening, charring marshmallows into gooey gobs, but there were no problem bears roaming the campground. In the women's washroom, a bulletin warned only of a mountain lion that had been spotted prowling the campground the week before. As I climbed into my sleeping bag that night, I pulled my bear spray nearer. It worked on cats, too, right?

THE NEXT MORNING I AWOKE with the sun and crawled out of my tent. I walked over to the bear locker and inspected the latch. Still secure. I scanned the ground for paw prints or any evidence that a bear may have tried to break in. Nothing. I retrieved some instant coffee and a granola bar from the locker and then headed out for the day to El Portal, a community just outside the park's boundaries partially under the administrative jurisdiction of the NPS.

Today, Yosemite is a global model for living with bears. But the park learned its lesson the hard way. Throughout the twentieth century, Yosemite was considered a national embarrassment, not a triumph of bear management. Up until the late 2000s, brainy bruins were running amok over the park, smashing minivan windows, raiding campgrounds, wandering into tents, and overturning garbage bins. "You'd drive your car to the park and then it got destroyed because you left a candy bar in the door," a former Yosemite superintendent told the *Mercury News*. In 1997, black bears broke into more than six hundred cars in the park. Hondas, Dodge Caravans, and old Toyotas were their favorite targets. As the Bay Area paper summarized, "It wasn't that long ago that a trip to see Yosemite's spectacular granite cliffs and splendid waterfalls was a descent into *bear mayhem*" (emphasis mine).

At the NPS compound in El Portal, a concrete multistory building surrounded by a chain-link fence that looked like a correctional facility stranded out on the scrubby landscape, I took the elevator up several floors and followed a maze of hallways to find Rachel Mazur sitting in her office, surrounded by reams of paper and field guides. She had a deep end-of-summer tan, and her dark brown hair, streaked with gray, was pulled back in a low ponytail. She was suffering from a migraine and thought some fresh air might help, away from ringing phones and chatty coworkers. So she led me down to a picnic table at the back of the building where staffers often ate their lunch. The dry hills of the Sierra rose around us. "Everyone likes bears," she said, pressing her palms on the picnic table as she sat down. "It's harder to find someone who *doesn't* like bears." But back in the 1990s, the park's bears were an even bigger headache for Mazur. "Yosemite had created an entire population of bears that was not just conditioned to human food, but habituated to human presence."

Mazur, a trained biologist, is chief of wildlife, visitor use, and social science at Yosemite, but she's also the park's unofficial bear historian. She grew up in Syracuse, New York—an area with its own booming population of black bears—and at the age of nineteen headed west to fill a seasonal job post at the nearby Kings Canyon National Park. She ended up staying thirty years. Mazur had spent decades on the ground contending with the Sierra Nevada's bears at a time when conflicts were at their worst. In 2015, she published *Speaking of Bears*, a book about the ursine crisis in American national parks and subsequent rewilding efforts.

To understand how Yosemite came to be such a hub for marauding bears, it's important to understand the park's history. The Indigenous Ahwahnechee inhabited the Yosemite Valley for at least three thousand years before settlers set eyes on the dramatic granite edifices that would one day transform the region into an international playground. Unfolding west to east, the valley opens with Elephant Rock, then the striking cliff of El Capitan, then rambles on to Bridalveil Falls—a sheer rock wall spliced by a cascading waterfall—the Three Brothers cliffs, Yosemite Falls, and finally the world-famous Half Dome at the eastern end of the valley, which hunches over at 4,800 feet, as if sliced cleanly in half.

These impossible sculptures captured the imaginations of the first Anglo-Americans who arrived in the valley around 1833. Thousands of miners would later pass through the area in search of gold, as would the Mariposa Battalion, laying siege to the Native inhabitants. Still, it wasn't until journalist James Mason Hutchings and draftsman Thomas

A. Ayres began publicizing the splendors of the valley in the 1850s that Yosemite attracted national interest. The United States Congress formally established Yosemite as a national park in 1890. With the construction of Yosemite Lodge, thousands of visitors were soon arriving in the park every summer, coaxed by the fantastical engravings made by Ayres and the idealistic writings of naturalist John Muir, who encouraged others to "Climb the mountains and get their good tidings. Nature's peace will flow into you as sunshine flows into trees." As city folk poured in, the native Ahwahnechee who remained on reservations had little choice but to perform for the tourists' entertainment.

By the time World War I began, the majority of Americans lived in cities, and nature had taken on a different hue. It offered a respite from the choking pollution and trappings of urban life. Yosemite's black bears were presumably delighted by the picnic baskets unwitting tourists toted into their valley. "At first, there weren't too many interactions between people and bears," Mazur said. "Garbage was mostly biodegradable back then, not like our plastic love affair of today." It wasn't until the early years of the last century, when visitation increased, that more bears started coming in. Perhaps park visitors should have paid more mind to some of John Muir's other, less romanticized writings:

> [The bear] breaks into cabins to look after sugar, dried apples, bacon etc. Occasionally he eats the mountaineer's bed; but when he has had a full meal of more tempting dainties he usually leaves it undisturbed, though he has been known to drag it up through a hole in the roof, carry it to the foot of a tree, and lie down on it to enjoy a siesta.

In 1915, park staff began hauling tourist trash to newly created dump sites within the park's boundaries. These aromatic spoils were a beacon for hungry bears. Tourists delighted in the sight of the real-life teddy bears. They flocked to the trash piles in hopes of encountering a black bear rummaging through their rotting leftovers. "At that time, there was a complete naivete about bears," Mazur told me. Black bears soon grew so used to the human intrusion that they were taking food right out of people's hands. Park managers grew concerned. A bear was a dangerous wild animal. It didn't understand the boundaries of human society. Something had to be done.

A logical next step would have been to close off the dump sites and issue fines to those caught feeding bears. Park staff could have even restricted certain food items from being brought into the park or asked that visitors take their trash out with them. But this was not the solution Yosemite managers devised. Incredibly, park management reasoned that the only way to gain the upper hand on the bear situation was to establish bear-feeding shows. Beginning in the 1920s, King Canyon and Yosemite converted their dumps into "feeding areas" that turned trash-loving bruins into performers. Standing among the stench of putrefying garbage, tourists gazed upon as many as a dozen bears eating their scraps. Staff argued that the shows would help to draw bears out of the campgrounds and contain them in a few centralized places where they were easily managed.

Yosemite's key concessionaire, the Yosemite National Park Company, later formalized the bear pits into a commercial enterprise. In 1923, they built a feeding platform near the river bend at Yosemite Lodge and baited bears to come in on cue for waiting guests who had paid 50 cents each for a coveted spot. Later, they scaled up the event, transporting as many as two thousand guests every night. The park earned money from this distraction-attraction, and with any luck, the bears would leave the campgrounds alone. What could go wrong?

Naturally, decades of feeding wild black bears eventually created an even bigger problem in Yosemite and nearby Sequoia and Kings Canyon. As Yosemite visitor and bear numbers ballooned, so did conflicts. In 1937, an astounding sixty-seven people were hospitalized due to injuries received at Yosemite's gluttonous bear shows (they were clawed, cuffed, or bitten). Two years later, an NPS report admitted that black bears in the region had become habituated to human food:

> The bear shows had grown to be a major attraction and the service found itself unable to abruptly discontinue them without tremendous public protest. Soon, bears began to invade

campgrounds, break into automobiles, and some bears that were unable to stand the competition around garbage pits became the pitiful "holdup" bears begging along the roadsides.

Yosemite had become a full-scale experiment of all the ways people and bears can clash. More than one hundred bears were killed in the Sierra's national parks in the 1930s. Besieged by bruins, park officials began to shut down the bear shows. Soon after, rangers began collecting and taking the trash out of campgrounds every evening to a central incinerator in the park. The bears still showed up. It was like playing whack-a-bear. "When they bear-proofed the dumps, they went into the campgrounds, and when they bear-proofed the campgrounds, they went into the cars, and then they went to people," Mazur said.

It would take decades before Yosemite finally had the tools at its disposal to deal with the park's garbage problem once and for all. Come the 1960s, trucks, dumpsters, and roads would allow staff to transport garbage far outside the park's boundaries—and far away from hungry bears. Still, progress lagged until one devastating night in the summer of 1967.

On August 12, college students Julie Helgeson and Michelle Koons were camping in Glacier National Park when they were attacked and killed by two different grizzly bears in separate incidents. Their deaths were later memorialized in Jack Olsen's 1969 book *Night of the Grizzlies*. Koons had grown up in San Diego and was working at the park's gift shop. Helgeson, a Minnesota native, had also arrived in Glacier that summer to work in the laundry room of East Glacier Park Lodge. On the day of the attacks, Koons and her friends had hiked up to Trout Lake; Helgeson and her partner Roy Ducat, meanwhile, had ventured about 20 miles east of the lake to a spot not far from the Granite Park Chalet.

Koons's group was camped out under the glow of a lightning storm when the grizzly arrived. It sniffed around the camp until it came to Koons, who awoke with a scream. Her friends bolted out of their sleeping bags and shimmied up a tree. But Koons's zipper was stuck and the bear was soon upon her. She yelled that the bear was tearing her arm off, then, "Oh my god. I'm dead." Ten miles away, Helgeson and

Ducat had fatefully chosen a spot close to a path frequented by bears feeding on food scraps disposed of by Granite Park Chalet. Ducat woke to Helgeson whispering there was a bear prowling nearby. All too suddenly, the bear was on top of her. Then it was Ducat's turn. When the grizzly finally released him, Ducat ran to a group of nearby campers. The bear then focused its attention on Helgeson, dragging her into the woods as her screams faded into the night.

Authorities later determined that some grizzlies had been "lured in intentionally" by garbage. The chalet had even advertised, "Come to Granite Park and see grizzly bears." Writing in his 1985 book *Bear Attacks: Their Causes and Avoidance*, biologist Stephen Herrero offered this prescription: "The most likely predisposing factor related to the attack on Julie Helgeson and Roy Ducat was garbage feeding and habituation. An even stronger confirmation of the role of garbage, human-food feeding, and habituation, however, is found in the death of Michele Koons."

The day before Koons was killed, an aggressive grizzly bear had treed a father and son hiking on a trail near Trout Lake, Herrero wrote. In the skirmish to get away, the son dropped his food-filled pack and the bear immediately tore into it. Though Herrero noted that several factors may have contributed to Koons' death—the hot weather and lightning may have agitated the bear; the friends were sleeping without the meager protection of tents; and Koons wore a lot of fragrant makeup—he believed that "the bear's personality combined with her garbage and human-food foraging experience predisposed her to attack. She was an aggressive individual encouraged to be so by the outcomes of her many interactions with people and their garbage and food." Koons's partially devoured body was found dragged 107 feet from the campsite.

At first, however, the NPS appeared to blame the attacks on the fact that both victims were women. An initial report by the NPS noted, "The Trout Lake girl was in her monthly menstrual period while the Granite Park victim evidently expected her period to begin at any time." An NPS and US Forest Service brochure about safety in bear country published soon after advised women to "stay out of bear country during their menstrual period." It also noted that bears were attracted to "human sexual activity." (Decades later, a study found that neither grizzly bears nor black bears showed a heightened interest in menstrual blood—but, terrifyingly, polar bears did.)

Eventually, the NPS was forced to reconcile with the role of garbage and food in the attacks. Shenandoah, Mount Rainier, Rocky Mountain, and the Grand Tetons permanently closed their dumps. In 1969 and 1970, Yosemite finally did the same. The dumps at Tuolumne Meadows, White Wolf, Wawona, Crane Flat, and Yosemite Valley were all retired. From that point on, all garbage was either incinerated or trucked out of the park to Mariposa County Landfill. Despite this earnest effort, Yosemite's bear problem didn't go away. "They closed the dumps kind of abruptly," Mazur explained. "The bears needed somewhere to go. So they went into the campgrounds." In *Speaking of Bears,* she wrote, "it was like a repeat of the closing of the bear pits—on steroids. The campgrounds still weren't bear-proof. In many parks, trash containers weren't bear-proof." Again, the parks attempted to deal with the chaos they'd created by killing a lot of bears.

"We had this mess that developed, in part, because we didn't have anywhere to put trash, and, in part, because we developed these bear-feeding areas," Mazur told me. "It took decades and decades to create this situation, and then it took the equivalent amount of time to fix." She recalled a holiday weekend back in the 1990s when she'd worked overtime, hauling six pickup trucks full of trash out of the park and chasing bears away. "During the years I was at Sequoia, I would literally work from before sunrise until well after midnight dealing with bears. I used to lock myself in a closet and cry." I asked Mazur when she felt that Yosemite had finally conquered the bear problem, once and for all. She settled on 2010. "To get to the point where we had lockers everywhere, things were bear-proof, education was in place . . ." She paused. "And, on top of that, we needed to get rid of a lot of bears that were beyond saving." A generation of bears that never learned how to forage for wild foods. Now, she said, the park is able to spend time and resources on restoring other species instead of dealing only with trash-addicted bears.

"It's a different park now. It's a truly different park."

THE YOSEMITE WILDLIFE MANAGEMENT OFFICES were a short walk down a dirt pathway from the valley's visitor center and museum, where sunscreen-smeared children and their parents were preparing to hike up the Mist Trail to Vernal Falls. The offices, a series of brown wooden cabins set amid a stand of oaks and poplars, blended in seamlessly with the autumnal landscape. Gray squirrels were in a foraging frenzy, diving headfirst into piles of leaves. I imagined the park's black bears were doing the same.

Inside, Caitlin Lee-Roney was carefully laying out an assortment of curiosities on her desk. Rubber bullets. Chewed-up plastic jars. A crushed beer can with tooth-puncture marks. "Bears love beer," she offered as an explanation. Retro bear posters drawn by Bay Area cartoonist Phil Frank decorated the office walls. In 1975, Frank created the comic strip *Farley,* set in the fictional Asphalt State Park. Ranger Farley was tasked with contending with a posse of black bears running a restaurant called the Fog City Dumpster. Sound familiar? Lee-Roney handed me a carved wooden plaque that sat next to her computer. "This is one of my favorites," she chuckled. It read: "At the root of the bear problem in Yosemite is the overlap in intelligence between the smartest bear and the dumbest camper."

Lee-Roney had grown up in El Portal—both of her parents worked for the NPS in Yosemite—and bears were in her blood. She went to high school in Mariposa, about 40 miles from Yosemite Valley, and during that time she began volunteering with the human-bear management program in the park. When she later went away to college in Santa Cruz to study ecology and evolutionary biology, she returned every summer to continue volunteering with the bear program. Her first paid job was at the Yosemite Conservancy's bookstore. "I just kept coming back here. It was pretty hard to leave." On the day I met her at the Yosemite Wildlife Management Offices, she was heavily pregnant, and a light blue T-shirt with the words BEAR TEAM stretched across her belly.

For more than a decade, Lee-Roney had led Yosemite's specialized bear force. Created in 1998 at the peak of bear-human conflict in the park—nearly 1,600 incidents were reported that year—the program had the mandate to fix the park's egregious bear problem. Today, no other park has a team of scientists and full-time staff dedicated solely to mitigating bear-human conflict.

To begin, the Bear Team had to ensure that no human food was ever within reach of a bear. Day and night, they collected garbage at campgrounds and drove it out of the park; they cracked down on improper food storage and fined campers; and, when the situation warranted it, they euthanized food-conditioned bears. Lee-Roney lifted up the showstopping piece she used at educational fairs—a pelt belonging to a black bear known as Orange-19, who had roamed the Yosemite Valley a decade ago. I swept my hand across the soft, bristling fur. "She had cubs that would jump on people's backs and try to get their food by pulling their packs off," Lee-Roney explained. Eventually, they had no choice but to euthanize her.

On the wall hung an old, verbose sign written in a campy font:

> Notice to Bears: Beware of Sabotage: We want to warn you that certain humans in this park have been passing the biscuits and soda pop to some of your brothers. Keep your self respect—avoid them. Don't be pauperized like your uncles were last year. You remember what happened to those panhandlers, don't you? Do you want gout, an unbalanced diet, vitamin deficiencies, or gas on the stomach? Beware of 'ersatz' food stuffs—accept only natural food and hunt these up yourself. These visitors mean well but they will ignore the signs. If they come too close, read this notice to them. They'll catch on after awhile.—THE COMMITTEE.

Happily, things had improved since then, and park staff no longer had to resort to pleading with illiterate animals. Within the park, bear-resistant infrastructure was everywhere. "One campground alone has over three hundred bear lockers," Lee-Roney told me. Every evening, the Bear Team led interpretative walks for campers to learn more about the park's three hundred to five hundred bears. And staff often conducted late-night patrols of Yosemite's thirteen campgrounds to ensure that all food was secured in lockers and that the dumpsters were empty. "If there's a bear in the campground, we'll do negative conditioning to chase it out. If there are bear jams, we'll manage traffic." There was even an impound lot in Yosemite Valley for unattended vehicles left with food inside.

Yosemite's progress was evident not just at the landscape level, with thousands of trash bins and lockers, but in the bears' behavior. During the twentieth century, Yosemite's bears had altered their schedules to be more active at night. Bears aren't nocturnal by nature, but darkness afforded them the perfect disguise for raiding campsites and avoiding people. As such, nearly 90 percent of the park's bear incidents occurred after dusk. As the availability of garbage in the park declined, Yosemite's bears had returned to keeping daylight hours, Lee-Roney said. Moreover, when park scientists analyzed snippets of bear fur to understand how the bears had changed their diet, they found that compared with a half century ago, bears were consuming about 63 percent less human food.

The Bear Team rarely had reason to euthanize problem bears now. "On average, it's between two and three per year," Lee-Roney told me. Incidents had been decreasing, too. There were just twenty-two that year—a record low. And the cost of bear-inflicted damage had dropped from $660,000 in 1998 to less than $5,000—a decline of 99 percent. But the team had to stay on top of the bears' evolving curiosity. "We have really smart bears," Lee-Roney observed. An adult female bear had been hanging around a backcountry campsite in the Snow Creek area, northeast of the valley. She had learned to break into backpackers' bear canisters—supposedly bear-proof jars used to store food—by batting them off a 400-foot-high cliff so that they shattered. The bear then scrambled down to the bottom to feast on its spilled contents. (Again, make that *bear-resistant.*)

"Some of our bears will figure out our lockers, too. We just finished replacing all the lockers in the valley and shortly after we noticed there were paw prints all over them. The bears were checking them out. The same thing happened when we replaced the trash cans." On Lee-Roney's desk sat the blanched skull of a bear with its two canine teeth ground down to dull stumps. "We think he got this way from gnawing on the metal bar of a food storage locker." She mentioned the lockers up at Hodgdon Meadows, where I was camping. They'd already been retro-fitted multiple times because the bears had figured out how to get into them. "If they're not latched correctly, the bears get their claws in and bend the door. We welded on an extra bar to prevent the bears from swatting them open, but they need to be replaced again." The park, she added, preferred to use models that required sticking a hand up inside a covered lever. Bear paws couldn't fit.

"It's just always a progression of bear-proofness, because, eventually, they do figure it out."

THERE WAS NO END POINT TO bear management in Yosemite. The park had solved the initial problem created over nearly a century, but with millions of people visiting the park each year and roughly five hun-dred smart and hungry bruins in their midst, coexistence was always going to be an ongoing process of innovation, determination, and, ulti-mately, compassion.

Yosemite's bears weren't urban bears. This meant the park had far more agency in how to deal with wildlife than cities or towns, whose first priority would always be the safety of human residents, not the health of the ecosystem. But the lessons learned in Yosemite through decades of mismanagement could still be exported to the rest of the country to help communities in the wildland-urban interface manage their relationships with neighboring bruins.

Still, this brought up another question I'd pondered long ago: Why was it so important that we learn to live with American black bears?

As I drove out of Yosemite the next morning, past the former dump-site at Crane Flat, I thought of the other five bear species I'd seen—or hadn't seen—around the world. The caged sun and moon bears. The spectacled bear in the shrinking cloud forests. The sloth bear roaming fractured wilderness. And the adorably pathetic 1,864 pandas. Amer-ican black bears were being killed for eating garbage. They were being hit by cars. And, in some cases, they were no longer hibernating. All terrible things. But at a landscape level, the American black bear population was doing just fine. There were nearly one million black bears roaming the world. From a pragmatic perspective, a few dozen deaths didn't come close to making a dent in the global population. So why was it so important to coexist?

I'd posed this question to Carl Lackey and Jon Beckmann when we'd met on that rainy day in Incline Village years earlier. Beckmann understood that perception of the situation. "Yeah, if people really want to worry about bears, then we need to be worrying about the seven other species," he had answered. But, he went on, black bears were the training wheels for truly threatened species.

"If we can't live with black bears, how the heck are we going to learn to live with grizzlies? It's one thing to have a black bear in your house, but it's a whole different ball game to have a grizzly in your house."

"And," he'd added, "that's starting to happen."

CHAPTER SIX

RETURN OF THE GRIZZLY

Brown bear, United States
Ursus arctos

Nathan Keane is an early riser. On most mornings, he'd let the dogs out to run around the yard at around 7:30. Then he'd make a pot of coffee and enjoy a few quiet minutes to himself before the kids woke up and the farmwork began. But his routine changed one early June day in 2020. First, he forgot to put the dogs out. Then, as he waited for the coffee to brew, he glanced out the kitchen window, across the winter wheat almost ready for harvest, toward the horizon. He did a double take. There—no more than 30 feet from the house— was a grizzly bear.

"There was no mistake about it. It had the big natural hump on the shoulder and the broad face," he recounted. Not to mention, "it was eating a chicken inside our coop."

Keane had lived on the plains 16 miles north of Loma, Montana, for fourteen years. He married into the farm and he and his wife grew small grains, mostly. Wheat. Canola. Flax. Mustard. Hemp. They kept chickens, but not cows. To the best of his knowledge at the time, grizzlies lived far away—some 150 miles west—in Glacier National Park. Certainly not in the wide-open ranchland of north-central Montana. The only connection his small plot of domesticated land had to such rugged wilderness was the Marias River. The tributary flows east from Glacier County, near the Blackfeet Indian Reservation, across the state, running along the edge of his property. The bear, he reasoned, must have followed the water. "I guess he happened to smell the chickens and came up out of the river bottom."

At the time, Keane's sighting was the farthest east a grizzly had been seen in the United States in more than a century. He had heard murmurings around town that the bears were moving closer, "but you just don't expect one to be in your backyard," he told me. As the grizzly pulverized his poultry, Keane dialed up the Montana Department of

Fish, Wildlife and Parks to report the brazen animal. But before the officer could make it out to his farm to apprehend the grizzly, a neighbor drove by in a loud pickup. The bear shot off. Keane was left to assess the carnage.

When the state's grizzly bear management specialist for the region investigated the crime scene, he determined the culprit to be a three-year-old male that had previously been spotted moving toward the area, traveling about 10 miles east every day. He set a trap next to Keane's coop, hoping the bear might come back for another free meal. But the bear was never caught.

After the encounter, Keane installed an electric fence around his chicken coop to protect the ruffled survivors. He started carrying a pistol with him on the tractor. "I catch myself looking over my shoulder now," he said. "It makes you think twice about what else is out there." He lowered his voice. "This *wildlife thing.*" After the incident made the local news, Keane started receiving harassing comments. "One guy said we should have known better to keep chickens, being in bear country and all. Well, we *aren't* in bear country. But maybe we're starting to be now."

GRIZZLIES ARE EXPANDING INTO AREAS WHERE they haven't been seen in generations. Keane's run-in is no longer shocking in the Mountain West. Just a year after his sighting, another grizzly was photographed roaming the Big Snowy Mountains, 30 miles farther east than the Keane farm. In the Yellowstone and Northern Continental Divide ecosystems, bears that have been isolated from one another for more than one hundred years are increasingly venturing out of their respective regions, slowly closing the gap and reclaiming old territory.

The grizzly bear, despite what most people think, isn't a species unto itself. Rather, it's one of two living subspecies of brown bear found in North America, the other being the Kodiak bear (*Ursus arctos middendorffi*) in Alaska. Grizzlies (*Ursus arctos horribilis*) once ranged as far south as central Mexico, where they were known as *oso plateado*, silvery bears, for their grayish fur. But these southerly bears were trapped, shot, and poisoned until they'd become scarce by the 1930s. Another fifty thousand grizzly bears were estimated to live in the contiguous United States when the Lewis and Clark Expedition passed through in the early 1800s. But European settlers decimated these bear numbers, too, until fewer than one thousand remained. The southern extent of the grizzly's range eventually contracted from Mexico to the southern border of the Greater Yellowstone Ecosystem.

Grizzlies also disappeared from the coast. In California, the bears saw a $10 bounty placed on their heads during the mid-1800s. Restaurants fried up greasy grizzly steaks that they served for less than a dollar. Seth Kinman, a Californian trapper who perhaps best embodied the attitudes of the Gold Rush era, gained notoriety for his bizarre furniture pieces fashioned from various grizzly parts. Kinman claimed to have personally shot eight hundred grizzlies in his time, and one of his resulting creations featured two grizzly arms encircling a rounded chair back. The furry seat was bolted onto four chopped up grizzly legs with clawed feet. Kinman gifted this chair to President Andrew Johnson, who kept it in the White House library. One biographer describes an interesting parlor trick: "The seat was soft and exceedingly comfortable, but the great feature of the chair was that, by touching a cord, the head of the monster grizzly bear with jaws extended, would dart out in front from under the seat, snapping and gnashing its teeth as natural as life." Ultimately, of the thirty-seven US grizzly populations still present in 1922, thirty-one would vanish within just fifty years. Survivors, driven out of the wide-open grasslands, sought refuge in only the most remote and wildest places—the forests of Montana, Wyoming, Idaho, and Washington.

The grizzly's gains in the past five decades have been the result of swift human intervention followed by natural expansion. In 1975, all grizzlies living in the Lower 48 of the United States were protected under the Endangered Species Act, a landmark piece of legislation that the federal government had introduced a few years earlier to conserve animals at risk of disappearing in the country. The grizzly, more charismatic than most, inevitably became the poster child of the act. Protection meant that bears responsible for killing cattle were no longer allowed to be killed by frustrated landowners. Trophy hunts in Wyoming and Idaho ceased. "It is now unlawful to kill, capture, harm, harass, import, or export a grizzly bear anywhere in the lower-48 states," the listing dictated. The US Fish and Wildlife Service later identified six ecosystems where grizzlies were thought to still exist, making them a priority for recovery: Greater Yellowstone, Northern Continental Divide, Cabinet-Yaak, Bitterroot, Selkirk, and the North Cascades.

Americans, whether through taxes or donations, spent millions of dollars to restore grizzlies—financing habitat protection, private land easements, and educational programs to teach people how to live with an animal capable of eating them. Critically, they also funded the relocation of bears. In the 1990s, scientists decided to augment the Cabinet-Yaak grizzly population in northwestern Montana by transplanting a handful of Canadian bears into the ecosystem. The descendants of those bears are now wandering down into the Bitterroot Range, near the Montana-Idaho border, which has been devoid of grizzlies for decades. Biologists had initially hoped to plop some foreigner bears into the Bitterroots, too. Now they think the grizzlies may repopulate the ecosystem without their help.

Today, grizzlies number just below two thousand in the Lower 48. Their population has more than doubled in half a century, and, as evidenced by Keane's encounter, the bears are no longer content to roam behind the contrived boundaries we've made for them. In 2021, USFWS released a report on the subspecies' status, noting that "Grizzly bear populations in the lower-48 states have expanded considerably, both in terms of size and range." Yellowstone's grizzlies are on the move. The bruins have tripled their range in recent years and are now moving north out of the national park and core of the protected area. Meanwhile, grizzlies that belong to the Northern Continental Divide recovery zone are heading south. About 50 miles are left separating the two populations—the closest they've been in more than a century. Scientists expect that the bears will join up in less than a decade—two islands becoming a continent.

For an animal that was flirting with extinction in the Lower 48 just fifty years ago, the return of the grizzly bear is one of America's unlikeliest comeback stories. The bears are among the slowest-reproducing mammals in North America; they require vast tracts of habitat (an adult male grizzly can have a home range of 600 square miles); and they kill people. Bringing back the grizzly required a profound shift in people's conception of wilderness and their place within it. Humans had to overcome genetic memory—the part of the primitive brain that drives our fear of predators—to champion the return of a known man-eater. The emergence of a new kind of environmental philosophy, underpinned by the writings of naturalists Edward Abbey and Aldo Leopold, undoubtedly popularized such restoration ethos.

In the centuries since the Lewis and Clark Expedition, the grizzly bear has evolved from a loathsome predator to a symbol of wilderness in the human mind, allowing us to cautiously extend the olive branch. The bear's hump rises like the mountain itself, gently sloping into a peak anchored in the rolling plains of its back that bristle with coarse fur like pine needles. Its dish-shaped face appears much like the harvest moon, rising over its forested body when the bear stands on its hind legs to peer over alders, reaching a height of 8 feet. Four heavy paws carve trails through undergrowth, joining rivers with woods. Without wilderness, the grizzly would cease to exist. And without the grizzly, wilderness is tamed, deprived of its monarch.

Still, as much as the grizzly is now an iconic animal, it remains a fearsome one. The bear is more than 800 pounds of muscle and fat, ending in sharp canines and 4-inch-long claws. It is extremely defensive, ready to neutralize a perceived threat in a moment's notice. A human being is little more than a rag doll in its immense jaws. Such attributes dictate that the grizzly is the ultimate test of human acceptance. Though the bear has veered from the path of extinction, public sentiment remains mutable. That the grizzly should continue to prosper in the American wilderness is far from a preordained right. And as grizzlies expand into places they haven't inhabited in more than a century, the bears aren't only crossing geographical boundaries, but thresholds of tolerance.

Along the Rocky Mountain Front, where the undulating eastern slopes meet the plains, ranchers bridle at the sight of a bear roaming among their cows. Elk hunters are increasingly wary of venturing into the bush to collect a kill. It's not uncommon to find an irascible grizzly bear claiming a carcass as its own. Even hikers and backpackers have reason to worry. In 2015, sixty-three-year-old Lance Crosby was attacked and killed by a 259-pound mother grizzly with two cubs while hiking in Yellowstone National Park. Officials made the decision to euthanize the bear based on the fact that "a significant portion of the body was consumed and cached with the intent to return for further feeding," the park said in a statement. It was strange behavior. "Normal defensive attacks by female bears defending their young do not involve consumption of the victim's body." The grizzly's two orphaned cubs were transferred to the Toledo Zoo in Ohio. But the fears of those living in communities around Yellowstone were far from quelled. They took the attack on Crosby as a sign: the grizzly bear population had grown too large for coexistence.

Grizzlies are undeniably a flashpoint species in North America. Only the wolf inspires more hatred and mistrust among those who earn their livelihood from the land. In much of the rural West, where economies hinge on farming and ranching, the recolonization of American forests by apex predators has been met with resistance. People lament being forced to live in a state of constant fear and suffer the financial losses caused by predation of cows. A chauvinistic desire to conquer nature has also returned as grizzlies gain ground and power. In the United States, this yearning has manifested as a push to open a legal trophy hunt for the grizzly bear if it were to lose federal protections.

Grizzlies have come so close to closing the gap. But whether they continue to expand in the coming decades will depend on us. Since 2015, federal scientists have documented more than four hundred grizzly bear deaths in the Greater Yellowstone Ecosystem. At least three-quarters of these were deemed to be caused, whether directly or indirectly, by humans. Around eighty-five resulted from wildlife managers euthanizing bears that fed on cattle. Another fifty or so were "self-defense" kills. Fewer than thirty bears were ruled to have died a natural death.

Tolerance is often an ever-changing boundary, subject to push and pull. But in some cases, it's a barbed wire cow fence. Though scientists expect that grizzlies in Yellowstone and the Northern Continental Divide will reconnect within the decade, elsewhere such reconnections remain elusive. The grizzly's eastward expansion may be limited not just by food—the bears that once thrived on the plains were dependent on a robust bison population—but also by societal acceptance. Though a few stray males may be moving out of the mountains and into the prairies, it's unlikely the bears will take up full-time residence there without greater support. The male grizzly seen in the Big Snowy Mountains a year after Keane's sighting was eventually killed by wildlife officials for eating cows. All of this raises the questions: How many grizzlies are people willing to live with as next-door neighbors? How many bears are truly enough to satisfy recovery efforts? And who should decide?

I ENCOUNTERED MY FIRST YELLOWSTONE GRIZZLY prowling outside the entrance of the Hotel Terra in Jackson Hole, Wyoming, several years ago. Next to the stone facade, a portly man wearing a brown furry onesie was waving at passing cars. The bear costume's head was perched above his own, and two fangs protruded over his mustachioed visage, almost as if the man had been partially consumed by the bear and was now helplessly peering out of its agape mouth. In front of his chest, clasped between toothpick claws, he held a placard that read: "I'm Worth More Alive Than Dead."

I approached the bear, notebook in hand.

"I got this costume just for this event," the man hiding under its fangs beamed, doing a small twirl. "Grizzlies are my absolute favorite species! I always feel more alive when I'm in grizzly habitat."

He introduced himself as Jim Laybourn, extending a paw, and said he had shown up on behalf of Wyoming Wildlife Advocates, a nonprofit dedicated to conservation in the state. Inside the hotel, dozens of federal, state, and tribal representatives were gathering for the Yellowstone grizzly subcommittee's annual meeting to discuss the possible removal of federal protections from the population. If management was passed over to the states—Wyoming, Montana, and Idaho—a legal trophy hunt was likely to kick off for the region's famous bears.

The debate over delisting Yellowstone bears from the Endangered Species Act has been dragging on in the Mountain West for more than a decade. In 2007, USFWS briefly removed protections from Yellowstone's grizzlies, deeming the population recovered with more than five hundred individuals. But environmental groups disputed the government's assessment that the population had adequately rebounded. Of concern, state agencies had a reputation for catering to ranchers and hunters while shrugging off conservation concerns. This, environmental groups lamented, would be catastrophic for grizzly recovery in the United States. So they took the agency to court, where they ultimately won their battle to restore the grizzly's threatened status. The judge ruled that USFWS had failed to adequately analyze the impact of climate change on whitebark pine, a key food source for Yellowstone's grizzlies. Temperatures in Yellowstone had increased by an average of 1.3°C (2.3°F) since the 1950s, with the greatest warming at elevations above 5,000 feet, where whitebark pine grows. In 2022, the tree would also be added to the Endangered Species list.

Federal scientists launched their own investigation into the grizzly's food sources. They agreed that whitebark's precipitous decline caused bears to forage at lower elevations, making run-ins with humans more likely. And reduced cub survival rates had begun to slow grizzly population growth in 2002, coinciding with whitebark pine mortality. However, the study team praised the bears' diverse diet and adaptability. Yellowstone grizzlies relied more on meat than other populations, the team wrote in their report, and many bears already lived in areas without much whitebark pine. The reason more cubs and yearlings were dying, the scientists proposed, was not because of mass whitebark pine die-offs, but because too many grizzlies were crowded into too small an area. "We have not observed a decline in the Yellowstone grizzly bear population, but only a slowing of population growth since the early 2000s, possibly indicating the population is near carrying capacity," they wrote.

Federal officials again recommended that protections be stripped from the Yellowstone population. Laybourn, a lifelong Wyoming resident, expressed concern over the grizzly's tenuous future in the state and the potential trophy hunt. Oddly, he identified as a hunter. "But I would never shoot a grizzly bear," he clarified. Still, he fretted that people might misconstrue him as a bear-hugger. I had to admit that his furry attire didn't necessarily run against such interpretation. Despite his love for the iconic bears, Laybourn said he was most concerned about the economic ramifications of a trophy hunt. "Our tourism economy here is based on bears. I work as a guide myself and I've taken hundreds of people to see grizzly bears," he said. Scientists funneled past us into the building, carrying hefty manila folders. Laybourn held the door open with his toothpick claws, an inadvertent ursine bellhop. "I want to make sure we have a robust population," he continued. "Whenever we take people out to see the wildlife and geysers, every single person asks me, 'Are we going to see a bear today?' "

THE BEAR-HUGGER PERSPECTIVE would appear to be the dominant one across the Mountain West. Tourist towns around Yellowstone lean heavily on the ursine motif, from the Three Bears Lodge to the Beartooth Barbeque to the Running Bear Pancake House. "Grizzly X-ing" mugs are well stocked at every souvenir stand. And bear claws—a sweet danish—are sold in almost every bakery within a 100-mile radius of the national park. But evidently, there were still those who lusted after an *actual* bear claw.

Though trophy hunting may seem an anachronism rooted in the colonial school of thought that wilderness should be conquered and sanitized to satisfy human ego, fragments of this worldview have prevailed into the twenty-first century alongside the vulnerable grizzly bear. To understand the future of human coexistence with grizzly bears in North America, I would need to gather perspectives beyond the readily available bear advocate groups who eagerly sounded off about the grizzly's natural prestige. I would need to talk to a hunter.

At his office in eastern Oregon, I met Steve West, the host of the TV show *Steve's Outdoors Adventures*. West was huge in both height and girth—the kind of man who might even stand a tiny chance against a grizzly in a fight. A trimmed sandy beard created the mirage of a jawline on his round face. On the day I met him, he wore a plaid shirt that pulled tightly across his chest and a camouflaged ball cap with his TV show's logo on it. West explained that he had started out hunting for meat—deer and elk, mainly—and made his first foray into trophy hunting in the 1990s with black bears and grizzlies in Alaska. Part of what had made bears so attractive was the risk. "Grizzlies are hunted because they're a challenge," he said.

West had killed a lot of bears in his lifetime. One of his champion bears was undone by a muzzleloader in a grassy estuary of British Columbia's Great Bear Rainforest before the province instituted a ban on trophy hunting. But he didn't discriminate between species. West was a connoisseur of charismatic megafauna, bumping off magnanimous beasts around the world one by one. Oryx in Namibia. Water buffalo in Australia. Musk ox in Canada. His exotic glass-eyed trophies decorated the wood-paneled walls of his office, located in a one-story building near La Grande's main street. I locked eyes with a mountain lion frozen on a log in this macabre menagerie. West followed my stare. "Ah yeah—that was a cat called 'Catzilla.' He was killing domestic sheep in Utah. That was a phenomenal hunt," he recalled wistfully. "My dogs tracked him down. Lost him twice. My feet were bleeding by the end of that one."

But the big cat paled in comparison to grizzlies.

"Stalking a grizzly bear is completely different than going after anything else," West observed as we moved through the halls of his office, taking in each lauded kill. "There's the man versus bear thing that comes into play. Yeah, I've got a rifle or a boat, I'm holding an advantage of weaponry, but there's still an element of danger," he insisted.

One of his show's episodes had featured him unloading on the champion British Columbia grizzly at low tide. The rain and reverberation of the gunshot masked what should have been the tremendous sound of the 900-pound body collapsing into the shallow water of the estuary. A camouflaged West had raised a triumphant fist in the air, shouting to his guide in the metal skiff floating behind him. "Ooh, Bob, that's a nice bear." He then reached down into the brackish water and hoisted the grizzly's head up by its wet ears, posing the conquered animal for the camera. "That's what it's all about right there!"

Hunting grizzlies provided West with an intense adrenaline rush. It required skill and focus. "It's something that will bite you back. Don't mess up. Don't make a bad shot. Then you have to chase a wounded bear." The stalk, he continued, was everything. "After you shoot a bear, it's anticlimatic." Evidence of this alleged anticlimax—the BC grizzly— was now mounted at the entrance of the office to greet visitors. Its face had been fashioned into a menacing snarl and its arms hung limply forward, like a T-Rex. It looked nothing like the grass-eating bear I'd seen on TV.

West told me he supported a mix of management approaches to brown bears. He thought there should be places off-limits to hunters, like Brooks Falls in Alaska, where thousands of tourists can watch brown bears fish for salmon from wooden viewing platforms. At the same time, bear hunting existed in other parts of the state. "Alaska is the perfect compromise," he said. But there were getting to be fewer and fewer places in the world where it remained legal to shoot a brown bear. With that in mind, I asked West about Yellowstone, the new locale on the horizon. Without pause, he replied:

"I'll buy the first tag."

🐾

IN EARLY 2017, the Yellowstone grizzly lost federal protections for a second time. Department of Interior secretary Ryan Zinke designated the delisting as "one of America's great conservation successes, the culmination of decades of hard work." Less than a year later, Wyoming and Idaho announced they were opening a trophy hunt. The states held a lottery for twenty-three tags; each one would enable the winner to bag a bear. It cost less than $20 to enter.

Trophy hunters salivated over the prospect of knocking off the park's most beloved animal, Grizzly 399. The female bear was often photographed ambling along the road with two or three cubs in tow. As such, world-renowned wildlife photographer Thomas Mangelsen entered the lottery in hopes of winning a tag to spare a bear's life by shooting it with a camera instead of a gun. More than seven thousand people entered the draw. In the end, twenty-two tags were allotted to hunters in Wyoming, and one in Idaho. Miraculously, Mangelsen was one of them. (Steve West was not.) Soon, it wouldn't matter.

Following the announcement of the grizzly's second delisting, environmental groups and Native American tribes again sued the government. One lawsuit took issue with the USFWS's decision to remove protections from the isolated Yellowstone grizzly population rather than prioritize reconnecting populations across the West. Another lawsuit alleged that the federal government ignored legal requirements to consult with tribes about the decision. Members of the Cheyenne, Blackfeet, Eastern Shoshone, and Northern Arapaho Tribes had previously held a resistance meeting near Jackson Hole in a lakeside lodge. At a large wooden table, representatives from Canada and the United States signed the Grizzly Treaty—only the third international agreement of its kind in 150 years—that committed to restoring and revitalizing the threatened grizzly bear across North America. More than one hundred tribal nations signed on. "Our people have been separated from the grizzly since we were forced onto reservations, but we have not forgotten," the then Crow Creek Sioux Tribe chairman Brandon Sazue wrote to me. "In our genesis, it was the great grizzly that taught the people the ability for healing and curing practices, so the grizzly is perceived as the first 'medicine person.' . . . It is no coincidence that the spiritual reawakening of Native people on this continent has coincided with the modest recovery of the grizzly since the 1970s—a recovery that will end with delisting and trophy hunting in a return to the frontier mentality of the 1870s."

Just before the trophy hunt was scheduled to begin, the judge presiding over the Yellowstone case brought down the gavel. He ruled that the federal agency had acted "arbitrarily and capriciously" and ultimately exceeded its legal authority when it removed protections from the Yellowstone grizzly. The judge wrote in his decision that it would be "simplistic at best and disingenuous at worst" to not take into account the five other populations of grizzlies outside of Yellowstone. With the bears so close to closing the gap, losing protections would be an enormous setback for the subspecies. If USFWS was going to succeed in delisting the iconic bears, it would need to focus on rejoining these island populations and creating genetic linkages that would ensure that grizzlies endured long into the future. So, there would be no trophy hunt. Protections were restored.

The ruling was a victory for the environmental groups and tribes who had fought hard to keep the magnanimous animal protected indefinitely. For others living in close proximity to America's growing grizzly population, it was anything but.

BLACK BART IS THE ONLY BEAR Trina Jo Bradley doesn't mind having around. The enormous jet-black grizzly, pushing 900 pounds, has lived on her ranch on Birch Creek for close to six years. He's well behaved and never gets into trouble. Plus, the resident bruin keeps the riffraff out. "Normally we get bears coming through here pretty thick in March, heading out from the mountains down to the prairie. Since he's been here, we've seen way fewer bears."

Ranching is in Bradley's blood. She was raised on a cattle operation some 16 miles south, near Dupuyer Creek in Montana. Her father was a hired rancher for the man who owned the land, which meant that Bradley and her brothers were put to work at a young age. They rode horses and herded cows. Any free time was spent mucking around outside—but always within shouting distance of the house, and with a guard dog. There were bears near Dupuyer, she said, even back then in the 1980s and 1990s. Glacier National Park wasn't too far away, and occasionally a grizzly from the Northern Continental Divide population would wander out and kill one of their cows.

Bradley went down to Casper, Wyoming, for college, where she studied agribusiness. At twenty-two, she was in a bad car accident and "crippled myself for a while," which forced her to return home to Montana where, while recuperating, she met her husband. Instead of going back to school like she'd planned, she moved onto his family farm, where she's now been for eighteen years, raising Angus cattle and quarter horses—and their daughter. When her father-in-law bought the Birch Creek ranch back in 1956, there were no grizzlies in the area, she said. The first bear returned in the 1990s and killed a calf. Authorities promptly trapped and removed it. "That was the last bear they saw until I moved here. I'm pretty sure the bears followed me from Dupuyer," she said.

As Montana's bears grow their numbers and range, ranchers like Bradley are growing frustrated. The bruins are occupying more private land, leading to more encounters with humans and livestock. Bradley's sage-green farmhouse is surrounded by some 3,500 acres of hayfield and private pasture, where they run their cows—about 250 of them—though Bradley admonished me when I asked how many she owned. "It's like asking someone how much money they make—none of your damn business," she scolded, half-joking. The house's living room window looks out over rolling hayfields, toward the snowcapped perimeter of the Rocky Mountains. From this vantage point, Bradley often watches the bears go by. "Grizzly bears are super cool, and I love seeing them," she said. "But I *don't* love seeing them in my yard or in my cows."

Mornings on the ranch begin with feeding the livestock—hay and "cake," a mineral and vitamin supplement. When I spoke with her, most of their cows were being kept in a pasture behind the house, following the spring calving. "That's where Black Bart was last time I saw him. He just hangs out there," she said. In the afternoon, Bradley walks through the cattle to make sure none are sick, injured, or dying. She always carries a gun. Grizzlies are around nearly every month of the year. Still, her ranch hasn't experienced severe depredation—the term used to describe domesticated animals killed by bears. "I think we're just lucky. Or maybe our cows are really mean." A neighbor less than a mile away, she said, lost between fifteen and twenty calves to bears annually.

A few years ago, Bradley was appointed to Montana's Grizzly Bear Advisory Council, a state-run initiative with the aim of "listening to Montanans" and "following their interests while also conserving bears." She was passionate about promoting and protecting agriculture in the state and hoped that future generations would be able to grow up on the land, as she had. Grizzlies were making that difficult. So, she started going to meetings. Talking to other ranchers. Getting to know all the grizzly officials in the state. Bradley wanted to ensure that people were receiving assistance to cope with the grizzlies in their midst. "Pretty much everybody here is just tired. We're tired of grizzly bears. We're tired of conflicts. We're tired of not letting our kids play outside. We're tired of having to sacrifice our paychecks for the public's wildlife." This was one of the most common arguments I heard from livestock producers: liberal urbanites are the ones who want predators back on the landscape, but they aren't the ones suffering the consequences of a grizzly in the backyard. "It's not like camping or backpacking," Bradley said. "We don't have a choice. We have to go outside. We have to take care of our cows. And there's probably going to be a bear there."

As long as grizzlies remain under the wing of the Endangered Species Act, state wildlife managers are unable to deal with cow killers—relocating or euthanizing bears—without first consulting the federal government. Ranchers believe this limits their ability to get rid of the bears causing problems. (Environmental groups and scientists have long questioned whether grizzlies are responsible for as many livestock deaths as states allege.) At committee meetings, there was some discussion about also removing protections from the Northern Continental Divide bears, but, perhaps chastened by the Yellowstone debacle, USFWS recommended in 2021 that grizzlies in the Lower 48 remain threatened under the Endangered Species Act.

Bradley disagreed with this assessment. "Grizzly bears no longer need to be protected. They're not unicorns," she said.

"How many bears do you think is enough, in an ideal world?" I asked.

"I think when the grizzly bears were put on the Endangered Species Act—there were only like [three hundred to] four hundred bears in the entire state then—that was enough."

Many ranchers want tougher punishments for encroaching bears. They want them removed from the population right away, not given multiple chances to redeem themselves after attacking livestock. They want more funding for conflict prevention measures. And, most of all, they want bears delisted. But until science proves that the bears have been unequivocally recovered across the United States, there isn't much that can be done. Bradley had set up an electric fence around the chickens and goats in the yard, but it wasn't feasible to put an electric fence around the entire ranch. For now, she'd have to rely on Black Bart to scare off the others.

"He's the best guard bear there is."

CHRIS SERVHEEN FIRST LAID EYES ON a grizzly in the Scapegoat Wilderness, near Helena, Montana. He was in his early twenties, backpacking with a few college friends, when they entered a meadow and caught sight of a bear tearing up a huge stump, looking for insects. "We stayed there for several hours, just watching him from the trees," he said. "Grizzlies have this ability to burn into your memory so that you remember everything that was happening when you saw them. It's really amazing how much you can remember, even years later. . . . That's the magic of grizzly bears."

Servheen is arguably the foremost grizzly expert in the United States, having served as the USFWS national grizzly bear recovery coordinator for thirty-five years until his retirement in 2016. In his heyday, he was the guy in charge of making sure bears didn't disappear from the Lower 48. And, evidently, he did a pretty decent job of it.

Servheen grew up on the East Coast, but moved out to Montana for school to study wildlife biology, inspired by the National Geographic wildlife specials that had captivated him as a young child. He began by researching bald eagles under the mentorship of John Craighead, one-half of the Craighead twins who gained fame as American conservationists focused on falcons and grizzlies. Craighead kept a small flock of captive eagles at his house, and Servheen often worked with the birds. But he later pivoted to grizzly bears for his PhD. It was a timely detour. The grizzly bear was a hot topic, having itself landed on the endangered species list just three years earlier. After finishing his doctorate in 1981, Servheen accepted the newly created position of grizzly bear recovery coordinator, though he wasn't optimistic about the bear's prospects. He assumed he would likely spend a few years documenting the species' demise before switching to another troubled animal. Around Yellowstone, there were just thirty breeding females left in the population at the time the bear was listed. "It's important to recognize we were *really* close to losing grizzly bears at that point," he said.

For more than three decades, Servheen was a constant presence at bear meetings. Whether in Yellowstone, in the North Cascades, or in the Cabinet-Yaak, his nearly bald head could be seen popping up from a corral of Stetsons. A bushy horseshoe mustache that turned from brown to gray as time passed drooped over his upper lip. In 2015, still working at the agency, he had been adamant it was time to remove protections from the Yellowstone bears. Though the legal wrangling had cast a long shadow on the case, he believed that the Yellowstone population, and possibly even the bears in the Northern Continental Divide population, should be delisted. The grizzly group had met its ecological recovery goals, and provided the population was managed carefully after delisting, the bears were guaranteed to be around for a long time.

"The objective of the Endangered Species Act is to get a species to the point where protection is no longer required," Servheen had told me at the time. "It's not like the Wilderness Act where a species must forever remain listed. The purpose is to fix the problem." In the case of the Yellowstone grizzly, he believed it had been.

Servheen was now spending his retirement backpacking with his family and fly-fishing in Missoula, Montana. Albeit, I learned that he didn't exactly view it as retiring when he left the agency. Rather, in his final years as the grizzly recovery coordinator, he was worried that the Feds were bending to the will of the states instead of doing what was in the grizzly's best interests. As the agency prepared for the second delisting, Servheen had written some guidance on how best to manage grizzly deaths once the population lost protections, essentially putting safeguards in place that would stem any future population decline. If too many bears died, for example, these measures would ensure that the population regained protections. But his document came back with such safeguards removed. This, he felt, eroded the credibility of the recovery program and made delisting "biologically incredible and legally indefensible." Knowing it would be up to him to defend such a plan in the face of a lawsuit—which was all but guaranteed—"I quit."

It wasn't the triumphant ending to his career that Servheen had imagined. "The grizzly bear recovery program is one of the most successful stories in the Endangered Species Act. They're a challenging species to recover and we did it," he told me, "but all the political bullshit that happened right at the end kind of spoiled it." He mentioned none of this at the time. And few questioned the premise of his retirement; he was sixty-five and had successfully stymied the grizzly's extirpation. Now, rather than spending his days idly fishing, Servheen had made it his mission to bring attention to the risks confronting grizzlies anew.

Given how things had changed since we last spoke in 2015, I wondered whether he thought grizzlies should still be delisted.

The answer was a decisive no. "For years I was an advocate for delisting," he admitted. He believed that the agency had gotten Yellowstone's bears to the point where protections were no longer needed. And he hoped states would take on this responsibility with maturity and grace. But lately, "the actions of Montana's legislature have proven that the states are no longer able to be trusted when it comes to managing large carnivores." Servheen pointed to a disconcerting trend in the West that he dubbed "anti-predator hysteria." In spring 2021, the Republican Montana legislature signed into law a bill that would allow hunters to trap and kill an unlimited number of wolves—unprotected in the state—on a single license, also permitting the use of spotlights and bait traps. Another bill extended the season for wolf hunters to use leg-hold traps and neck snares, coinciding with when bears are out of their dens. And lastly, the legislature approved a spring hound hunting season for the state's black bears—a practice that had been banned in Montana for a century. Though such hysteria was largely centered around wolves, Servheen believed that all other predators would suffer the consequences, including grizzlies. It was an unprecedented slide backward toward the Manifest Destiny mindset of eliminating every danger that threatened human safety. "It's really horrifying to me to see this. If they weren't still [federally] protected, one can only imagine what Montana would do to grizzlies."

I asked Servheen how many grizzlies he thought the United States could feasibly handle. It was a question I'd put to almost everyone I met who had some skin in the grizzly game in the American West. There were conservation advocates who denounced the human-centered worldview and believed we could happily live with tens of thousands, no matter the cost to humans. They lobbied for the bears to be returned to California, the Grand Canyon, and the Southern Rockies in hopes of tripling the population. And then there were people like Trina Jo Bradley, who wanted far fewer bears than were currently wandering around. Most people weren't willing to give a numerical answer, focusing instead on the genetic health and connectivity of the populations. However, Servheen—the scientist—was ready with a precisely calculated answer: three thousand to thirty-four hundred grizzlies.

He broke that number down. The habitat of the Yellowstone ecosystem and Northern Continental Divide, he explained, could support two thousand. The Bitterroot could hold three hundred to four hundred. The Selkirks and Cabinet-Yaak could take another 150 bears. And the North Cascades could support up to four hundred bears—though there were none present at the moment. It would therefore take a sincere human effort to nearly double the grizzly population in the Lower 48. And, worryingly, Americans seemed to be moving in the other direction. Servheen warned that we could begin to see an overall population decline, not an increase. "Grizzly bears are special animals," Servheen said. "They have low resilience. They live in special, remote places. And if we're going to maintain grizzly bears, we have to behave and treat them in a special way."

In early 2023, the USFWS said it would again review whether to remove federal protections from the grizzly bears in both Greater Yellowstone and the Northern Continental Divide ecosystems. Whether or not grizzlies continue to grow their numbers in the Lower 48 and eventually close the gaps that exist between populations depends now on our behavior. Can we share the landscape with a known predator, even if it's an inconvenience to us? Still, thinking of the bears that had wandered down from the Cabinet-Yaak and into the Bitterroot, I had to acknowledge that nature did not always require permission nor adhere to our politics. And while some bears were moving south and east in the Lower 48, perhaps even more notably, another group of grizzly bears was heading north.

CHAPTER SEVEN

THE ICE WALKERS

Polar bear, Canada
Ursus maritimus

Whiteout conditions blotted out the banks of Canada's Hudson Bay. It was mid-November, and sea ice had been slowly forming a frozen jigsaw puzzle over the dark open water. It would soon reach the shoreline, bridging the terrestrial and marine worlds. The region's six hundred or so polar bears would then head out onto the ice to hunt ringed seals, where they would lead an enigmatic existence until they returned to the rocky tundra next spring. Inside Tundra Buggy One, the official research vehicle of the conservation group Polar Bears International, I scanned the monotone landscape for the camouflaged ice-pilgrims to no avail. Out here, one had to be adept at discriminating between shades of white: porcelain, bone white, eggshell, milky white, pearl. Spotting a polar bear, particularly in a snowstorm, was an ocular feat. Gusts of wind lacerated the saltwater coastline as the buggy pushed forward. The bears had likely taken refuge among the low-lying willows that fringed the shore.

"Buggy" is a benign word for the armored monstrosity we were using to navigate this part of the Canadian Shield, where large gray boulders broke through the tundra grasses like breaching whales. The snow-white vehicle, driven by a polar bear biologist named BJ Kirschhoffer, was reminiscent of a stretch Land Cruiser balanced on gigantic tires with some 6 feet of clearance above the permafrost—and curious polar bears. It felt less like a truck and more like a boat as it pitched over rocks and lurched into deep craters carved by the buggies that had passed before us. A native of the region, Len Smith, developed the first iteration of the Tundra Buggy in 1980, blending together equal parts gravel truck and school bus to safely transport tourists and film crews over the fragile tundra. The buggies followed a network of trails created by the military in the 1950s. Wind-scoured flag trees—black spruces with the branches on the windward side destroyed by strong gusts—stood as a testament to the severity of the landscape. So fierce was the wind that even their tree rings huddled to one side when cored. Black gulls squawked above us. The buggy's wipers struggled across the windshield, trying in vain to divert the hammering snow. A colorful assortment of bear cracker shells and bullets jittered on the dashboard with each rotation of the tires. I checked the temperature on my phone, which I had tucked into the inside pocket of my parka to keep the battery from dying: $-23°C$ ($-9°F$) with wind chill. No wonder the polar bears weren't out and about.

Fortunately, the inner chamber of the wood-paneled buggy was cozy—not least of all because those of us huddled inside were surreptitiously sipping Irish cream mixed into our coffee at eleven in the morning. Unlike the dozen or so bear-viewing tourist buggies with coach seating humming along through the blizzard, this one was designed to allow a team of researchers to stake out on the tundra for days, even weeks, during the polar bear migration, observing the habits of the ice walkers. The back of the buggy was equipped with bunk beds, a working fireplace, a whiskey stash (count on Arctic scientists to always have the good stuff), and, on the exterior, four surveillance cameras connected to a live-stream channel that transmitted images of Hudson Bay's bears around the world.

I had long dreamed of this journey north. Whenever people had asked me which bear was my favorite, I had dithered and hedged. "I like them all equally," I would say, diplomatically. Sun bears were cute with lolling tongues. Grizzlies were emblematic of the American wilderness. And who could pass up the panda? What a jolly fellow. That, however, was all a lie. My favorite bear was unequivocally the polar bear. It was singular in its magnetism. An all-white bear, with translucent fur and black skin. It ate seals! Males could weigh more than 1,000 pounds! Never mind that it split off from the grizzly bear a few hundred thousand years ago, the ice bear was a novelty and we were lucky to be in its presence. Or, very near its presence, I hoped.

The day before, dozens of bears had been spotted padding along this stretch of frigid tundra pockmarked by shallow kettle lakes that formed when glaciers retreated thousands of years ago. In the nearby town of Churchill, Manitoba, tourists dressed in expensive parkas gabbed about their good fortune between bites of Arctic char at the Tundra Inn restaurant. Churchill is one of the easiest places in the world to see polar bears. What other northern locale has a group of polar bears that shows up, on a predictable schedule, near an airport, train station, and grocery store? Indeed, the sign posted along the desolate road into town proclaimed Churchill to be "Polar Bear Capital of the World." How much longer, I wondered, would this hold true?

Around twenty-six thousand polar bears are believed to exist worldwide. That estimation would make them the fourth-most populous bear species, and compared with many of their relatives whose numbers are slowly ticking down, most polar bear populations appear to be doing okay. Many Inuit even purport that the population is growing and that there are too many bears roaming the Arctic. But the species is heading toward an inevitable cliff: the point on a population chart where the red line chugging along uninterrupted suddenly nose-dives and disappears entirely below the x-axis, submerged much like the polar bear in an ice-free ocean. In the past two decades, climate change has devastated the sea ice that bears use for a hunting platform. Without ice, the bears starve. Those visitors who had made the long journey to Churchill were last-chance tourists, much like those who had sailed the undammed Yangtze in its final weeks or who now snorkel at the bleaching Great Barrier Reef. All of this could come to an end in as little as forty years. Churchill's southerly location in the subarctic means not only that the region is more accessible to researchers and visitors, but that the bears living here are likely to be among the first wiped out by climate change.

Hudson Bay is a large inland sea bordering three Canadian provinces and one territory, though technically the waters are considered the property of the Nunavut territory alone. At low tide, locals joke you can walk out along the sandy shore and find yourself standing in the northern territory. English explorer Henry Hudson, who built up his seafaring credentials near Greenland and Svalbard, discovered the bay in 1610 while searching for the fabled Northwest Passage, as was the thing to do if you were a brazen man with a penchant for exploration in the seventeenth century. But like his ambitious forefathers, he, too, was led astray. Mistakenly, Hudson believed he had discovered a route to Asia when he happened upon the large saltwater body smack-dab in the middle of what would later become Canada. After three months of searching the bay's edges, Hudson could find no outlet. By November, his ship was trapped in ice. He stubbornly demanded that his crew spend an abysmal winter on the shore of the bay before forging westward. (The polar bears were out on the ice by this point—a small comfort.) Fed up with Hudson's orders and the cold, the crew mutinied the following spring and set him and his teenage son adrift in a small shallop boat on the bay's waters. No one ever heard from Hudson again.

Hudson Bay does not connect to the Northwest Passage, but it does eventually empty out of the aptly named Hudson Strait into the Labrador Sea, an arm of the North Atlantic Ocean. In late autumn, as Hudson and his crew unfortunately discovered, ice grows over the surface of the bay. Though this may have filibustered Hudson's grandiose plans and led to his untimely demise, it's also given rise to a unique population of polar bears that inhabit the bay's shores. In other parts of the Arctic, sea ice may shrink in the summer but persists year-round, and polar bears spend most of their lives on the ice, rarely coming ashore. (At least, this was the case before climate change entered our vernacular.) The sea ice of Hudson Bay, however, freezes and thaws according to the season. The region's polar bears endeavor to stay on the ice as long as possible, but at some point they must decamp. During the summer and early fall, they bide their time on land as they wait for the ice to return. The patch of tundra around Churchill has become particularly populous with bears, in part because it's the place where the sea ice breaks up last in spring and returns first in the fall. Migrating bears from around Western Hudson Bay are getting on and off the ice here, often passing through town as they do so.

Forced ashore for months at a time, there is little else to do but get to know the neighbors. Young male bears spar on the slushy shores to stave off boredom in late autumn. Others munch on kelp washed in by the tide. Pregnant females den in the soft peat banks of Wapusk National Park, the only place in North America outside of the Mackenzie River delta where all three species of bears—black bears, polar bears, and brown bears—mingle. Though grizzlies were thought to have disappeared from Manitoba, they began showing up again in Wapusk in the 1990s. Scientists believe the bears—barren-ground grizzlies—are dispersing southward from Nunavut. Grizzlies have been seen in the park every year since 2008. For polar bears, the impermanence of ice means that they must pack on as much weight as possible during winter and spring when they can hunt blubbery ringed seals. A polar bear stomach can hold the food equivalent of as much as 20 percent of its body weight. Upon returning to land, the bears will fast for more than four months—pregnant females for eight—with rarely a pinniped in sight. Remarkably, during these lean months, a bear sheds about 2 pounds every single day until the ice returns.

Today seemed to be that day. In the twelve hours that had passed between me eavesdropping on the tourists' conversations and heading out in pursuit of bears, the thick ice edge had connected to the shoreline. Nearly every single bear spotted on land yesterday had departed for the winter season, finally satisfied that the ice could support their tremendous weight. Though it was bad news for me, it was good news for the bears. In recent years, Hudson Bay has been freezing up later in the season, extending the bears' tenuous fasting period. A sudden shift in weather patterns that week had spurred a surprisingly early freeze-up, and the bears would have extra time to fatten up.

Trying to appear patient despite this bedeviling change of fortune, I took a seat next to Andrew Derocher, a towering Canadian with a gray-streaked beard dressed in a puffed-out parka that doubled his stature. Still, it was difficult to make out anyone's physical characteristics under several layers of jackets, scarves, and toques. I was nearly as keen to meet Derocher as I was a polar bear. He was one of only a handful of scientists who had been studying polar bears before climate change hijacked the research agenda. Back in the mid-1980s, while Derocher was working on his master's of science, polar bears were doing well in Canada. It had been over a decade since the Canadian government began limiting the number of bears that could be harvested and restricting hunting permits to Indigenous people or to sport hunters with an Indigenous guide. (Canada is the only nation that still allows for the international export of polar bear hides and the only nation that permits the sport hunting of polar bears.) With these restrictions in place, many bear populations were recovering. "Our focus back then was just on basic ecology. We wanted to know about the lingering effects of the harvest and how many bears there were," he told me as we rumbled over the tundra.

In the mid-1990s, Derocher moved to Norway to study the emerging threat of pollutants accumulating in high levels in the unhunted population of polar bears living in the Svalbard archipelago. But things soon began heating up. "I love learning how animals make a living in a place like this. But now it's vainglorious to study the natural history of polar bears in a time when it doesn't seem to be that relevant. Seeing how much they're screwed up . . . it's not as much fun," he said with sad frustration. Derocher now leads the Polar Bear Science Lab at the University of Alberta in Edmonton and is a volunteer scientific adviser to Polar Bears International. Most of his spring field season is spent in Western Hudson Bay, traveling the tundra by helicopter to count the bears—a far smoother ride than the buggy.

Derocher first arrived in Churchill in the summer of 1984, a fresh-faced university student from rainy Vancouver who had never been to the subarctic before. Snow, in his view, was for downhill skiing. Despite such inexperience, he was handed a tranquilizer gun on his first time out in the chopper. The scientific mission was to dart and deploy radio collars on female bears (male bears can't wear radio collars because their necks are wider than their skulls). It wasn't long before Derocher spotted a pregnant female. He pulled the trigger and made contact. Success! The great bear swayed, but wouldn't go down. Instead, she began staggering toward a shallow lake as Derocher watched in horror. The bear collapsed in the water, nearly unconscious and partly submerged. The pilot turned to him and sternly told him to get out. "Next thing I knew I was standing on the skids and jumping into the lake." Immersed in waist-high frigid water, Derocher struggled to keep the bear's nose in the air. "She was heavy. And she was still swaying." The pilot flew back to camp to get help while Derocher was left alone in the water with the bear. When he returned, they dragged the soaked and now slumbering bear back onto the land. "She was fine," Derocher shrugged. "She went off and had her cubs." Sometimes he saw her family around and wondered if she remembered him.

Finally, in the early afternoon, we spotted a lone female bear the color of limestone. Bears will appear white when they first come off the ice, freshly rinsed from the pristine seawater. But eventually, dirt or tannins from the peat tinge their fur a creamy yellow. We were just past No Pants Lake—named for the man who once had to push his Tundra Buggy out of the water, losing his trousers in the process—and she appeared to be coming in from the bay. The quality of the ice must not have been up to her standards. Idle conversation was instantly abandoned. I jostled to the other side of the buggy and pressed my face against the glass, squinting through the driving snow to see the majestic animal of my Arctic imagination. Derocher hardly moved. He'd spent his life hand-to-paw with these bears, and seeing one from the buggy must have been like Jane Goodall seeing an animatronic gorilla on the Jungle Cruise in Disney's Magic Kingdom. He calmly lifted a pair of binoculars up to his eyes, observed the bear for a moment, then deemed her to be in good condition—though, he added, that wasn't indicative of how things were going across the Arctic. The yearlings he had seen earlier in the week were looking a bit smaller than was normal for the time of year. Moreover, the physical size of Western Hudson Bay polar bears had declined since the 1980s. The buggy inched closer to the bear padding across the tundra. I held my breath. Her black eyes and nose formed a dark triangle in a sea of white. What would she do? Roll in the snow? Break into a run? I raised my camera, ready for whatever charismatic polar bear behavior came next. She was about 30 feet away when she shrank behind a small willow, looked around, and emptied her bowels.

THE WORLD'S POLAR BEARS ARE SPREAD OUT across nineteen populations in five nations that range from the unforgiving icescapes of Svalbard, to the Chukchi Sea off the coast of Siberia, to Greenland, to

Alaska's North Slope, notable for its prodigious oil fields. However, the majority of polar bears—approximately sixteen thousand—live in the Canadian Arctic. Western Hudson Bay, Davis Strait, and Southern Hudson Bay, in the subarctic, constitute the southernmost latitudes of the polar bear's range.

Borne of ice and sea, polar bears, *Ursus maritimus*, branched off from the brown bear lineage a few hundred thousand years ago. Scientists have a few hypotheses for how an ocean-dependent bear—an impossibility of the mind—came to be during a time when much of the earth was in flux between a frozen and unfrozen state. Many brown bear groups were extinguished by the excruciating cold and shrinking food supply during these glaciated periods. Some marched south in search of hospitable ground as ice gripped the northern realm. But others sought refuge near the ocean, where, encouraged by warmer coastal air, they eked out a tenuous existence. In the Admiralty, Baranof, and Chichagof (ABC) Islands of Southeast Alaska, this gave rise to a unique subspecies of brown bear, *Ursus arctos sitkensis*, which exhibits mitochondrial DNA revealing a close match to polar bears. Along northern seacoasts, however, it's believed that brown bears became isolated from others of their kind. They turned to the sea for food. And the sea changed them forever.

"Not only had [the polar bear] gone from brown to white, from land to sea, from omnivore to carnivore, he had completely reversed the seasons of the bear year. Winter is a time of activity, summer is for fasting, resting and conserving energy," geologist Charles T. Feazel wrote in *White Bear*, which chronicles memorable encounters with polar bears. Despite this radical transformation, clues of the polar bear's ancestry are still present if you look closely—the slight shoulder hump and the long sharp claws.

The great white bear would later traverse this extreme environment with the Dorset, a Paleo-Eskimo culture that preceded the Inuit, lasting from 500 BCE to 1000 CE. The Dorset hunted almost entirely on the sea ice, waiting for seals to pop up at their breathing holes in the ice and harpooning whales and walrus. They weren't as fond of hunting land animals, such as the polar bear, as the Dorset did not use bows and arrows. Like the bear, their survival relied entirely on the sea ice. The Thule people, who rose to prominence after the disappearance of the Dorset, are believed to have begun spreading out from modern-day Alaska and, by the eleventh century, dominated the eastern Arctic, with some groups traveling as far as Hudson Bay. The Inuit were the descendants of the Thule, and within their culture the polar bear gained greater recognition. Some stories say that the Inuit learned to hunt seals from the polar bear. Two animals are believed to have isuma, a shared way of thinking, with the Inuit: the raven and the polar bear. The Inuit have many names for the polar bear, *nanuq*, including "the great white one" and "the ever-wandering one." Unlike the Dorset, the Inuit hunt polar bears. But killing a bear is seen as a far different experience than hunting seal, whale, caribou, and walrus. It is not just a deliberate, organized hunt, but a fortuitous and serendipitous moment.

Around the same time that the Thule were moving out across the North American Arctic, Norse travelers were making the acquaintance of the bears in Scandinavia and writing them into sagas. Most notably, in 1252, King Haakon of Norway gifted England's monarch, Henry III, a polar bear. Haakon was an expansionist ruler who had brought both Greenland and Iceland under Norwegian control. King Henry, meanwhile, was renowned for the menagerie of wild beasts that he kept locked in the Tower of London. Initially, Henry's sheriffs were to provide food for the bear at the stingy rate of 4 sous a day. Later, he boldly—and perhaps frugally—decided that the bear should be able to fend for itself. Writing in a letter to the bear's handler, Henry instructed:

> Greetings. We commend you that for the keeper of our white bear, recently arrived from Norway . . . ye cause to be had one muzzle and one chain to hold that bear without the water, one long, strong cord, to hold the same bear fishing or washing himself in the river Thames.

His court hastily fashioned a muzzle and chain for the bear so that the great animal could be walked, like a dog, down to the riverbank. Here, the polar bear was affixed to a long, staked rope and allowed to swim in the river and fish for himself. For three years, the polar bear was the icy diamond in Henry's crown. Alas, in 1254, the king of France one-upped Haakon: he gifted Henry an African elephant.

During Europe's Little Ice Age, between the fourteenth and nineteenth century, polar bears likely crossed the Arctic ice pack with enough frequency to populate mainland Norway and Iceland, though they were later exterminated by the demand for live cubs and skins. When men later began sailing to the seas around Svalbard and Greenland in pursuit of whale oil and walrus ivory, they encountered far greater numbers of the pale predators. Crew members were only familiar with the brown bears of their homeland, and so they often returned to Europe with shackled white cubs. Adult bears were another matter. On William Barents's 1595 Arctic expedition, the Dutch navigator's crew had a deadly encounter. While searching for diamonds on an islet near Russia's Vaygach Island, two of his sailors were resting in a wind-protected depression when "a great leane beare came sodainly stealing out, and caught one of them fast by the necke." The bear killed and devoured both men, despite the crew's attempt to drive the animal away. The incident, recounted in Dutch officer Gerrit de Veer's diary, became the first account of a polar bear attacking humans in recorded history. (The crew later shot the bear between the eyes.) These attacks must have weighed heavy on the minds of Renaissance cartographers, who depicted polar bears as if they were fierce mythical beasts. One early Arctic map warned *hic sunt ursi albi*— here are white bears. Bears, in the view of Europeans, were yet another obstacle to overcome in the harsh and mysterious north.

Polar bears have persisted as a cultural icon that dwells largely in the realm of imagination. Unlike American black bears, brown bears, and sloth bears, few people will ever encounter a polar bear unless they seek them out. The unique animals have been co-opted as commercial mascots—white bears guzzling Coca-Cola—and it is through these renderings that we have largely come to understand the polar bear. Our relationship to the polar bear is one of abstracted interaction, not only in conception, but in how we are driving it to extinction. We are not locking up polar bears in cages to extract bile. Nor are we entering their habitat and bulldozing their home. Rather, the polar bear is imperiled due to our own geographical biases. The melting Arctic is a distant afterthought as we emit an endless stream of greenhouse gases into the earth's atmosphere, paying little mind to the denizens of the ice.

↙

THE POLAR BEAR IS UNDOUBTEDLY one of the Anthropocene's most charismatic victims. Greenhouse gases emitted by human activity trap heat in our atmosphere. This heat melts the glossy white Arctic sea ice that reflects solar radiation. Instead, without this ice cover, the sun's rays are absorbed by the dark waters. This heats up the ocean and quickens the overall warming of the Arctic. As air temperatures increase, sea ice is melted from above and below.

The Arctic is unraveling at a pace no scientist could have imagined half a century ago, warming at roughly three times the rate of the rest of the world. Satellite records show we've lost roughly one-third of summer sea ice cover since 1979. Moreover, today's ice is thinner and fractured— only 1 percent of the remaining sea ice is thick and sturdy multiyear ice. In the seasonal ice zone around Hudson Bay, the ice-free period grows longer with each passing year. Across the Arctic, it's expected that summer sea ice cover could disappear completely as early as 2035.

Sea ice is to the Arctic as soil is to a forest. Rhythms of northern marine life are dictated by ice. Zooplankton and algae thrive on the underside of the sea ice like moss and lichen. Millions of polar cod come to nibble at this overturned dining table. Hungry seals feed on the fish. And polar bears keep vigil over seal breathing holes during the winter and spring, waiting hours for blubbery meals to pop up for air. When a seal finally makes an appearance, the bear will snap its jaws, hoisting the helpless seal onto the icy platform and shredding it apart—bears only eat the blubber—creating a gory anatomical display on the pale landscape. A single adult ringed seal weighs about 150 pounds, providing enough energy for a polar bear to go eight days without eating before it needs to feed again.

But the polar bear cannot adequately hunt without sea ice. In the High Arctic, bears that once spent their lives out on the sea ice are increasingly driven ashore during the summer as the sea ice melts out. Whatever food they might be able to scrounge up on land—snow geese, eider ducks, eggs, berries, kelp—is nowhere near enough to sustain them indefinitely. Though polar bears are masters of fasting, eventually they will reach a point when survival rates drop. In Western Hudson Bay, scientists think this is around 210 days—or about seven months—of fasting for male bears. (Females can go without food for longer.) Four decades ago, the region's bears spent 120 days on shore. At that time, less than 3 percent of adult male bears would die of starvation, and most were old bears past their prime. Scientists recently found that if the ice-free period were to extend to 210 days, between nearly a third and a half of all adult males could starve to death.

It's not an outlandish scenario. Winter sea ice in Western Hudson Bay is already breaking up about one week earlier and forming two weeks later than it did in the past, meaning that adult bears are spending an additional three to four weeks on land. In 2015, the bears fasted for approximately 177 days. This extreme diet has taken a toll on the population, which has declined by around 50 percent since 1987 and dropped roughly 27 percent just since 2016. In nearby Southern Hudson Bay, the population slipped from 943 individuals to 780 in just five years. Other southern populations are in trouble, too. In 2021, the US Fish and Wildlife Service announced that the population in Alaska's Southern Beaufort Sea had declined by almost 50 percent—from 1,526 animals to just 780—since 2010.

Péter Molnár, an ecologist at the University of Toronto Scarborough, and scientists with Polar Bears International recently created a time line for when different polar bear populations might reach their critical physiological limit. They found it's "very likely" some of the world's polar bear groups will begin to experience reproductive failure as early as 2040, leading to local extinctions. By 2080, polar bears in much of Alaska and Russia will be in serious trouble. And, under this business-as-usual emissions scenario, polar bears will likely remain only in the Queen Elizabeth Islands—the northernmost cluster in Canada's Arctic Archipelago—beyond the end of this century. Even if we mitigate emissions, some populations of polar bears will still go extinct before the end of this century. "It's important to highlight that these projections are probably on the conservative side," Steven Amstrup, chief scientist for Polar Bears International, told me. The models they developed, he explained, may assume a better-than-reality body condition of the bears at the start of the fasting period. "The impacts we project are likely to occur much more rapidly."

¥

NOBODY LOCKS THEIR DOORS IN CHURCHILL. The prefabricated houses, painted drab shades of gray and blue, are left unsecured at all times should some unlucky person need to take emergency shelter from a prowling polar bear. Bears, evidently, are of greater concern than crooks. The same thing holds true for the rusted pickup trucks and cars. All unlocked. "You're just always aware," said Joan Brauner, a long-time Churchill resident who works as the local helicopter dispatcher. "I always have a cocker pistol on me whenever I go out. I've had [bears] right up on my porch." Signs in the town's restaurants remind patrons to "look both ways" before exiting the establishments—not for cars, but for bears.

The edges of Churchill, much as they are hemmed by Precambrian boulders crudely tagged by tourists and graduating high school seniors, are also bordered by blue and white rectangular signs warning pedestrians to stay away. At the peak of the polar bear migration, few people venture out into Churchill's snowy streets. Residents rely on their cars for nearly everything. When dawn breaks over the tundra, armed officers patrol the town by vehicle, scouting out alleyways for concealed bears before people head to work and children to school. And every night at 10 p.m., an air raid siren sounds—a hangover from wartime. Locals have co-opted it as an alarm for a voluntary polar bear curfew.

Humans have invented a number of salacious ways to describe the aggression of bears, often to indulge macabre fascination rather than for scientific purpose. Sloth bears could be considered the world's deadliest bear because they kill the most people on an annual basis. Brown bears, which mostly roam the unpopulated northern forests of Canada and Russia, kill about six individuals every year and often relent once a perceived threat has been beaten into submission. Polar bears kill even fewer people, with only a handful of fatalities over 150 years. But when the ice bear strikes, with forty-two serrated teeth and dinner plate–sized paws that measure 12 inches across, few people live to tell the tale. Brown bears kill 14 percent of those they attack. Polar bears kill nearly double that.

Several of the documented fatal polar bear attacks in North America during the twentieth century occurred in zoos. These tragic incidents occurred when mentally ill or drugged men jumped into captive bear enclosures. Lafayette Herbert, a forty-three-year-old man with a history of mental illness, was mauled by three polar bears—Moe, Mollie, and Tillie—when he climbed over the fence at the Baltimore Zoo in 1976. It took officers three hours to retrieve his shredded body with grappling hooks, using tear gas canisters to keep the bears at bay. Among the exceptions to these zoo attacks was the killing of Hattie Amitnak, near Rankin Inlet, after she tried to distract a polar bear that had already injured two others at a Hudson Bay camp. And two more attacks took place in Churchill, Manitoba.

In 1968, Paulosie Meeko, a nineteen-year-old Inuit man, surprised a bear on the tundra near Churchill. It leapt up and grabbed him, slashing his throat. Police later arrived and shot the bear. Fifteen years later, in November 1983, forty-six-year-old Tommy Mutanen snuck into the charred remains of the Churchill Motel to scavenge what was left after a fire had torn through the place. The meat locker remained intact, and Mutanen set about stuffing his parka's pockets with raw flesh. Locals weren't sure what happened next, but whether in the kitchen or out on the street, a polar bear attacked Mutanen, biting into his skull and dragging him over a snowbank to the doorstep of a nearby shop. People tried to save Mutanen from the bear's jaws, throwing whatever they could find at the bear, until one man shot the polar bear dead over his body. He was too late. Local media reported that the townspeople swiftly "shuttered their homes and stayed inside to guard against further attacks by the polar bears." In both instances, officials blamed a lack of sea ice on Hudson Bay for the attacks.

That Churchill should end up directly in the path of hundreds of hungry polar bears migrating to the ice edge is rather unfortunate. The site, located near the confluence of the freshwater Churchill River and saltwater bay, was initially scouted by the Hudson's Bay Company, a North American fur trading giant, in the seventeenth century. Connecting to the Atlantic, it was an ideal location for shipping harvested furs from the boreal forest back to Europe. Profits evidently won out over the propensity to be polar bear prey. Moreover, between 1682 and 1900, 4,093 polar bear skins were shipped out of Churchill and nearby York Factory.

Overzealous hunting brought the fur trade to its knees in the late 1800s, but Churchill managed to fight off obsolescence—first as a base for the US Air Force during World War II, then by reinventing itself as a tourism hub to capitalize on the area's deadly megafauna. The danger was an irresistible attraction, akin to cage diving with great white sharks. Today, about nine hundred people live in the town year-round, with most employed in the tourism industry, working as hotel managers, chefs, buggy guides, dogsled operators, aurora chasers, and souvenir shop cashiers.

When she's not teaching yoga, Erin Greene works the till at the Fifty Eight North gift shop at the end of Kelsey Boulevard, peddling bear-themed trinkets to Tundra Buggy tourists. It was here that I met her one evening while tourists browsed polar bear T-shirts and chocolates labeled as bear droppings. Her highlighted brown hair was tucked under a mustard-yellow toque that gave her a relaxed vibe, but her huge brown eyes remained vigilant. Greene had moved to Churchill from Montreal in the summer of 2013 for a waitressing gig at Gypsy's, the local bakery owned by a friend's aunt and uncle. She wasn't sure how long she would stay in the subarctic town, but when summer turned to fall, she chose to stick around. It was a decision that would define the rest of her life.

In the early hours of November 1, 2013, Greene was walking home from a late-night Halloween party with two friends. Halloween is a complicated affair in Churchill. The holiday inconveniently falls right in the middle of the annual polar bear migration. So, before any trick-or-treating can begin, helicopters survey the town for stealthy bears and

secure the area before sunset. Then, volunteers from the Royal Canadian Mounted Police, fire department, and local hydro utility patrol the
town in their vehicles as tiny ghouls and goblins go from door to door
begging for Tootsie Rolls and Snickers. (As if monsters were the thing
to fear in Churchill's streets.) By the time Greene left the party, it was
nearly 5 a.m. The curfew siren had sounded long ago. Patrol teams had
gone home. No pumpkins glowed in the predawn darkness. As the three
friends moved silently through the snowy streets, they caught sight of
a ghostly white shape hurtling itself down an alley toward them. The
three friends ran. But they weren't fast enough. At top speed, a polar
bear can cover 25 miles per hour. In a matter of seconds, the animal
caught up with thirty-year-old Greene, sinking its teeth into her scalp.

She'd often thought about what she would do if a polar bear
attacked. She'd seen the warning signs around Churchill. She'd had
nightmares. But now it was actually happening. When the bear had
fixed its black eyes on her, Greene instinctively knew it would choose
her. In the middle of a Churchill street, Greene was locked in the jaws of
one of the world's top predators. She flailed and punched the bear, helpless to do anything else. When it briefly dropped her, she tried to hide
her face under her arms, hoping the bear would go for her limbs instead.
The bear bit down again, picking her up by the shoulders and shaking
her like a rag doll. Warm blood flowed down her face. She screamed for
her friends, but could hear nothing but the sound of the bear gnawing
on her flesh.

Nearby, retired water plant operator Bill Ayotte was already awake
and settling into an armchair in front of his television when he heard the
commotion. Clad only in pajama bottoms, a sweater, and slippers, the
sixty-nine-year-old early bird ran out of the house where he saw a polar
bear "wagging" a woman around in its mouth. He reflexively grabbed
a snow shovel from his porch, worried she was close to death, and took
aim at the bear's head, beating the animal until it turned its attention
to him. The bear dropped Greene's bloody body and lunged for the
back of Ayotte's left leg. It sank its powerful teeth through his pajamas
and into the flesh behind his knee. Greene had stumbled away and ran
to a house for help. Meanwhile, the bear was now unleashing its fury

on Ayotte, ripping through the cartilage of his ear. The sounds stirred everyone on the street. They rushed out in their socks and underwear, screaming and throwing shoes at the bear—anything to make the brutal assault on Ayotte stop. But it didn't. Not until one quick-thinking neighbor jumped into his truck and drove straight for the bear, honking the horn and shining the headlights into the bear's black eyes. The animal released Ayotte and fled into the bush.

Greene felt like the attack had lasted forever. In reality, it was only minutes. When the bear finally ceased its assault, it had torn off part of her scalp. Sliced open her knee. Severed three arteries. And Ayotte had lost an ear. Authorities later shot the bear—though, to give an idea of just how many polar bears are lingering around Churchill at any given moment, they initially shot the wrong one. The battered pair were airlifted to a hospital in Winnipeg, where Greene received twenty-eight staples to her head and several blood transfusions. A plastic surgeon reattached Ayotte's ear. Today, Greene and Ayotte are part of a very small and very exclusive club of people who have not only been attacked by a polar bear, but survived.

"Before that experience, I had respect for bears," she told me at Fifty Eight North. "Now it's even greater. I know what it's like to be the meal. To have to fight for your life." After the attack, Greene left Churchill and returned to Montreal. But being in the big city made the experience seem surreal and harder to process. Her wounds healed. Her mind did not. "When I was back [there] I felt this sense of detachment. People there couldn't understand what I had been through," she said. The isolation overwhelmed her. Eventually, she decided to return north to be among those who could empathize with her trauma and who had supported her after the incident. "Being back here was part of my healing."

It seemed a bit ironic, maybe even distasteful, that Greene spent her workday surrounded by hundreds of objects made in her attacker's likeness. Plushies. Magnets. Jewelry. Chocolates. They stared at us from the shelves with their inky black eyes. But it didn't bother her. "At first, everything made me scared," she admitted, "but I don't harbor any hard feelings toward the bear; he was just doing what bears do." Still, most people couldn't fathom why she would want to stay in Churchill, especially since she'd only lived there for a few months prior to the attack. "I guess it takes a certain type of personality," she said, resting her elbows on the counter. "Maybe it's weird, but I'd rather get attacked by a bear than a human." Next to the cash register, I noticed a small cardboard box filled with needle felted polar bear ornaments. They'd been made by the Quechua women in Peru, and Greene had arranged to sell them in the gift shop. The proceeds would go to help fund spectacled bear research in the Andes. Greene saw it as a silver lining. "I didn't even know these bears existed until after the attack. Now, because of the polar bear, I know about a bear in Peru!"

As the Arctic melts out, attacks like the one on Greene are happening more frequently. Biologists recently cataloged 145 years' worth of recorded polar bear attacks on humans in an effort to learn what drove the bears into conflict. Hungry adult male bears, they found, were the most common perpetrators, often invading field camps or causing trouble in towns. Between 1960 and 2009, there were forty-seven attacks (again, most weren't fatal) around the circumpolar Arctic. When researchers looked at the last decade, a disturbing picture emerged. Between 2010 and 2014, when sea ice extent reached record lows in many parts of the Arctic, polar bears attacked fifteen people—the greatest number ever recorded in a four-year period. Moreover, almost all of the attacks since 2000 had occurred in the months between July and December, coinciding with when sea ice is largely absent or thinned out. "We're just getting more reports of bears, and bears occurring, too, in places they historically haven't been seen before," one of the bear biologists who worked on the project told me. "At the same time, because of that same sea ice loss, we're seeing more shipping, more tourism, more research, and more industrial activities bringing people into the Arctic. It really is creating that perfect storm of potential for human-bear conflict." Compared with the 1980s, Churchill's polar bears are spending about an extra month on shore waiting for the ice to return. An extra month without food. And an extra month to get into trouble. People like Greene and Ayotte, I realized, weren't merely victims of the polar bear. They were victims of climate change.

THE HELICOPTER FLEW LOW ON THE HORIZON, hovering mere feet above the craggy shore of Hudson Bay. I watched as a bearded man in an orange fluorescent snowsuit waved his arms and made a series of hand signals to the pilot, who was evidently close enough to decipher the man's coded script. The chopper suddenly shot toward the ground like an attacking hornet, scaring up a furry white shape hiding among the boulders. The snowy blob bounded toward the thin crust of ice on the outer edge of the bay in confused and desperate retreat. Then it plunged into the open water. The metal machine whirred menacingly overhead.

It had been less than an hour since I'd arrived in Churchill on a chartered flight from Winnipeg and I'd already seen a bear. When my previous visit had failed to turn up any ice bruins besides the defecating female, I knew I needed to return to the tundra town. This time I hedged my bets and headed north three weeks earlier in the migration, before Halloween, to catch the bears before they departed for the bay. On the road toward Cape Merry, a national historic site near where a new marine observatory was being built, I happened upon a conservation officer's truck parked at the side of the road. Then I heard the sound of the chopper.

It can be difficult to deter a resolute polar bear. While trained dogs might work on grizzlies, and clattering pots and pans can keep a black bear treed, polar bears often necessitate the use of the big guns—a helicopter, rifles loaded with rubber bullets, snowmobiles, and flares. On this particular morning, the six conservation officers patrolling the shoreline were dealing with a two-year-old male who had left his mother's side earlier that year. He was still trying to figure out his place in the bear world, steering clear of the larger adult males on the offensive for territory and mates.

The young bear had chosen his refuge poorly. He was far too close to town, in an area wildlife managers had designated as the highest priority response zone, after the immediate townsite. It was less than a 2-mile walk to Churchill's main street from here. The young polar bear could cover that distance in just five minutes. Plus, the construction crew was already on the ground, working on the marine lab. Their privately contracted bear guard—the bearded man shouldering a rifle and directing the chopper—had spotted the animal and called the town's 24/7 polar bear hotline to report it. (Conservation officers receive up to three hundred tips every year about bears around town.)

Through binoculars, I watched as the helicopter dove again. The stubborn bear had reemerged and was dithering between going back into the bay or making a beeline for the adjacent Churchill River, which was covered in thick ice. A snowshoe hare bolted from the rocks before he could decide. The bear guard shot off a series of flares toward the animal in hopes of pushing him toward the river, where he would be able to move farther away from Churchill. With any luck, the bear not only would run away, but would remember this unpleasant experience and permanently associate it with humans. The chopper turned again, harassing the bear. It was organized chaos. With nearly one polar bear for every Churchill resident, this was what it took to coexist.

THE HEADQUARTERS OF CHURCHILL'S Polar Bear Alert Program is housed in an angular, pale green building that also contains the town's only bank and only post office, where tourists can get their passports stamped to brag to future border agents that they've been to the "Polar Bear Capital of the World." I had arranged to meet with one of the conservation officers here who had been out at Cape Merry the day before to discuss polar bear management. Given that it was still daylight and only a few blocks from my hotel over to the office, I decided it was probably safe to walk.

The freshly fallen snow squeaked under my boots as I plodded past the Northern Store grocery, where watermelons sold for more than $20, the Seaport Hotel, the charred wreckage of Gypsy's bakery, which had burned down in 2018, and the hardware store, then into the grid of residential streets. The sides of whole apartment blocks, reminiscent of 1970s socialized housing, were painted with 25-foot-tall murals of geometric and whimsical polar bears. A bushy silver fox was denning under one of the cabins elevated above the permafrost. I glanced nervously toward the dark bay in the distance. The cobalt sky concealed the secrets of the muskeg. A stirring white shape could be either a bear or the wind gusting over a snowbank. The fur fringe of my parka obscured my peripheral vision and muffled my hearing. A feeling of unease settled over me. The streets were empty. I was easy prey for a rogue bear. I picked up my pace.

Andrew Szklaruk was just pulling up in his pickup truck when I arrived, unmauled, at the office. A middle-aged man with pale skin and thinning ginger hair, he led me into the building, past the coffee break station where the other officers were warming up from the cold, and into a small conference room. Glass display cases ran along its walls, showcasing relics from past management regimes—leg snare traps, guns, and sedatives. The Polar Bear Alert Program is the government body tasked with handling Churchill's boldest ice walkers. Typically, six officers staff the unit, but Szklaruk told me they were shorthanded this year. He'd been sent in from another northern Manitoba district to take charge for the season. "What happened to the bear yesterday?" I asked. "Did he go to jail?" Jail, in this context, was the government-run Polar Bear Holding Facility, D-20, located in an old military aircraft hangar out on the tundra. It opened in the early 1980s with twenty cells to house offending bears while they awaited the formation of the sea ice. "Nah, we didn't immobilize any bears yesterday, but it was a really busy day," Szklaruk answered. "Busiest so far this year. We had five calls the night before. There were three different bears in town and we were up from midnight until eight in the morning chasing them away. That one bear returned so we had to deploy the helicopter." He told me it had taken them more than three hours before the bear finally took off for good.

When the Polar Bear Alert Program, then called the Polar Bear Control Program, was first established in the 1960s, it had the mandate of shooting and killing almost any bear that came into Churchill to feed at the town's dump. (Polar bears, like their southern relatives, appreciate a good landfill.) When that solution grew unpopular, the program evolved to deal with bears in a nonlethal manner. Enter the polar bear jail. "We've reached capacity maybe every other year," explained Szklaruk, sorting through a stack of statistics on the conference table. He swiveled idly in his chair, positioned in front of a very large polar bear skin on the wall. I found it hard to look at Szklaruk and not at the bear's still-attached head. The jail, he continued, had held more than twenty-three hundred polar bears since its inception. Eight additional cells were later added to make room for more bears, and five of those were air-conditioned to help the bears cope with Churchill's rising temperatures. "We try not to fill up because we never know how many bears are going to show up." Bears are given clean wood shavings for bedding and drinking water during their incarceration, but no food. Officers don't want the bears to associate food with people. Plus, the bears are fasting anyway.

Journalists aren't allowed entry to the polar bear jail. No matter how much you beg—and I speak from experience—the best media relations will do is send you some government stock footage of the facility and an FAQ packet addressing questions like, "What are the cells constructed of?" The riveting answer: "steel reinforced cinder block brick walls and steel bar ceilings and doors. The floor is concrete and has a drainage trough built in." From reviewing the footage—and staring longingly at the Quonset hut hangar from the roadside (painted to resemble a huge sleeping polar bear)—I gleaned that the inside of the jail looks something like a cavernous horse barn. Some bears are locked up for just a few days, while others are held captive for weeks, depending on when they're captured. Shortly before the ice freezes, the Polar Bear Alert team tranquilizes the inmates and transports them by helicopter about 50 miles north of Churchill, where they're released onto the bay's incoming ice edge. Any released bear is branded with a green cattle marker on their shoulder hump. Locals often come out to see the bears off for the winter, waving and drinking hot chocolate. "Generally, we handle anywhere from thirty to fifty bears every season," Szklaruk told me. (Handled is defined as anyone touching a bear.) Yet in contrast to a few decades ago, officers rarely killed bears. Conflicts between humans and bears in Churchill increased between 1970 and 2004, but there hadn't been any obvious trend since 1999 to suggest that conflicts were still going up. That's likely due to a few factors. First, in 2006, a waste disposal site that drew bears into town was shut down. Second, the polar bear population declined significantly. And lastly, wildlife managers improved management tactics. By intervening early—as with helicopters—the town was able to get ahead of most bears. With hungry bears hanging around town longer, and the tundra of Hudson Bay likely to become a refugee camp for gaunt bears in the coming decades, getting a head start was critical.

IN THE BACK OF TUNDRA BUGGY ONE, Geoff York, senior director of conservation for Polar Bears International, was squinting through rectangular glasses at a large computer monitor displaying a satellite map of the area. He had a lean athletic build, which helped him maintain balance when the buggy suddenly lurched forward without warning. His fingers, chapped from the cold, hovered over the controls. Several colored squares inched along the map, representing the six or so tourist buggies nearby. "It came from the military," he said as a way of explanation. "We call it 'BEARDAR.'"

York had spent most of his career studying Alaska's polar bears, but he traveled to Churchill every year for the annual polar bear migration. His specialty of late was studying human–polar bear conflict; York is one of the coauthors of the study that summarized 145 years of conflict, and he formerly chaired the Polar Bear Range States Conflict Working Group, an international effort to reduce conflicts. He was always looking for new solutions. This is how he came across the renamed BEARDAR, a novel radar system developed by the military to identify threats. He was retraining it to detect polar bears on the landscape. Over time, it should be able to pick out a polar bear and begin tracking the animal, sending its location to wildlife managers, who could spring into action and scare the bear away from Churchill before it got any closer. The system was presently mounted on the roof of the Tundra Buggy Lodge, a high-end hotel for tourists parked out on the tundra, along with a camera that could zero in on whatever the radar detected.

York was teaching it to discriminate common objects on the tundra—foxes, bears, tourist buggies. It was having some trouble identifying caribou and smaller animals—"then again, we're not too worried about false alarms for caribou." The radar had previously been put up at Churchill's community center, where it learned to identify people, snowmobiles, and dogs. The key benefit to the radar was that it had a range of 1,300 feet. "When you can only see 30 feet with your naked eye, you're going to miss bears," York explained to me. Snow, darkness, wind—the radar system could cut through all that. He and his team were even toying with the idea of rigging up the system to trigger flashing lights or loud noises to scare any curious bear—and notify nearby pedestrians of its presence. If such a system had been in place when Greene was leaving the Halloween party, she might have made it home unscathed. And two bears would still be alive.

York's long-term goal is to deploy the BEARDAR, or similar technology, to other Arctic communities. Churchill was ground zero simply because it has so many polar bears passing through, not because it has the most attacks. In 2018, polar bears attacked and killed two men in two separate incidents in Nunavut. In the weeks that followed, five of the region's polar bears were killed and left unharvested near Arviat, in Nunavut, near where the first man had been killed. Local hunters had already used up the twelve tags the government allocated to the Kivalliq region for the year, which meant the bears were shot illegally. The attacks had spurred an upwelling of pain and resentment in the community. Inuit groups urged that the government relax hunting restrictions and increase quotas. Many Inuit communities in Canada allege that polar bear populations are increasing, which has created tension with Western scientists who have found the opposite. The BEARDAR could help to bridge that divide. York hopes that communities like Arviat could benefit from such technology, as well as Longyearbyen, on the Norwegian archipelago of Svalbard, which has seen two fatal attacks since 2011.

Saving polar bears from extinction can't be done on the ground. The

BEARDAR is a solution to a smaller problem. By reducing management kills and revenge kills, York may be able to spare the lives of a few dozen polar bears, but climate change is the real threat to their survival. "Their frozen habitat is disappearing forever," York sighed as the wind howled outside the buggy. "We're watching this slow-motion train wreck." To save polar bears, humans must rapidly change course this decade or else it will be too late for the polar bear. Even if we ceased all greenhouse gas emissions tomorrow, it would still take decades for the heat-trapping gases already in the atmosphere to wash out and for the ice to regrow to historical levels. The flow of bile can yet be stemmed. Forests can be saved or replanted. Mines can be blocked. But it will take a truly monumental effort to save the ice, and thus the bear.

WHAT, THEN, IS TO BECOME OF the polar bear?

An animal forged from ice and snow whose presence defines the Arctic. This is a truth not of allegory but of etymology. "Arctic" originates from *arktos*, the Greek word for bear. The bear defines the rhythms of life: the ebb and flow of fish, seals, and walrus. Without the white bear, the food chain will not summit in a sharp point, but rather plateau and eventually collapse. Prey will not prosper in the predator's absence, for they, too, depend on ice and cold.

The polar bear will likely not persist much beyond the end of this century. In the present moment, the animal is in the high pitch of its swan song—one final hurrah before it disappears from our world forever. A great white bear that roamed the High Arctic will soon be an impossibility once more.

True, some will remain in zoos as a diaspora of melted homelands. Those who visit the caged bears, swinging their heads to and fro in monotony, will never know the Arctic as it once was, a frozen refuge for some of the most magnanimous and specially adapted species on our planet. The Arctic of tomorrow seems destined to have superhighway shipping routes and monolith mines, whose glaring lights cleave through the polar night, threatening the last vestige of northerness—the eternal dance between light and darkness. And the polar bear will remain frozen in our collective memory, as if trapped in ice.

This does not mean that the Arctic will be without bears. Tundra mosses and lichen will give way to taller shrubs as the world warms. If unleashed, the boreal forest could stampede northward to conquer new lands, laying tangled roots in thawed permafrost. Larches and spruce could claim the fading tundra as their own. That is, until they burn. And the brown bears will follow this greened path toward the pole, much as they did hundreds of thousands of years ago when they first sought refuge by the sea. Yet the sea, now void of ice and seal, will not alter them.

This migration has already begun. "Grizzlies are expanding their range in all directions right now, after going through a couple hundred years of range retractions," Andrew Derocher had told me when we spoke in the Tundra Buggy. Much as the grizzly is moving into the plains of Montana and closing the gap between Yellowstone and the Northern Continental Divide, the grizzly is also invading the Arctic tundra. Derocher recalled recently seeing a grizzly bear out on the edge of the sea ice during fieldwork just east of Churchill. "This was the first time I've seen a grizzly bear in that part of the world," he said. Between 2010 and 2014, sixteen grizzly bears were harvested, captured, or seen in the western Arctic islands of the Northwest Territories—including one bear 15 miles offshore on the sea ice. A remote camera trap on Russia's Wrangel Island, located at 71 degrees north in the Arctic Ocean, also captured the first photographic evidence of a brown bear wandering the island in July 2019. Early explorers had never reported brown bears in this remote and icy region.

In April 2012, scientists had an even more peculiar sighting. Two government scientists were flying near Victoria Island, high above the Arctic Circle, as part of a project to place satellite collars on polar bears, when they looked out the window and saw a grizzly traveling along the sea ice with what they initially perceived to be a polar bear. It wasn't.

The grizzly's expansion has led to another intriguing phenomenon.

In 2006, Jim Martell, a sixty-six-year-old hunter from Idaho, embarked on a polar bear hunting trip with a guide on the southern tip of Banks Island in Canada's Northwest Territories. Here, they encountered the most unusual bear. Its creamy white fur was tinged brown in patches. It had long claws and a humped back that met with a concave, dish-shaped face. Martell pulled the trigger. Eighty miles south, Derocher was at a research camp when he overheard an Inuk hunter chatting on the bush radio with the guide of the hunt. The guide knew instantly what Martell had shot—a pizzly bear.

Because brown bears and polar bears diverged fairly recently, the two species are able to interbreed, creating hybrids, much like a lion or tiger can produce a "liger" or a horse and donkey can create a mule. But the female offspring of polar bears and grizzly bears are fertile; two pizzly bears can mate and produce more little pizzlies, or "grolars," if you prefer. Martell's specimen—the first-ever evidence of a wild hybrid—spurred some people to theorize that we could soon see widespread hybridization as grizzly bears move northward, encouraged by warmer temperatures. Since the first pizzly bear was documented in 2006, several other hybrids have been found roaming the Arctic tundra. The "polar bear" that the government scientists spotted tagging along with the brown bear was also suspected to be of pizzly origin. However, when scientists later examined these hybrid bears, they were surprised to find that the wave of hybridization sweeping across the Arctic was due entirely to one female polar bear's unusual sexual preoccupation with male grizzlies; four of the pizzly bears were her children, and the rest her grandchildren. Clearly, she had a type.

Derocher is doubtful of a future Arctic dominated by hybridized bears. Males, he said, are almost always the vanguard of any expanding species, and that's essentially what scientists are witnessing as male grizzly bears wander into the Arctic and mate with female polar bears. But polar bears are likely to disappear at a rate that far outpaces such interbreeding. Moreover, he explained that because polar bears evolved from brown bears, if pizzly bears and grizzlies were to continue breeding, eventually the brown bear genes would dominate. Hybrids would revert back to grizzlies. This phenomenon already occurred among the polar bears who once lived in Alaska's ABC Islands. "Once the climate warmed, most of the polar bears left or died, and any individuals that remained saw their genes flooded with brown bear genes," Derocher explained.

Ultimately, "it's a bit of a race to see whether the polar bear range will contract faster than the grizzly bear range expands," he said. "But I think polar bears are going to be the big loser here, and I think grizzly bears will take over the High Arctic."

EPILOGUE

[Exit, Pursued by a bear.]

—WILLIAM SHAKESPEARE, *THE WINTER'S TALE*

At some point in early history, humans and bears arrived at a fork in the road. We went one way. Bears chose another. Based on the footprints left behind in the earth, it would be difficult to distinguish the route taken by either group. But from there on, our stories diverged. Human populations boomed. Bear populations faltered and crashed. Where humans have crossed paths with bears since, the animals have largely suffered for it.

Though bears have accompanied us for thousands of years, there's no guarantee they will continue to walk alongside us. By 2100, the world will reach nearly eleven billion humans. Every new person exacerbates the crises faced by the natural world. More forests will be cleared for the expansion of agriculture. More planet-warming carbon dioxide and methane will enter our atmosphere. And new generations may adopt the same expunging fear of big and predatory animals.

Certainly, humans can be incredibly compassionate and altruistic toward wildlife when they wish to be. They've built forested overpasses along highways to help grizzlies cross safely. They've designed dozens of models of bear-resistant food bins to help keep black bears out of trouble. And they've built artificial water points, termite mounds, and dens to help meet the habitat needs of sloth bears. I went in search of bear champions around the world and I found them. Zhang Hemin had dedicated his life to figuring out how to breed pandas and reintroduce them into the wild. This could prove critical in years to come if climate change withers bamboo forests. Nishith Dharaiya and Arzoo Malik were determined to map the water needs of sloth bears in Gujarat. Boulder's bear-sitters gave up their weekends to look after hungry black bears. The Vietnamese staff at Animals Asia's Tam Dao Bear Rescue Center far outnumbered the bear farmers I met in Phung Thuong. And Geoff York hadn't given up on trying to save what bears he could through tinkering with a military radar system.

But climate change, population growth, and habitat loss are harder issues to address. We can't easily bring back the ice or the clouds once they're gone. And while we might stymie the flow of bear bile yet, scientists have found that moon bears are likely to lose a significant portion of their habitat in the Hindu Kush Himalaya by century's end due to a warming climate. Similarly, the sun bear may be able to evade the wildlife trade, but palm oil plantations will continue to destroy its forest home to satisfy the demands of the global supply chain if we don't change consumption.

At the end of my odyssey from cloud forest to sea ice, only three bear species seemed destined to prosper beyond the end of this century—the American black bear, the brown bear, and the panda. Indeed, the future itself reads much like a fairy tale: The Three Bears.

If we fail to make room for bears, we will solidify a future where many of the world's bears exist only behind glass. Losing bears would mean we lose a beautiful and complex relationship that has paralleled our own journey in this world. We would lose a grandfather, an uncle, a mother, a medicine man, and a teacher. And in some ways, we would lose a part of our own wildness. Without bears, the woods, and our stories, would be empty.

ACKNOWLEDGMENTS

Though there may only be eight bears, there are hundreds of people who care about them and I was fortunate enough to cross paths with many in the reporting and writing of this book.

I am deeply indebted to the experts who shared their research and wisdom with me, and allowed me to follow them following bears. Among them are Santiago Molina Proaño, Becky Zug, Rodrigo Cisneros, Rodrigo Tapia Castro, Manuel Antonio Morales Mite, and Francisco Sanchez Karste, who guided me through the Ecuadorian Andes in search of the spectacled bear. In Peru, Russ Van Horn, Denisse Mateo Chero, and Karina Vargas made for wonderful scientific companions in the cloud forests. I'm grateful to Nishith Dharaiya, Harendra Bargali, Zeenal Vajrinkar, Arzoo Malik, Tahir Ali Rather, and the staff at Wildlife SOS in India for their diligent fact-checks and their kindness over many cups of chai. Thanks to Jill Robinson, one of my childhood inspirations, Tuan Bendixsen, and the staff at Animals Asia in Vietnam; Johanna Painer, Claire LaFrance, and the staff at Four Paws International; Rod Mabin, Dung Nguyen Van, Nev Broadis, Brian Crudge, and Nga Loung of Free the Bears not only for their assistance with this book but for their insurmountable compassion and perseverance in ensuring all of the world's farmed sun and moon bears make it to sanctuary. Zhang Hemin, Wang Dajun, Marc Brody, Ron Swaisgood, and Gretchen Daily shared their knowledge of pandas and conservation in China. Geoff York, Andrew Derocher, Steve Amstrup, and Annie Edwards held the polar frontline. Thanks also to Chris Serveheen, Peter

Alagona, Jeff Miller, Noah Greenwald, Jack Oelfke, Jasmine Mishbanian, Trina Jo Bradley, Fabian Rodas, Matthew Clark, Louisa Willcox, David Mattson, Susanna Paisley, Michael Moen, Peter Molnar, Steve West, Carl Lackey, Jon Beckmann, Steve Michel, Bill Hunt, Jennifer Vonk, and Heather Johnson for all our ursine conversations.

In Colorado, Brenda Lee, founder of the Boulder Bear Coalition, introduced me to the city's backyard bears and facilitated many fondly remembered stakeouts with the Boulder Bearsitters. Bryan Peterson in Durango helped provide early guidance on how trash affected black bears while I was working on my master's at the University of Colorado Boulder.

Michael Kodas had a profound impact on my life and career. In addition to serving as my adviser on my master's project at the University of Colorado Boulder, he allowed me to shadow him on his own book reporting trips to Arizona and taught me how to be a journalist. His continued support and friendship mean the world to me.

Many others strongly encouraged the pursuit of this book early in its conception—James Balog was a friend, role model, and wonderful mentor early in my career and pushed me toward writing a book. Sarah Musgrave, a gifted editor, expressed boundless enthusiasm for the eight bears—"a very manageable number"—and sent me on assignment to China to report back on pandas. Tom Yulsman and Kevin Moloney helped oversee my master's work at the University of Colorado Boulder. And Susan J. Tweit granted me my first writing residency (Terraphilia) in Salida, Colorado, in 2016 to begin developing this idea.

I was fortunate to be supported and aided by many friends over the years it took to report and write this book. Algirdas Bakas and Kyle Obermann kept my spirits high while navigating Sichuan culture and roads. Kyle, a master of Mandarin, was instrumental in speaking with 'papa panda' Zhang Hemin and providing translation for this book. Many others supported my book-induced transience by offering up a spare room and kind words—my Victoria bureau friends Erica Gies and Peter Fairley (and Chairman Mao); Jess Chamberlain in Seattle; Svavar Jonatansson in Reykjavik; and Alisha Somji and Anish Bhide in San Francisco.

Others helped review copy—Leyland Cecco, Jean-Marc Perelmuter, Alex Carmona, Kelsey Simpkins, Shaun Swingler—shared their own authorship experience—Ben Goldfarb, Lyndsie Bourgon, David Baron, and Scott Carney—offered travel and editorial guidance—Sharon Guynup, Rachel Nuwer, Kumar Sambhav, and Katy Daigle—or helped overcome writer's block with a bottle(s) of wine, pub quizzes, and movie nights—Naomi Flis and Maisha Moon.

Among the most influential experiences in shaping this book was my participation in the Banff Centre for Arts and Creativity Mountain and Wilderness Writing residency in November 2019. My mentor, Harley Rustad, shared a deep love for the natural world and provided thoughtful and eloquent feedback that set a smooth course. He remained a close confidant and cheerleader throughout the writing process and granted me time at the Port Renfrew Writers' Retreat to work on the book. I am forever grateful to my fellow Banff writers Tony Whittome, Marni Jackson, Maria Coffey, Brian Hall, Louise Blight, Michael Kennedy, Kate Rawles, Rhiannon Russell, Martina Halik, and Katherine Leonard. Our friendship and creative collaboration did not end with the residency and persisted through monthly Zoom meetings during pandemic lockdowns to workshop our books. They helped hold me to task and offered up encouragement to persevere when the world seemed to be shutting down.

Thanks to the *Walrus* magazine, *National Geographic*, Yale Environment 360, BioGraphic, *Adventure Journal*, *EnRoute* magazine, and *High Country News* for publishing and supporting my previous ponderings on bears.

To Amy van den Berg, thank you for your hard work and friendship that followed across the Atlantic.

My heartfelt thanks to my agent, Wendy Strothman, who believed in this book from its first inklings and championed it to publishers.

My greatest gratitude to my editor, Matt Weiland, who was the perfect partner for bringing this "ursine odyssey" to life. I knew immediately that he possessed a shared vision for this book, and his kindness, eloquence, and love for the eight bears made writing and refining it a joy. Thank you.

My grandparents helped inspire and nurture my love of mountains and all the wild creatures they contain.

Finally, I want to thank my mom and dad, who surrounded me with fictional and literary bears as a child—from the Berenstain family to Yogi to Winnie—and my brother, who took delight in tormenting me with stories of marauding grizzlies while camping in the Rockies. These dueling narratives of killers and cartoons undoubtedly fed into a lifetime fascination that led to *Eight Bears*. Their love, support, and enthusiasm was behind me throughout this journey.

NOTES

PREFACE

x **bear sleeping in the tree on campus:** Brittany Annas, "Bear Tranquilized after Climbing Tree at CU-Boulder's Williams Village Dorms," *Daily Camera*, April 26, 2012.

x **mountain lion trading glares with a house cat:** Kieran Nicholson, "Boulder Mountain Lion, House Cat Face Off," *Daily Camera*, October 18, 2011.

x **bobcat roaming through backyards:** Mitchell Byars, "Neighborhood Bobcat Has (So Far) Charmed West Boulder," *Daily Camera*, November 16, 2015.

x **operating under a "two-strike" policy:** Jonathan Lewis et al., "Summarizing Colorado's Black Bear Two-Strike Directive 30 Years after Inception," *Wildlife Society Bulletin* 43, no. 4 (2019): 599–607.

x **a male black bear was dozing:** Charlie Brennan and Joe Rubino, "Wildlife Officers Kill Boulder Bear Near Columbia Cemetery," *Daily Camera*, September 6, 2013.

xi **590 pounds:** Erika Strutzman, "The Bears' Problem," *Daily Camera*, September 10, 2013.

xi **known to wildlife wardens:** Associated Press, "2nd Bear Euthanized Near Boulder Elementary School," as appeared in *The Denver Post*, September 9, 2013.

xi **fat bear's stomach:** Strutzman, "The Bears' Problem."

xi **pushed council members to pass an ordinance:** https://bearsandpeople.com/ordinance/.

xi **first time a large city:** Established after multiple discussions with Brenda Lee, founder of the Boulder Bear Coalition, and Valerie Matheson, senior urban wildlife coordinator at City of Boulder. While smaller mountain towns, including Snowmass, Aspen, and towns around Lake Tahoe, had passed ordinances, none had human populations larger than Boulder.

xi **Boulder Bearsitters:** Mitchell Byars, "Bear Necessities: Sitters Help Keep an Eye on Boulder's Furry Visitors," *Daily Camera*, October 28, 2016; Gloria Dickie, "Out of the Wild," University of Colorado Boulder Master's Project, 2015.

xi **"Bears are all I do":** Dan Glidden, Aspen police department bear specialist, author interview, October 2014.

xii **off-duty cop had even been attacked:** Associated Press, "Bear Swipes at, Injures Woman in Aspen Alley," as appeared in *The Denver Post*, July 28, 2014.

xii **killed a hiker:** "Bear kills New Jersey Student in Nature Preserve," BBC, September 22, 2014.

xii **napping in a backyard hammock:** Ruby Gonzales, "Bear Bites Woman Sleeping in Her Backyard; She Hits It with a Laptop," *Mercury News*, June 17, 2020.

xii **mountain biker:** Gaby Krevat, "Big Sky Man in Stable Condition after Grizzly Bear Attack Last Week," 7KBZK Bozeman, June 1, 2020.

xii **Yellowstone's Old Faithful geyser:** Eric Grossarth, "Grizzly Bear Attacks Woman at Yellowstone," *East Idaho News*, June 24, 2020.

xii **Five others in the Yellowstone area:** Mike Koshmrl, "Grizzly Attacks in 2020 Run at Record High," *Jackson Hole Daily*, July 23, 2020.

xiii **polar bear populations to crash:** Peter Molnar, author interview, July 2020; Steven Amstrup, author interview, July 2020.

xiii **brown bears likely still roamed:** Bears went extinct in Germany in the mid-nineteenth century, with the last bear photographed in the Bavarian Alps Mountains in 1835. The Brothers Grimm lived from the 1780s to 1863. *Grimms' Fairy Tales* was published in 1812.

INTRODUCTION

1 **among our closest relatives:** Michel Pastoureau, *The Bear: History of a Fallen King* (Cambridge, MA: Harvard University Press, 2011); A. Irving Hallowell, "Bear Ceremonialism in the Northern Hemisphere," *American Anthropologist* 28, no. 1 (1926).

1 **share the same estuaries:** Lauren Henson et al. "Convergent Geographic Patterns between Grizzly Bear Population Genetic Structure and Indigenous Language Groups in Coastal British Columbia, Canada," *Ecology & Society* 26, no. 3 (2021).

1 **eat everything a bear does:** Conversation with Heiltsuk elders; "Skunkcabbage Is a Bear's BFF," *Pique Newsmagazine*.

1 **"old man with the fur garment":** Bernd Brunner, *Bears: A Brief History* (New Haven, CT: Yale University Press, 2007), 4.

1 **"grandfather" and "uncle":** Edward B. Tylor, *Primitive Cultures: Researches into the Development of Mythology, Philosophy, Religion, Art, and Custom, Vol. II* (London: John Murray, 1871), 231.

1 **move on their hind legs:** R. M. Alexander, "Bipedal Animals, and Their Differences from Humans," *Journal of Anatomy* 204, no. 5 (2004): 321–30.

2 **tastes considerably like human flesh:** Ian Wei, *Thinking about Animals in Thirteenth Century Paris* (Cambridge, UK: Cambridge University Press, 2020).

2 **la va-nu-pieds:** Remy Marion, *On Being a Bear* (Vancouver, BC: Greystone Books, 2021), 16.

2 **"Bears are made of the same dust as we":** John Muir, *A Thousand Mile Walk to the Gulf* (Boston: Mariner Books, 1998).

2 **not lost on the Greek philosopher Aristotle:** Aristotle, *History of Animals, Volume I: Books 1–3* (Cambridge, MA: Harvard University Press, 1965).

2 **the monkey, the pig, and the bear:** Pastoureau, *The Bear*.

2 **"This is why, although doctors knew":** Pastoureau, *The Bear*.

3 **diverged around thirty million years ago:** Bruce McLellan and David Reiner, "A Review of Bear Evolution," International Association for Bear Research and Management, 1994.

4 **Around twenty-five thousand years ago:** Giant short-faced bears began to go extinct between ten thousand and eleven thousand years ago. Cave bear extinction time line is more uncertain; however, the youngest valid radiocarbon date for a cave bear is about 24,200 years old; Correspondence with Hervé Bocherens, paeleobiologist at University of Tübingen; Borcherens et al., "Chronological and Isotopic Data Support a Revision for the Timing of Cave Bear Extinction in Mediterranean Europe," *Historical Biology* 31, no. 4 (2019): 474–84.

4 **cave bear mitochondrial genomes:** Joscha Gretziner et al., "Large-Scale Mitogenomic Analysis of the Phylogeography of the Late Pleistocene Cave Bear," *Scientific Reports* 9, article no. 10700 (2019).

4 **first bear species humans managed to push:** Gretziner et al., "Large-Scale Mitogenomic Analysis" ; Author correspondence Hervé Bocherens; Rhys Blakely, "Cave Bear Was First Species Made Extinct by Humans, Study Suggests," *The Times*, August 16, 2019.

4 **Clovis hunted short-faced bears:** Donald Grayson and David Meltzer, "Clovis Hunting and Large Mammal Extinction: A Critical Review of the Evidence," *Journal of World Prehistory* 16, no. 4 (2002): 313–59.

5 **belong to the Ursidae family:** McLellan and Reiner, "A Review of Bear Evolution."

5 **"Pandas have been 'uniquely pandas'":** "Pandas' Lineage Traced Back Millions of Years," *New York Times*, June 19, 2007.

6 **discovered to be two distinct species:** Yibo Hu et al., "Genomic Evidence for Two Phylogenetic Species and Long-Term Population Bottlenecks in Red Pandas," *Science Advances* 6, no. 9 (2020).

6 **"circumpolar bear cult tradition":** Lydia T. Black, "Bear in Human Imagination and in Ritual," *Ursus* 10, no. 43 (1998): 343–47.

6 **"unique among other-than-human persons":** "Bear Ceremonialism," Exchange for Local Observations and Knowledge of the Arctic. https://eloka-arctic.org/bears/bear-ceremonialism

7 **"A previous version of this story":** Andrew Chamings, "Behold the Wrath of Mei Mei and Squirt. Two Tiny Terriers Chase a Very Large Bear Out of California Home," *SFGate*, April 15, 2021.

7 **twelve hundred seedlings:** Kris Millgate, "What Happens When You Plant a Pile of Bear Scat?" *Nature* blog, May 10, 2017.

7 **dire assessment:** IUCN, "Seventy-Five Percent of Bear Species Threatened with Extinction," November 12, 2007.

8 **Viking berserkers:** Arwen van Zanten, "Going Berserk: In Old Norse, Old Irish, and Anglo-Saxon Literature," *Amsterdamer Beiträge zur älteren Germanistik* 63 (2007): 43–64; Ruarigh Dale, "The Viking Berserker," University of Nottingham blog, March 11, 2014. https://blogs.nottingham.ac.uk/wordsonwords/2014/03/11/the-viking-berserker/

8 **known as the Ursari:** Von Pelin Tünaydın, "Pawing through the History of Dancing Bears in Europe," Frühneuzeit-Info blog, the Research Institute for Early Modern Studies in Vienna, 2013; George Soulis, "The Gypsies in the Byzantine Empire and the Balkans in the Late Middle Ages," *Dumbarton Oaks Papers*, 1961.

9 **parade through village streets:** Imogen Tilden, "Romania's New Year Bear Dancers—Alecsandra Raluca Drăgoi's Best Photograph," *The Guardian*, January 8, 2020.

9 **as he presides over:** Joint Secretariat,"Inuvialuit and Nanuq: A Polar Bear Traditional Knowledge Study. Inuvialuit Settlement Region," 2015; Lorraine Brandson, curator of the Itsanitaq Museum in Churchill, Canada, author interview, November 2018.

9 **Bear Mother:** "Bear Mother," Bill Reid Centre at Simon Fraser University. https://www.sfu.ca/brc/imeshMobileApp/imesh-art-walk-/bear-mother.html

9 **cultural keystone species:** Douglas Clark et al., "Grizzly and Polar Bears as Nonconsumptive Cultural Keystone Species," *Facets* 6 (2021): 379–93.

9 **rite of passage known as *arkteia*:** Richard Hamilton, "Alkman and the Athenian Arkteia," Bryn Mawr College; Jessica Ward, "The Cult of Artemis at Brauron," Women in Antiquity blog, March 20, 2017. https://womeninantiquity.wordpress.com/2017/03/20/the-cult-of-artemis-at-brauron/

10 **the *bestiarius*:** "*Bestiarius*," University of Chicago. https://penelope.uchicago.edu/~grout/encyclopaedia_romana/gladiators/bestiarii.html

10 **twenty-nine Saxon prisoners:** Symmachus Epistulae 2:46; Jillian Mitchell, "The Case of the Strangled Saxons," paper presented at the Classical Association Conference, University of Exeter, 2012.

10 **leopard had to be called in:** K. M. Coleman, "Fatal Charades: Roman Executions Staged as Mythological Enactments," *Journal of Roman Studies* 80 (1990): 59.

11 **thirty-five hundred "African wild beasts":** Caroline Wazer, "The Exotic Animal Traffickers of Ancient Rome," *The Atlantic*, March 30, 2016.

11 **created superior to all other creatures:** Sean Nee, "The Great Chain of Being," *Nature* 435 (2005): 429; Tylor, 1871; Marion, *On Being a Bear*.

11 **Bearbaiting found even greater success:** Pelin Tünaydın, "Pawing through the History."

11 **Master of the Bears:** Pelin Tünaydın, "Pawing through the History."

11 **"a very pleasant sport":** The Langham Letter. http://www.oxford-shakespeare.com/Langham/Langham_Letter.pdf

12 **"a verry large and a turrible looking animal":** Journals of the Lewis and Clark Expedition, University of Nebraska. https://lewisandclarkjournals.unl.edu/item/lc.jrn.1805-05-05

12 **Governments issued bounties:** US Fish and Wildlife Service, "Grizzly Bear in the Lower-48 States: Five-Year Status Review," March 2021, 3.

12 **1.1 billion acres to less than 741 million:** FAO, "State of the World's Forests 2012," 14.

13 **fewer than twelve individuals remained in Mississippi:** Stephanie Simek et al.,

"History and Status of The American Black Bear in Mississippi," *Ursus* 23, no. 2 (2012): 159–67.

13 **Florida population plummeted:** Florida black bear abundance study, Florida Fish and Wildlife Conservation Commission, 2017.

13 **forest cover had declined to 10 percent:** FAO, "State of the World's Forests 2012," 12.

13 **"The last word in ignorance":** Aldo Leopold, *A Sand County Almanac* (Oxford, UK: Oxford University Press, 2020).

14 **"The government trapper":** Leopold, *A Sand County Almanac*.

14 **lacking in sportsmanship:** National Park Service, "The Story of the Teddy Bear." https://www.nps.gov/thrb/learn/historyculture/storyofteddybear.htm

14 **"Drawing the Line in Mississippi":** Clifford Berryman, "Drawing the Line in Mississippi," *Washington Post*, November 16, 1902, accessed in Library of Congress digital archives.

15 **"From all quarters of the globe":** Jon Mooallem, *Wild Ones* (New York: Penguin Books, 2013), 69.

15 **when they went out to tea:** "The Teddy Bear's Birthday," *Washington Post*, November 12, 2002.

15 **occupy 6 percent:** USFWS 5-year grizzly status review, 2021.

15 **into Yonkers:** Paul Owen, "Hungry Bear's Three-Day Trashcan Picnic Ends 12 Miles from Manhattan," *The Guardian*, May 20, 2015.

15 **10 million acres of primary forest:** Global Forest Watch, "Forest Loss Remained Stubbornly High in 2021," April 28, 2022.

CHAPTER ONE: THE CLOUD DWELLERS

21 **"Please look after this bear":** Michael Bond, *A Bear Called Paddington* (New York: Dell, 1958).

21 **"I have now read your novel":** Harper Childrens, interview with Michael Bond, January 2002. https://web.archive.org/web/20020129134454/http://www.harperchildrens.com/hch/author/author/bond/interview2.asp

21 **The Atlas bear:** Some sources note that the last Atlas bear was killed in the Tetouan Mountains of northern Morocco in 1870. However, Sebastien Calvignac et al., "Ancient DNA Evidence for the Loss of a Highly Divergent Brown Bear Clade during Historical Times," *Molecular Ecology* 17, no. 8 (2008): 196 –70, notes that the Atlas bear "is thought to have disappeared during the mid-19th century, although the most recent skeletal remains were recently radiocarbon dated back to 1600 Before Present."

21 **capture and trade for Rome's arena games:** Calvignac et al., "Ancient DNA Evidence."

22 **Westminster Public Library:** Harper Childrens interview.

23 **warming climate could shrink and dry:** E. H. Helmer et al., "Neotropical Cloud Forests and Páramo to Contract and Dry from Declines in Cloud Immersion and Frost," *PLoS ONE* 14, no. 4 (2019).

24 **first victim of climate change:** Leticia M Ochoa-Ochoa et al., "The Demise of the

Golden Toad and the Creation of a Climate Change Icon Species," *Conservation & Society* 11, no. 3 (2013): 291–319; IPCC WGII Sixth Assessment Report, 2–29.

24 **90 percent of western cloud forests:** Helmer at al., "Neotropical Cloud Forests and Páramo."

26 **one-third of the 270 native birds:** Nature and Culture International, "Andean Cloud Forests."

27 **there weren't many spectacled bears left:** IUCN Red List of Threatened Species Assessment, Andean Bear, assessed by I. Goldstein, X. Velez-Liendo, S. Paisley, and D. Garshelis (Bear Specialist Group).

29 **migrating upslope:** C. Tovar et al., "Diverging Responses of Tropical Andean Biomes under Future Climate Conditions," *Plos ONE* 8, no. 5 (2013).

33 **El Lanzón is the supreme deity:** Susanna Paisley and Nicholas Saunders, "A God Forsaken: The Sacred Bear in Andean Iconography and Cosmology," *World Archaeology* 42, no. 2 (2010): 245–60.

33 **the jaguar:** Paisley and Saunders, "A God Forsaken."

33 **a jaguar cult:** James B. Richardson III, *People of the Andes* (Montreal: St. Remy Press, 1994).

34 **taboo emerged:** Paisley and Saunders, "A God Forsaken."

34 **"potent ritual symbols":** Lydia T. Black, "Bear in Human Imagination and in Ritual," *Ursus* 10, no. 43 (1998): 343–47.

35 **"El Lanzón dwells at the centre of the centre":** Paisley and Saunders, "A God Forsaken."

36 **Ukuku is a mythical creature:** Paisley and Saunders, "A God Forsaken."

36 **"strongly associated with human fertility":** Paisley and Saunders, "A God Forsaken."

36 **Qoyllur Rit'i:** Paisley and Saunders, "A God Forsaken"; Alan Taylor, "Peru's Snow Star Festival," *The Atlantic*, June 7, 2016.

37 **ravages of climate change:** Danielle Villasana, "Witnessing Peru's Enduring, If Altered, Snow Star Festival," *New York Times*, October 26, 2020; Russ Van Horn, author interview, July 2019.

37 **curtailing the collection:** Jean Chemnick, "When a Melting Glacier Is Seen as the Apocalypse," *E&E News*, November 1, 2011.

38 **largest concentration of orchids:** Vibeke Johannessen, "Where to See Ecuadorian Orchids," *The Culture Trip*, October 19, 2017.

39 **radically restrict mining:** "Ecuador's Moves against Foreign Investors," Reuters, June 18, 2009.

39 **exploratory mining concessions:** Roo Vandegrift et al., "The Extent of Recent Mining Concessions in Ecuador," report prepared for the Rainforest Information Centre, January 17, 2018.

40 **additional 10 percent:** Bitty Roy et al., "New Mining Concessions Could Severely Decrease Biodiversity and Ecosystem Services in Ecuador," *Tropical Conservation Science* 11, no. 2 (2018).

40 **fell within Indigenous territories:** Vandegrift et al., "The Extent of Recent Mining," Table 1.

40 **the country's abundant mineral reserves:** Stephanie Roker, "Ecuador to Grow Mining Industry to 4% GDP by 2021," *Global Mining Review*, November 2, 2018; Matthew DuPee, "Ecuador Has Big Plans for Its Mining Industry. But at What Cost?" *World Politics Review*, August 12, 2019.

40 **291,000 acres in the surrounding Cuenca Canton:** "Ecuador: Cuenca Says 'No' to Mines in El Cajas National Park," *Telesure*, July 21, 2018.

40 **a third were actively being explored:** Francisco Sánchez-Karste correspondence, June 2021.

40 **shamanic rituals:** Eduardo Franco Berton, "Poaching Threatens South America's Only Bear Species," *National Geographic*, May 31, 2019.

41 **where five bears:** Francisco Sánchez-Karste, author interview, July 2019.

41 **more than 90 percent of the land:** Vandegrift et al., "The Extent of Recent Mining," Table 1; Ana Cristina Basantes, "Mining Company Pressing to Enter Ecuador's Los Cedros Protected Forest," *Mongabay*, May 22, 2020.

43 **children trudging through Reading Station:** Michelle Pauli, "Michael Bond: 'Paddington Stands Up for Things, He's Not Afraid of Going to the Top and Giving Them a Hard Stare,' " *The Guardian*, November 28, 2014.

CHAPTER TWO: DANCING WITH DEATH

49 **Night was falling on Bandhavgarh National Park:** Gloria Dickie, "How to Make Peace with the World's Deadliest Bear," *National Geographic*, May 12, 2020.

50 **fewer than twenty thousand:** IUCN Red List of Threatened Species Assessment, "*Melursus ursinus*, Sloth Bear," 2016.

50 **attack more than 100 people:** Sloth bear attacks aren't tracked at a national level. However, Thomas Sharp et al., "Sloth Bear Attack Behavior and a Behavioral Approach to Safety" (2017), notes that 735 people were mauled by sloth bears in Madhya Pradesh alone between 1989 and 1994, of which 48 died. Around 150 attacks per year would therefore be on the lower end of any estimate.

50 **six people on average:** G. Bombieri et al., "Brown Bear Attacks on Humans: A Worldwide Perspective," *Scientific Reports* 9, no. 1 (2019), finds that brown bears attack 39.6 people on average per year globally. Between 2000 and 2015, there were 95 fatal attacks, or 6.3 per year on average.

50 **India contains more of the world's bear species:** India contains four of the world's bear species—sun bears, Asiatic black bears, sloth bears, and brown bears.

50 **"They [sloth bears] have a reputation":** Kenneth Anderson, *Man-Eaters and Jungle Killers* (London: Allen and Unwin, 1957).

51 **survey of more than five thousand households:** Sumeet Gulati et al., "Human Casualties Are the Dominant Cost of Human-Wildlife Conflict in India," *Proceedings of the National Academy of Sciences* 118, no. 8 (2021).

51 **"the probability of human injury":** Gulati et al., "Human Casualties Are the Dominant Cost," 3.

51 **"the most dangerous wild animal in India":** Aniruddha Dhamorikar et al., "Dynamics of Human–Sloth Bear Conflict in the Kanha-Pench Corridor, Madhya Pradesh, India: Technical Report," 2017.

51 **killed four people and injured three others:** Ritesh Mishra, "Man Climbs Tree to Escape Bear Attack, Waits for 5 Hours for Help," *Hindustan Times*, December 7, 2020.

51 **"I climbed the tree at around 4 p.m.":** Mishra, "Man Climbs Tree to Escape Bear Attack."

51 **442 villages in this corridor:** World Wildlife Fund, "Assessment of Fuelwood Consumption in Kanha-Pench Corridor, Madhya Pradesh, Factsheet," 2014.

51 **255 sloth bear attacks in the corridor:** Sharp et al., "Sloth Bear Attack Behavior."

51 **they can run faster than most humans:** Sloth bears can run at a pace of about 20 miles per hour. Usain Bolt, for comparison, can run at 27 miles per hour.

52 **European zoologist George Shaw:** Global Biodiversity Information Facility, "*Melursus ursinus*, Shaw, 1971." https://www.gbif.org/species/144098885

52 **some distance away:** Andrew Laurie and John Seidensticker, "Behavioural Ecology of the Sloth Bear (*Melursus ursinus*)," *Journal of Zoology* 182 (1977): 198.

54 **$3,234 per victim:** Gulati et al., "Human Casualties Are the Dominant Cost," 7.

54 **Retaliatory killings of sloth bears:** Harendra Bargali and Nishith Dharaiya, author interviews, February 2019.

54 **killed the cubs with an axe:** "Six Arrested in Killing of Two Sloth Bear Cubs in Akot," *The Hitavada*, June 16, 2020.

54 **betel leaf plantation:** Shivakumar Malagi, "Gudekote Pleads: We Can No Longer Grin and Bear It," *Deccan Chronicle*, September 16, 2018.

54 **716 sloth bear attacks on people:** Mayukh Chatterjee and Rudra Prasanna Mahapatra, " 'Bear'ing the Brunt," *Down to Earth*, March 25, 2019.

54 **more forgiving of wildlife:** Ravi Chellam, program director of the Foundation for Ecological Society and formerly with the Wildlife Institute of India, author interview, February 2019.

54 **decline by more than 30 percent:** Nisthi Dhariaya, Harendra Bargali, and Thomas Sharp, "*Melursus ursinus*," IUCN Red List of Threatened Species Assessment 2016, 2.

55 **"Baloo, the sleepy brown bear":** Rudyard Kipling, *The Jungle Book* (New York: Century Company, 1920), 19.

56 **"yet three or four days' rail to Lahore":** Rudyard Kipling, *Something of Myself* (London: Macmillan, 1937).

56 **snowy Vermont:** Victoria Villeneuve, "Rudyard Kipling Wrote 'The Jungle Book' in this Snowy Vermont House," *National Trust for Historic Preservation*, September 26, 2017.

56 **nursery stories he heard:** "Rudyard Kipling; An Anglo-Indian Icon or an Agent of Empire?" *Newstalk*, February 8, 2016.

58 **during tendu leaf collection:** Aniruddha Dhamorikar et al., "Characteristics of Human–Sloth Bear (*Melursus ursinus*) Encounters and the Resulting Human Casualties in the Kanha-Pench Corridor, Madhya Pradesh, India," *PLoS One* 12, no. 4 (2017).

63 **form their own state:** Dharmendra Kumar, *Rethinking State Politics in India* (London: Routledge India, 2011).

65 **pain-filled trance:** Tana Mewada, "How Sloth Bears Were Trained to Dance to the Beat of a Drum," *International Bear News* 21, no. 3 (2012): 24–25.

65 **"A Kalandar was forcing her to perform":** Abishek Madan and Shreya Dasgupta, "The Swan Song of India's Dancing Bears," *Mongabay*, November 20, 2013.

66 **1,200 rupees:** "India's 'Dancing Bears' Retire in Animal Rights Victory," *Bangkok Post*, December 2, 2012.

66 **into their communes every year:** Seshamani and Satyanarayan, "The Dancing Bears of India," 28.

67 **Kalandars punctured its nose:** Geeta Seshamani and Kartick Satyanarayan, "The Dancing Bears of India," World Society for the Protection of Animals report, 1997, 24–25.

68 **"the cubs have a high mortality rate":** Seshamani and Satyanarayan, "The Dancing Bears of India," 27.

69 **Raju is touted as the last dancing bear:** Bosky Khanna, "India's Last Dancing Bear Celebrates 9 Years Of Freedom," *Deccan Herald*, December 18, 2018; Wildlife SOS, "Drawing a Curtain on the Age-Long Practice of Dancing Bears," December 18, 2018.

69 **50,000 rupees:** "Dancing Bears Given Sanctuary," *Economic Times*, September 12, 2007.

69 **Rangila, a nineteen-year-old male:** Rachel Bale, "Nepal's Last Known Dancing Bears Rescued," *National Geographic*, December 22, 2017.

73 **wild animal attacks in Gujarat:** Himanshu Kaushik, "It's a Jungle Out There as Animal Attacks Rise," *Times of India*, June 9, 2019, notes "After a drought in 1987–88 there were 125 attacks on humans."

73 **nine attacks per year since 2009:** Nisthith Dharaiya, author correspondence, July 2022.

CHAPTER THREE: SOFT POWER

79 **at least 130 descendants:** Maggie Koerth, "The Complicated Legacy of a Panda Who Was Really Good at Sex," *FiveThirtyEight*, November 28, 2017.

80 **a fifth of the world's captive-bred pandas:** "World's Captive Panda Population Hits 633," *Xinhua*, January 3, 2021. 130 of 633 is about one-fifth.

80 **Ninety-nine percent of the bear's diet:** Rachel Kaufman, "How Do Giant Pandas Survive on a Diet of Bamboo?" *National Geographic*, October 17, 2011.

81 **little more than one thousand bears:** Stephen O'Brien and John Knight, "The Future of the Giant Panda," *Nature* 325 (1987): 758–59.

81 **dozen protected panda reserves:** O'Brien and Knight, "The Future of the Giant Panda."

81 **1,864 pandas living in the wild:** Henry Nicholls, "Yes, We Have More Pandas," *The Guardian*, February 28, 2015.

82 **crushed to death under the rubble:** Associated Press, "Panda Killed in China Earthquake Mourned," CBS News, June 10, 2008.

82 **Gu Gu jumped him:** Kang Yi, "Tourist's Affection Enrages Panda," *ChinaDaily*, September 20, 2006.

83 **"global cultural value"**: Fuwen Wei et al., "The Value of Ecosystem Services from Giant Panda Reserves," *Current Biology* 28, no. 13 (2018): 2174–2180.e7.

84 **"We wanted an animal that is beautiful"**: "WWF's History." https://wwf.panda.org/discover/knowledge_hub/history/

84 **Empress Dowager Bo:** Jianguo Liu et al., eds., *Pandas and People: Coupling Human and Natural Systems for Sustainability* (Oxford, UK: Oxford University Press, 2016).

85 **Père Armand David:** George B. Schaller, *The Last Panda* (Chicago, IL: University of Chicago Press, 1994), 135.

85 **"[The panda] came to be considered"**: Hallett Abend, "Rare 4-Pound 'Giant' Panda to Arrive in New York Soon," *New York Times*, December 20, 1936.

85 **Ruth Harkness arrived in Shanghai:** Vicki Constantine Croke, *The Lady and the Panda* (New York: Random House, 2005), 27.

86 **"She had, of course, her sex going against her"**: Croke, *The Lady and the Panda*, 57.

86 **"There was a shout from ahead"**: Croke, *The Lady and the Panda*, 126.

86 **"a little bit of something very cute"**: Croke, *The Lady and the Panda*, 133.

86 **"The futile search"**: Croke, *The Lady and the Panda*, 149.

87 **"One dog, $20.00"**: Croke, *The Lady and the Panda*, 155.

87 **draped in luxurious otter furs:** Croke, *The Lady and the Panda*, 165.

87 **Su Lin debuted:** Croke, *The Lady and the Panda*, 176.

87 **Shirley Temple, Eleanor Roosevelt:** David Owen, "Bears Do It," *New Yorker*, August 26, 2013.

87 **Helen Keller:** Croke, *The Lady and the Panda*, 177.

87 **Su Lin died of pneumonia in 1938:** Croke, *The Lady and the Panda*, 254.

87 **Chicago's Field Museum of Natural History:** Field#: FMNH 47432. https://collections-zoology.fieldmuseum.org/catalogue/2546658

88 **noticeable dearth of sparrows:** Jemimah Steinfeld, "China's Deadly Science Lesson: How an Ill-Conceived Campaign against Sparrows Contributed to One of the Worst Famines in History," *Index on Censorship* 47, no. 3 (2018).

88 **ban on foreign hunters:** World Wildlife Fund, "History of the Giant Panda." https://wwf.panda.org/?13588/History-of-the-Giant-Panda

88 **two men were handed death sentences:** Associated Press, "Two Chinese Peasants Get Death Sentence for Selling Panda Skins," May 31, 1993.

88 **sentenced to twenty years in prison:** Associated Press, "Chinese Man Gets 20 Years in Prison for Poaching Giant Pandas," November 26, 1998.

88 **"not less than 10 years or life"**: Criminal Law of China (2017), China Laws Portal - CJO (chinajusticeobserver.com).

89 **bodies of 138 pandas:** Lifeng Zhu et al., "Genetic Consequences of Historical Anthropogenic and Ecological Events on Giant Pandas," *Ecology* 94, no. 10 (2013): 2346–57.

89 **80 percent of pandas were lost:** John MacKinnon and Robert De Wulf, "Designing Protected Areas for Giant Pandas in China," in *Mapping the Diversity of Nature*, ed. Ronald I. Miller (Dordrecht, Netherlands: Springer, 1994), 128.

89 **taken into captivity:** Zhang Hemin, author interview, July 2021.

89 **thirty lone cubs:** Zhi Lu, Wenshi Pan, and Jim Harkness, "Mother-Cub Relationships in Giant Pandas in the Qinling Mountains, China, with Comment on Rescuing Abandoned Cubs," *Zoo Biology* 13, no. 6 (1994): 567–8.

89 **leave young cubs behind:** Lu, Pan, and Harkness, "Mother-Cub Relationships in Giant Pandas," 567–8.

89 **longest separation:** Lu, Pan, and Harkness, "Mother-Cub Relationships in Giant Pandas," 567–8.

89 **giant panda was very much a bear:** Stephen O'Brien et al., "A Molecular Solution to the Riddle of the Giant Panda's Phylogeny," *Nature* 317 (1985): 140–144.

90 **"Pragmatism had won out":** Schaller, *The Last Panda*, 11.

90 **"Having transcended its mountain home":** Schaller, *The Last Panda*, xvi.

90 **fallen by nearly half since 1974:** John Ramsay Mackinnon, "National Conservation Management Plan for the Giant Panda and Its Habitat: Sichuan, Shaanxi and Gansu Provinces, the People's Republic of China: Joint Report," WWF & China's Ministry of Forests, 1989.

91 **abolished the presidential term limit:** Chris Buckley and Steven Lee Myers, "China's Legislature Blesses Xi's Indefinite Rule. It Was 2,958 to 2," *New York Times*, March 11, 2018.

91 **"serious effort to undermine the dignity":** Benjamin Haas, "China Bans Winnie the Pooh Film after Comparisons to President Xi," *The Guardian*, August 7, 2018.

92 **panda biology following the starvation deaths:** Zhang Hemin, author interview, July 2021, translated by Kyle Obermann.

93 **panda pornography:** Jennifer Holland, "Pandas: Get to Know Their Wild Side," *National Geographic*, August 2016.

93 **female genital stimulator:** Holland, "Pandas: Get to Know Their Wild Side."

93 **three problems that Zhang:** Zhang, author interview, 2021.

94 **Zhang was present for every single birth:** Zhang, author interview, 2021.

95 **"hedonic mechanisms":** Sam Howe Verhovek, "So Why Are Pandas So Cute?" *New York Times*, May 11, 1987.

96 **stage considered premature:** Peishu Li and Kathleen Smith, "Comparative Skeletal Anatomy of Neonatal Ursids and the Extreme Altriciality of the Giant Panda," *Journal of Anatomy* 236, no. 4 (2020): 724–36.

96 **Half of all panda cubs are twins:** Zhang, author interview 2021; Alfie Shaw, "The Panda Who Didn't Know She Had Twins," BBC.

96 **more than two hundred bears have been born:** "Brief Introduction to Chengdu Research Base of Giant Panda Breeding." http://www.panda.org.cn/english/about/about/2013-09-11/2416.html

96 **most genetically diverse endangered species:** Holland, "Pandas: Get to Know Their Wild Side."

97 **twelve captive-bred bears:** This figure is somewhat elusive. Zhang Hemin told me that eleven captive-bred pandas had been released and nine had survived. However, Mingsheng Hong et al., "Creative Conservation in China: Releasing Captive Giant

Pandas into the Wild," *Environmental Science and Pollution Research* 26 (2019): 31548–9, notes that twelve were released.

97 **"Congratulations to all of us"**: Associated Press, "Chinese Pandas Get Zoo Enclosure Fit for a Queen's Reception," April 10, 2019.

97 **"For such an iconic animal"**: Lisa Abend, " 'Panda Diplomacy': A $24 million Zoo Enclosure Angers Some," *New York Times*, April 12, 2019.

98 **"panda diplomacy"**: Kathleen Buckingham et al., "Diplomats and Refugees: Panda Diplomacy, Soft 'Cuddly' Power, and the New Trajectory in Panda Conservation," *Environmental Practice* 15, no. 3 (2013): 1–9.

98 **"friendship envoys"**: Zhang Yunbi, "Pandas 'Envoys of Friendship,' " *China Daily*, July 5, 2012.

98 **seventy bears dispatched from mainland China**: Giant Panda Global, "Zoos and Breeding Centers." https://www.giantpandaglobal.com/zoos/

98 **shipping two musk oxen to China**: Alexander Burns, "When Ling-Ling and Hsing Hsing Arrived in the U.S.," *New York Times*, February 4, 2016.

98 **China dispatched two dozen pandas**: Buckingham et al., "Diplomats and Refugees."

99 **banned the short-term import of pandas**: UPI, "Panda Imports Suspended While Policy Reviewed," December 20, 1993.

99 **"deep trade relationships characterized by trust"**: Buckingham et al., "Diplomats and Refugees," 1.

99 **repatriated to China**: Buckingham et al., "Diplomats and Refugees," 5.

100 **butted heads with a young Zhang Hemin**: Schaller, *The Last Panda*, 156.

100 **"home for the living dead"**: Schaller, *The Last Panda*, 156.

100 **"had been unable to develop"**: Schaller, *The Last Panda*, 156.

100 **"doesn't need three hundred pandas"**: Christine Dell'Amore, "Is Breeding Pandas in Captivity Worth It?" *National Geographic*, August 28, 2013.

100 **walked into the wild for the first time**: Meng Qingsheng, "Two Captive-Bred Pandas Released into Wild," CGTN, December 30, 2018.

101 **"naughty, active, and lively"**: Meng, "Two Captive-Bred Pandas Released into Wild."

101 **fell off a cliff and died**: James Owen, "First Panda Freed into Wild Found Dead," *National Geographic*, May 31, 2007.

101 **two more have died**: Hong et al., "Creative Conservation in China," Table 1.

102 **downgraded the panda's population status**: Christine Dell'Amore, "Giant Pandas, Symbol of Conservation, Are No Longer Endangered," *National Geographic*, September 4, 2016.

102 **Some experts questioned the validity**: Jane Qiu, "Experts Question China's Panda Survey," *Nature*, February 28, 2015.

103 **warned that another large-scale bamboo flowering**: Zhaoxue Tian et al., "The Next Widespread Bamboo Flowering Poses a Massive Risk to the Giant Panda," *Biological Conservation* 234 (June 2019): 180–87.

103 **"bamboo flowering could be a disaster for them"**: Zhaoxue et al., "The Next Widespread Bamboo Flowering."

103 **Giant Panda National Park:** Gloria Dickie, "Green Glove, Iron Fist," *BioGraphic Magazine,* December 18, 2018.

103 **"temporary captivity until the bamboo recovers":** Zhaoxue et al., "The Next Widespread Bamboo Flowering."

CHAPTER FOUR: LIQUID GOLD

110 **in traditional medicine for thousands of years:** Yiben Feng et al., "Bear Bile: Dilemma of a Traditional Medicinal Use and Animal Protection," *Journal of Ethnobiology and Ethnomedicine* 5, article 2 (2009).

110 **colds, cancer, even hangovers:** Rachel Fobar, "Bear Bile, Explained," *National Geographic,* February 25, 2019.

111 **reduce inflammation and lower cholesterol:** Feng et al., "Bear Bile."

111 **rich in omega-3 acids:** Cynthia Graber, "Snake Oil Salesmen Were on to Something," *Scientific American,* November 1, 2007.

111 **preclinical trials:** T. Achufusi et al., "Ursodeoxycholic Acid," National Library of Medicine, updated January 2022. https://www.ncbi.nlm.nih.gov/books/NBK545303/; URSO Prescribing Information, US Food and Drug Administration, November 2009.

111 **produce useful quantities of it:** Lee Hagey et al., "Ursodeoxycholic Acid in the Ursidae: Biliary Bile Acids of Bears, Pandas, and Related Carnivores," *Journal of Lipid Research* 34, no. 11 (1993): 1911–17.

111 **40 percent of the bile pool:** Hagey et al., "Ursodeoxycholic Acid," 1912. *Ursus americanus.*

111 **surge by over 10 percent:** Hagey et al., "Ursodeoxycholic Acid," 1912.

112 **semisynthetic ursodeoxycholic acid:** Fabio Tonin and Isabel Arends, "Latest Development in the Synthesis of Ursodeoxycholic Acid (UCDA): A Critical Review," *Beilstein Journal of Organic Chemistry* 20, no. 14 (2018): 470–83.

112 ***Tan Re Qing:*** "Notice on Printing and Distributing the Novel Coronavirus Pneumonia Diagnosis and Treatment Plan," Office of the Chinese Medicine Bureau of the General Office of the Health Commission, March 3, 2020. http://www.gov.cn/zhengce/zhengceku/2020-03/04/5486705/files/ae61004f930d47598711a0d4cbf874a9.pdf

114 **world's widest-ranging bears:** The moon bear can be found in roughly eighteen countries, second to the brown bear found in more than thirty.

114 **Cambodia, Myanmar, and Laos:** Lalita Gomez and Chris Shepherd, "Trade in Bears in Lao PDR with Observations from Market Surveys and Seizure Data," *Global Ecology and Conservation,* July 2018; Lorraine Scotson, "The Distribution and Status of Asiatic Black Bear *Ursus thibetanus* and Malayan Sun Bear *Helarctos malayanus* in Nam Et Phou Louey National Protected Area, Lao PDR," 2010, 28; Kaitlyn-Elizabeth Foley et al., "Pills, Powders, Vials, and Flakes: The Bear Bile Trade in Asia," TRAFFIC Southeast Asia report, 2011, vi, 7.

114 **"nursery with the children":** Sir Thomas Stamford Raffles, *Transactions of the Linnean Society, Vol. XIII,* March 1823, in the *Monthly Review,* 232.

114 **"The only time I knew him to be out of humour":** T. Raffles, *Transactions of the Linnean Society*, 232.

115 **"The only loss in our family":** Lady Sophia Raffles, *Memoir of the Life and Public Serves of Sir Thomas Stamford Raffles, F.R.S.* (London: Gilbert and Rivington Printers, 1830), 446.

115 ***Helarctos* genus:** S. Raffles, *Memoir of the Life*, 634.

115 **Europe's Etruscan bear:** Stephen Herrero, "Aspects of Evolution and Adaptation in American Black Bears (*Ursus americanus Pallas*) and Brown and Grizzly Bears (*U. arctos Linne.*) of North America," Panel 4: Bear Behaviour, in Vol. 2, *A Selection of Papers from the Second International Conference on Bear Research and Management, Calgary, Alberta, Canada, 6–9 November 1970.* IUCN Publications New Series no. 23 (1972), 221–231. Published by the International Association for Bear Research and Management.

115 **most talkative bears:** Liya Pokrovskaya, "Vocal Repertoire of Asiatic Black Bear (*Ursus thibetanus*) Cubs," *Bioacoustics* 22, no. 3 (2013): 229–45; Jill Robinson, author interview, March 2021.

115 **world's least studied bear:** IUCN SSC Bear Specialist Group et al., "Sun Bears: Global Status Review & Conservation Action Plan, 2019–2028," 2019, 4.

116 **helicopters to dart bears:** Gabriella Fredriksson, author interview, May 2021.

116 **first cub to arrive was Ganja:** Fredriksson, author interview, 2021.

116 **their playmate's open-mouth facial expressions:** Derry Taylor et al., "Facial Complexity in Sun Bears: Exact Facial Mimicry and Social Sensitivity," *Scientific Reports* 9, article no. 4961 (2019).

117 **about 8 percent:** Hagey at al., "Ursodeoxycholic Acid," 1912.

117 **164 of them:** Author interviews in March 2019; Animals Asia, "Convincing Vietnam's Most Notorious Bile Farm Village That Now Is the Time for Change," April 19, 2019.

117 **a quarter of the country's remaining:** During 2019 reporting in Vietnam, NGOs estimated that around four hundred bears remained on farms, though this number has since declined, as some bears have died or been rescued.

118 **had ever surrendered a single bear:** Tuan Bendixsen, author interview, March 2019.

118 **twenty thousand bears are believed to be kept:** A definite number on this is difficult to obtain. Animals Asia estimates that over ten thousand bears are kept on farms in China, with another ten thousand elsewhere in Asia. "Cruel Cures: The Industry Behind Bear Bile Production and How to End It," World Animal Protection report, 2020, 9, notes that twenty thousand bears are being legally held on bile farms in China, citing C. Iwen and G. Shenzhen, "Research on the Current Situation of Chinese Bear Bile Industry and Strategies for Transition," investigation report for Central State Council, Beijing, 2016. This report was not formally published, but via author correspondence, WAP established that they had briefly collaborated with the Development Research Centre of the State Council of China to get this number.

118 **gain a foothold:** "Bear Bile Farming—2022 Status," Free the Bears report. https://freethebears.org/blogs/news/bear-bile-farming-2022-status

118 **developed a tortuous method:** Peter J. Li, "China's Bear Farming and Long-Term Solutions," *Journal of Applied Animal Welfare Science* 7, no. 1 (2004): 71–80.

118 **"free-dripping fistula technique":** Feng et al., "Bear Bile."

118 **bile equivalent of forty or fifty poached wild bears:** Susan Mainka and Judy Mills, "Wildlife and Traditional Chinese Medicine: Supply and Demand for Wildlife Species," *Journal of Zoo and Wildlife Medicine* 26, no. 2 (1995): 193.

119 **spiked consumer interest:** Foley et al., "Pills, Powders, Vials, and Flakes," 6.

119 **"liquid gold":** Peter Li, "China's Bear Farming and Long-Term Solutions," *Journal of Applied Animal Welfare Science* 7, no. 1 (2004): 71–81.

119 **busloads of Korean tourists:** Author interviews; Moon Gwang-lip, "Vietnamese Urge Koreans Not to Travel for Bear Bile," *Korea JoongAng Daily*, October 27, 2009.

119 **valued at $1 billion:** WAP, "Cruel Cures," 4.

119 **fanciest cars:** Tuan Bendixsen, author interview, March 2019. "Some of them are so rich that you couldn't pay them for their bears, anyway . . . in Phuc Tho some of the bigger farms have bigger houses and fancy cars."

119 **"coffin" or "crush" cages:** Animals Asia, "Five Things You Need to Know about Bear Bile Farming," November 1, 2021.

120 **starve to death:** Animals Asia, "What Is Bear Bile Farming?" 2017.

120 **ketamine, an illegal anaesthetic in Vietnam:** Animals Asia, "Six Horrific Ways Bear Bile Is Extracted for Traditional Medicine," January 10, 2018.

120 **between 80 and 100 milliliters of bile:** Animals Asia, "Six Horrific Ways."

120 **outlawed the practice:** Animals Asia, "Why Bear Bile Farming Persists in Vietnam," October 7, 2014.

120 **forty-three hundred at the industry's peak:** Animals Asia, "From 4,300 Caged Bears on Bile Farms in Vietnam to a Future with None," July 19, 2017.

121 ***keeping* existing bears was still perfectly fine:** Animals Asia, "From 4,300 Caged Bears."

121 **get them microchipped:** Animals Asia, "Bear Numbers Fall on Vietnam's Bile Farms," January 8, 2015.

121 **most live nowhere near as long on farms:** Animals Asia, "Bear Numbers Fall."

122 **Fewer than five hundred of the forty-three hundred:** Correspondence with Rod Mabin and Matthew Hunt of Free the Bears. No centralized tally exists, and hundreds more bears have been rescued in other Asian countries, but in Vietnam they estimate between three hundred and five hundred bile bears have been rescued.

122 **lowering bile demand:** World Animal Protection, "End in Sight for Cruel Bear Bile Industry in Vietnam," January 9, 2017.

122 **$4 a month on food:** Shreya Dasgupta, "Vietnam's Bear Bile Farms Are Collapsing—But It May Not Be Good News," *Mongabay*, July 11, 2018.

126 **only eight respondents:** Brian Crudge et al., "The Challenges and Conservation Implications of Bear Bile Farming in Viet Nam," *Oryx* 54, no. 2 (2018): 256.

126 **missing paws:** Animals Asia, "These Broken Paws Have Become a Symbol of Bile Farm Cruelty," January 20, 2017.

126 **152 smuggled live bruins in Vietnam:** Elizabeth Burgess et al., "Brought to Bear: An Analysis of Seizures across Asia, 2000–2011," TRAFFIC report, 2014, 19.

126 **"many bear farms in [Vietnam]":** Daniel Willcox et al., "An Assessment of Trade in Bear Bile and Gall Bladder in Vietnam," TRAFFIC report, 2017, 30.

127 **classified as vulnerable to extinction:** IUCN Red List of Threatened Species Assessment, *Helarctos malayanus* and *Ursus thibetanus.*

127 **declined by as much as half:** IUCN Red List of Threatened Species Assessment, Asiatic black bear.

127 **plummeted by more than a third:** IUCN SSC Bear Specialist Group et al., "Sun Bears: Global Status Review & Conservation Action Plan, 2019–2028," 17.

127 **edges of these plantations:** Roshan Guharajan et al., "Does the Vulnerable Sun Bear *Helarctos malayanus* Damage Crops and Threaten People in Oil Palm Plantations?" *Oryx* 53, no. 4 (2019): 1–9; Thye Lim Tee et al., "Anthropogenic Edge Effects in Habitat Selection by Sun Bears in a Protected Area," *Wildlife Biology*, 2021.

127 **caught and maimed in snares:** Guharajan et al., "Does the Vulnerable Sun Bear *Helarctos malayanus* Damage Crops," 17; G. C. Tan, "Sun Bear Found Caught in Snare Near Oil Palm Plantation in Kedah," *The Star*, July 10, 2021.

127 **"reliable estimates of sun bear populations":** IUCN SSC Bear Specialist Group et al., "Sun Bears: Global Status Review," 17.

127 **villagers reported that they thought:** Brian Crudge et al., "The Status and Distribution of Bears in Vietnam, 2016," Free the Bears and Animals Asia Technical Report, 2016.

127 **"poaching free-for-all fueled by heightened demand":** Crudge et al., "The Status and Distribution of Bears," 6.

128 **rescued more than 630 bears:** Jill Robinson, author interview, March 2021.

128 **Born in Saigon:** Tuan Bendixsen, author interview, March 2019.

129 **a maximum of five years in jail:** Tuan Bendixsen and Trinh Huyen Trang, author interviews, 2019 and 2021.

130 **Poachers had killed Layla's mother:** Animals Asia, "Poachers Left This Sun Bear Orphaned and Alone—Now Heroes Have Rebuilt Her Life," August 28, 2017.

130 **Malaysian pop star Zarith Sofia Mohd Yasin:** Bella Peacock, "Malaysian Popstar Thought Pet Bear Was a Dog," 9News Australia, June 13, 2019.

130 **"If Bruno [the bear] could talk":** Peacock, "Malaysian Popstar."

131 **"Laos is getting big":** Also see Scotson, "The Distribution and Status of Asiatic Black Bear *Ursus thibetanus*," 28.

131 **Asia's wellspring of wild bears:** Vincent Nijman et al., "Assessing the Illegal Bear Trade in Myanmar through Conversations with Poachers: Topology, Perceptions, and Trade Links to China," *Human Dimensions of Wildlife* 22, no. 2 (2017): 172–82, notes that Myanmar "has significant wild populations of two globally threatened bears and is economically and geopolitically connected to China and other East Asian consumer countries."

131 **moved into a sanctuary:** Animals Asia, "Vietnam Agrees Plan to Close All Bear Bile Farms," July 19, 2017.

132 **petition in 2019 calling for an end:** Vietnam News Agency, "Thousands of Hanoians Call for End to Bear Farming," February 13, 2019.

132 **stop all prescriptions for bear bile:** Animals Asia, "Report: 97% of Traditional Medicine Doctors No Longer Prescribe Bear Bile in Vietnam," May 30, 2019.

132 **Wild sun bears are turning up:** Brian Crudge, author interview, March 2021.

132 **proposal to end bear farming by 2035:** Simon Denyer, "China's Bear Bile Industry Persists Despite Growing Awareness of the Cruelty Involved," *Washington Post*, June 3, 2018.

CHAPTER FIVE: OUT OF THE WILD

137 **grabs a bag of Tostitos:** Matthew Wright, "Bear Wanders into a California Grocery Store, Grabs a Bag of Tostitos," *Daily Mail Online*, August 21, 2020.

137 **breaks into a gas station:** Rachel Sharp, "Hungry Bears Break into California Gas Station and Supermarket and Eat Candy and Crackers," *Daily Mail Online*, September 1, 2020.

137 **24 pounds of pure butter:** Oliver Millman, "No Picnic: Americans Face Encounters with Black Bears as Population Rebounds," *The Guardian*, October 30, 2018.

138 **Yonkers:** "Wildlife Officials Tranquilize Black Bear in Yonkers," CBS News, May 20, 2015.

138 **his first dog, Stryker:** Carl Lackey, author interview, March 2015; Marie Baca, "Near Lake Tahoe, There's a Bear So Tough, Bullets Bounce Off His Head," *Wall Street Journal*, August 16, 2010.

139 **second-highest density of black bears:** Jon Beckmann and Joel Berger, "Using Black Bears to Test Ideal-Free Distribution Models Experimentally," *Journal of Mammalogy* 84, no. 2 (2003): 597, notes that the estimated density of urban-interface bears in the study area around Lake Tahoe, which includes Incline Village, Stateline, and South Lake Tahoe, was "2nd highest in North America."

139 **Beginning around 1990:** Jon Beckmann and Carl Lackey, "Lessons Learned from a 20-Year Collaborative Study on American Black Bears," *Human-Wildlife Interactions* 12, no. 3 (2018): 172–82, notes that conflicts began rising in the mid-1990s.

139 **Bears were no longer hibernating?:** Jon Beckmann and Joel Berger, "Rapid Ecological and Behavioral Changes in Carnivores: The Responses of Black Bears (*Ursus americanus*) to Altered Food," *Journal of Zoology* 261, no. 2 (2003): 207–212; Kendra Pierre-Louis, "As Winter Warms, Bears Can't Sleep. And They're Getting into Trouble," *New York Times*, May 4, 2018.

140 **tracked thirty-eight urban bears:** Beckmann and Berger, "Rapid Ecological and Behavioral Changes in Carnivores."

140 **reset bears' biological clocks:** Heather Johnson et al., "Human Development and Climate Affect Hibernation in a Large Carnivore with Implications for Human–Carnivore Conflicts," *Journal of Applied Ecology* 55, no. 2 (2018): 663–72.

140 **abandoning their dens weeks ahead:** John Hopewell, "Warning to Visitors, Yellowstone Grizzly Bears Emerge Weeks Early Due to Warm Weather," *Washington Post*, March 10, 2016.

140 **hibernating for six fewer days:** Johnson et al., "Human Development and Climate Affect Hibernation."

140 **"population sinks and ecological traps":** Heather Johnson, David L. Lewis, and Stewart W. Breck, "Individual and Population Fitness Consequences Associated with Large Carnivore Use of Residential Development," *Ecosphere* 11, no. 5 (2020): 1.

141 **drastically contracted their ranges:** Beckmann and Berger, "Using Black Bears to Test," 602.

141 **15 and 30 percent of their body weight:** National Park Service, "Denning and Hibernation Behavior."

141 **collective weight was a third more:** Beckmann and Berger, "Using Black Bears to Test," 602.

141 **interactions . . . skyrocketed by 1,000 percent:** Beckmann and Berger, "Using Black Bears to Test," 602.

141 **450 instances of an animal getting into trash:** "Bear Boxes in the Lake Tahoe Region," Tahoe Regional Planning Agency report, 2017, 4.

141 **euthanized 132 bears:** Rae-Wynn Grant et al., "Risky Business: Modeling Mortality Risk Near the Urban-Wildland Interface for a Large Carnivore," *Global Ecology and Conservation* 16 (2018).

142 **no longer repopulating the backcountry:** Beckmann and Lackey, "Lessons Learned."

142 **a phenomenon known as delayed implantation:** Andrea Friebe et al., "Factors Affecting Date of Implantation, Parturition, and Den Entry Estimated from Activity and Body Temperature in Free-Ranging Brown Bears," *PLoS One* 9, no. 7 (2014); Zhang Hemin et al., "Delayed Implantation in Giant Pandas: The First Comprehensive Empirical Evidence," *Reproduction* 138, no. 6 (2009): 979–86; Cheryl Frederick et al., "Reproductive Timing and Seasonality in the Sun Bear (*Helarctos malayanus*)," *Journal of Mammalogy* 93, no. 2 (2012): 522–31. Correspondence with Dave Garshelis, July 2022, notes that this is still not definitively known for sun bears, though if it occurs it would be quite short.

143 **a bear and its perceived meal:** Stephen Herrero et al., "Fatal Attacks by American Black Bear on People, 1900–2009," *Journal of Wildlife Management* 75, no. 3 (2011): 596–603.

143 **living, playing, and working:** Herrero et al., "Fatal Attacks by American Black Bear."

143 **mauled, swiped, or charged:** Alexandra Yoon-Hendricks and Ryan Sabalow, "California Man Had a Destructive Bear Killed. Then His Tahoe Neighbors Went on the Attack," *Sacramento Bee*, January 6, 2020; Travis Hall, "Black Bear Walks into California Home and Attacks Woman," *Field & Stream*, June 29, 2022.

143 **"I blast the [blow] horn":** Claire Cudahy, "Man Jump Kicks Bear in Chest after It Breaks into Cabin at Fallen Leaf Lake," *Tahoe Daily Tribune*, July 2, 2018.

143 **attacked teenager Anna Knochel:** Arthur Rotstein, "Bear Mauls Camp Counselor," Associated Press, July 26, 1996; UPI, "Bear Killed after Mauling Girl," July 25, 1996.

143 **for $2.5 million:** Tim Vanderpool, "Bruin Trouble," *Tucson Weekly*, February 17, 2000.

144 **chronicling twenty years of lessons:** Beckmann and Lackey, "Lessons Learned."

144 **large brain:** Valeria Zamisch and Jennifer Vonk, "Spatial Memory in Captive American Black Bears (*Ursus americanus*)," *Journal of Comparative Psychology* 126, no. 4 (2012): 372–87.

144 **smell about two thousand times better:** Experiments by Dr. George Stevenson, a retired neurosurgeon who specialized in bear physiology, found a grizzly bear had seven times as many nerve endings in its nose as a hound dog, and hound dogs have about three hundred times as many nerve endings as people.

144 **captive American black bears:** Jennifer Vonk, author interview, March 2021.

144 **"horse manure rolling behaviors":** Wenliang Zhou et al., "Why Wild Giant Pandas Frequently Roll in Horse Manure," *Proceedings of the National Academy of Sciences* 117, no. 51 (2020): 32493–98.

144 **complex mental inventories:** Peter Thompson et al., "Time-Dependent Memory and Individual Variation in Arctic Brown Bears (*Ursus arctos*)," *Movement Ecology* 10, article no. 18 (2022).

145 **polar bears using tools:** Ian Stirling et al., "Do Wild Polar Bears (*Ursus maritimus*) Use Tools When Hunting Walruses (*Odobenus rosmarus*)?" *Arctic* 74, no. 2 (2020): 175–87.

145 **most authoritative bodies of research:** These works include Jennifer Vonk, Stephanie E. Jett, and Kelly W. Mosteller, "Concept Formation in American Black Bears (*Ursus americanus*)," *Animal Behaviour* 84, no. 4 (2012): 953–64; Zamisch and Vonk, "Spatial Memory in Captive American Black Bears (*Ursus americanus*)"; Jennifer Vonk and Moriah Galvan, "What Do Natural Categorization Studies Tell Us about Apes and Bears?" *Animal Behavior and Cognition* 1, no. 3 (2014): 309–330; Jennifer Vonk and Zoe Johnson-Ulrich, "Social and Non-Social Category Discrimination in a Chimpanzee (*Pan troglodytes*) and American Black Bears (*Ursus americanus*)," *Learning and Behavior* 42, no. 3 (2014): 231–45; Vonk et al., "Manipulating Spatial and Visual Cues in a Win-Stay Foraging Task in Captive Grizzly Bears (*Ursus arctos horribilis*)," in *Spatial, Long-and Short-Term Memory: Functions, Differences and Effects of Injury*, ed. Edward A. Thayer (New York: Nova Biomedical, 2016), 47–60.

145 **Brutus, Dusty, and Bella:** Jennifer Vonk, author interview, March 2021.

145 **simple discrimination between objects:** Jennifer Vonk and Michael Beran, "Bears 'Count' Too: Quantity Estimation and Comparison in Black Bears (*Ursus americanus*)," *Animal Behaviour* 84, no. 1 (2012): 231–38.

146 **could distinguish and understand numbers:** Vonk and Beran, "Bears 'Count' Too."

146 **different arrays of dots:** Vonk and Beran, "Bears 'Count' Too."

146 **"The pattern of performance":** Vonk and Beran, "Bears 'Count' Too."

148 **Yet, they had:** Caitlin-Lee Roney, author interview, September 2019.

148 **retrofit old lockers:** Roney, author interview, 2019.

149 **running amok over the park:** Rachel Mazur, author interview, September 2019.

149 **"a candy bar in the door"**: Paul Rogers, "Conflicts with Yosemite Bears Fall Dramatically as People, Bears Learn New Lessons," *Mercury News*, August 12, 2016.

149 **six hundred cars**: Rogers, "Conflicts with Yosemite Bears Fall."

149 **favorite targets**: Suzanne Charle, "To Bears in Yosemite, Cars Are Like Cookie Jars," *New York Times*, November 30, 1997.

149 **descent into *bear mayhem***: Rogers, "Conflicts with Yosemite Bears Fall."

150 **Ahwahnechee inhabited the Yosemite Valley**: Kate Nearpass Ogden, *Yosemite* (London: Reaktion Books, 2015), 45.

150 **arrived in the valley around 1833**: Ogden, *Yosemite*, 32.

150 **Mariposa Battalion**: Ogden, *Yosemite*, 32–33.

150 **Thomas A. Ayres began publicizing**: Ogden, *Yosemite*, 36–42.

151 **thousands of visitors were soon arriving**: Rachel Mazur, *Speaking of Bears: The Bear Crisis and a Tale of Rewilding from Yosemite, Sequoia, and Other National Parks* (Guilford, CT: Falcon Guides, 2015).

151 **"Climb the mountains and get their good tidings"**: John Muir, *Our National Parks* (Boston and New York: Houghton, Mifflin and Company, 1901).

151 **little choice but to perform**: Ogden, *Yosemite*, 54–58.

151 **"[The bear] breaks into cabins"**: Mazur, *Speaking of Bears*, 24.

151 **flocked to the trash piles**: Mazur, *Speaking of Bears*, 25–26.

152 **establish bear-feeding shows**: Mazur, *Speaking of Bears*, 30–31.

152 **draw bears out of the campgrounds**: Mazur, *Speaking of Bears*, 29.

152 **formalized the bear pits**: Mazur, *Speaking of Bears*, 31.

152 **paid 50 cents each for a coveted spot**: Mazur, *Speaking of Bears*, 32.

152 **sixty-seven people were hospitalized**: Mazur, *Speaking of Bears*, 33.

152 **"The bear shows had grown"**: Mazur, *Speaking of Bears*, 33.

153 **one hundred bears were killed**: Mazur, *Speaking of Bears*, 36.

153 **shut down the bear shows**: Mazur, *Speaking of Bears*, 36.

153 **attacked and killed by two different**: Sarah Dettmer, "Night of the Grizzlies: Lessons Learned in 50 Years Since Attacks," *Great Falls Tribune*, August 3, 2017.

153 **Koons's zipper was stuck**: Dettmer, "Night of the Grizzlies."

153 **"Oh my god. I'm dead"**: Dettmer, "Night of the Grizzlies."

154 **her screams faded into the night**: Dettmer, "Night of the Grizzlies."

154 **"lured in intentionally"**: Dettmer, "Night of the Grizzlies."

154 **"Come to Granite Park and see grizzly bears."**: Dettmer, "Night of the Grizzlies."

154 **"The most likely predisposing factor"**: Stephen Herrero, *Bear Attacks: Their Causes and Avoidance*, 3rd ed. (Guilford, CT: Lyons Press, 1985), 53.

154 **had treed a father and son**: Herrero, *Bear Attacks*, 53.

154 **fragrant makeup**: Herrero, *Bear Attacks*, 54.

154 **"the bear's personality"**: Herrero, *Bear Attacks*, 54.

154 **Koons's partially devoured body**: Herrero, *Bear Attacks*, 55.

154 **"The Trout Lake girl"**: Margaret Seelie, "Nature Is a Woman's Place: How the Myth That Bears Are a Danger to Menstruating Women Spread," *Jezebel*, May 25, 2017.

154 **"stay out of bear country"**: *Grizzly, Grizzly, Grizzly*, US National Park Service and US Forest Service brochure. https://archive.org/details/grizzlygrizzlygr239unit/mode/2up

155 **"human sexual activity"**: *Grizzly, Grizzly, Grizzly*.

155 **heightened interest in menstrual blood**: Kerry Gunther, "Bears and Menstruating Women," Yell 707, Information Paper BMO-7, February 2016.

155 **permanently closed their dumps**: Mazur, *Speaking of Bears*, 73.

155 **"it was like a repeat of the closing of the bear pits"**: Mazur, *Speaking of Bears*, 56.

156 ***Farley*, set in the fictional Asphalt State Park**: Bill Van Niekerken, "An Ode to Phil Frank: When 'Travels with Farley' Moved to SF Full Time," *San Francisco Chronicle*, February 25, 2020.

156 **She went to high school in Mariposa**: Caitlin Lee-Roney, author interview, September 2019.

157 **1,600 incidents were reported that year**: National Park Service, "Human-Bear Incidents Reach Record Low in Yosemite National Park," November 19, 2015.

157 **fix the park's egregious bear problem**: Caitlin Lee-Roney, author interview, September 2019.

157 **a black bear known as Orange-19**: Lee-Roney, author interview, 2019.

158 **returned to keeping daylight hours**: Lee-Roney, author interview, 2019. "Night bear activity has decreased substantially. In the last few years we've barely had any night-active bears at all, which used to be 90 percent of our issues."

158 **63 percent less human food**: John B. Hopkins et al., "The Changing Anthropogenic Diets of American Black Bears over the Past Century in Yosemite National Park," *Frontiers in Ecology and the Environment* 12, no. 2 (2014): 107–114.

158 **$660,000 in 1998 to less than $5,000**: National Park Service, "Human-Bear Incidents Reach Record Low"; Yosemite National Park Bear Facts, August 25 to August 31, 2019.

158 **batting them off a 400-foot-high cliff**: Lee-Roney, author interview, 2019.

CHAPTER SIX: RETURN OF THE GRIZZLY

163 **Nathan Keane is an early riser**: Nathan Keane, author interview, May 2021.

163 **glanced out the kitchen window**: Keane, author interview, 2021.

163 **lived on the plains 16 miles**: Keane, author interview, 2021.

163 **farthest east a grizzly had been seen**: Aaron Bolton, "Pioneering Grizzly Bear Spotted East of Great Falls," Montana Public Radio, June 20, 2020.

164 **report the brazen animal**: Keane, author interview, 2021.

164 **The bear shot off**: Keane, author interview, 2021.

164 **determined the culprit**: Bolton, "Pioneering Grizzly Bear Spotted"; Wesley Sarmento, author interview, 2021.

164 **installed an electric fence**: Keane, author interview, 2021.

164 **haven't been seen in generations**: Nathan Rott, "As Grizzlies Come Back, Frustration Builds over Continued Protections," NPR Weekend Edition, February 2, 2019; Jim Robbins, "Grizzlies Return, with Strings Attached," *New York Times*, August 15, 2011.

164 **roaming the Big Snowy Mountains:** Associated Press, "Grizzly Bear Photographed in Big Snowy Mountains," as appeared in *Great Falls Tribune*, May 6, 2021.

164 **isolated from one another for decades:** Craig Miller and Lisette Waits, "The History of Effective Population Size and Genetic Diversity in the Yellowstone Grizzly (*Ursus arctos*): Implications for Conservation," *Proceedings of the National Academy of Sciences* 100, no. 7 (2003): 4334–39; Sylvia Fallon, "No Room to Roam—New Top Ten Report Highlights the Isolation of Yellowstone Grizzly Bears," NRDC blog, November 18, 2015.

164 *oso plateado:* "Mexican Grizzly (Extinct)," Bear Conservation.

165 **trapped, shot, and poisoned:** "Special Status Assessment for the Grizzly Bear (*Ursus arctic horribilis*) in the Lower-48 States: A Biological Report," prepared by the US FWS Grizzly Bear Recovery Office, Missoula, January 2021, 50.

165 **Lewis and Clark Expedition:** "Grizzly Recovery Program," University of Montana. https://www.cfc.umt.edu/grizzlybearrecovery/about/default.php

165 **fewer than one thousand remained:** "Grizzly Recovery Program."

165 **disappeared from the coast:** Jeremy Miller, "Awakening the Grizzly," *Pacific Standard Magazine*, June/July 2018.

165 **a $10 bounty:** Karin Klein, "Orange County's Grizzly Past," *Los Angeles Times*, September 29, 2010.

165 **greasy grizzly steaks:** Miller, "Awakening the Grizzly."

165 **Seth Kinman:** "The Pacific Coast Nimrod Who Gives Chairs to Presidents," *New York Times*, December 9, 1885.

165 **"The seat was soft":** Marshall R. Auspach, "The Lost History of Seth Kinman," in *Now and Then* (Muncy, PA: Muncy Historical Society, 1947), 180–202; "The 'Pacific Coast Nimrod' Seth Kinman and His Snapping Grizzly Bear Chairs Fit for Presidents," *Flashbak*, April 6, 2014.

165 **thirty-one would vanish:** "Special Status Assessment," 51.

165 **swift human intervention followed by natural expansion:** "Special Status Assessment," 51.

165 **protected under the Endangered Species Act:** "Special Status Assessment," 4; Amendment listing the grizzly bear of the 48 Conterminous states as a threatened species (*Ursus arctos horribilis*), US Fish and Wildlife Service, Vol. 40, No. 145, July 28, 1975, Washington, DC, 31734–36.

166 **no longer allowed to be killed:** "Special Status Assessment," 4.

166 **Wyoming and Idaho ceased:** A small hunt did continue in northwestern Montana until the early 1990s: Associated Press, "Montana Grizzly Hunt Delayed," September 28, 1991.

166 **"It is now unlawful to kill":** "Grizzly Bear Listed as Threatened Species," Department of Interior News Release, July 28, 1975.

166 **identified six ecosystems:** "Special Status Assessment," 76; "Grizzly Bear Recovery Plan," prepared by Chris Servheen, approved by USFWS on September 10, 1993.

166 **private land easements:** "Special Status Assessment," 8.

166 **augment the Cabinet-Yaak grizzly population:** "Special Status Assessment," 178–179; Gloria Dickie, "Return of the Grizzly?" *High Country News Magazine*, February 21, 2017.

166 **wandering down into the Bitterroot Range:** "Grizzly Detected in Montana's Bitterroots Last Week," *Spokesman-Review*, July 23, 2019; Justin Housman, "Lone Grizzly Makes a Home in Bitterroot Ecosystem—First Time in 80 Years," *Adventure Journal*, July 22, 2019.

166 **Biologists had initially hoped:** Michael Dax, *Grizzly West: A Failed Attempt to Reintroduce Grizzly Bears in the Mountain West* (Lincoln: University of Nebraska Press, 2015); Rob Chaney, "Grizzly Biologists Release Bitterroot Studies," *Missoulian*, June 17, 2021.

166 **number just below two thousand:** "Special Status Assessment," 61, notes at least "1,913" individuals in Lower 48.

166 **doubled in half a century:** "Special Status Assessment," 4, notes seven hundred or eight hundred Lower 48 grizzly bears in 1975.

166 **"Grizzly bear populations":** "Grizzly Bear in the Lower-48 States (*Ursus arctos horribilis*) 5-Year Status Review: Summary and Evaluation," US Fish and Wildlife Service, 4.

166 **tripled their range:** "Special Status Assessment," 4–5, notes increase in occupation of historical range from 2 percent to 6 percent.

166 **About 50 miles are left:** Chris Servheen, author correspondence, July 2022.

166 **join up in less than a decade:** Chris Servheen, author interview, May 2021. "Within five to ten years we will see robust connectivity."

167 **home range of 600 square miles:** "Grizzly Bear Biology," University of Montana Grizzly Bear Recovery Program.

168 **Elk hunters are increasingly wary:** There have been six self-defense kills of grizzly bears by elk hunters since 2015, per USFWS data.

168 **Lance Crosby was attacked:** Yellowstone National Park, "Identity of Victim in Grizzly Attack Released," August 10, 2015.

168 **"a significant portion of the body":** Yellowstone National Park, "Hiker's Death Confirmed as Grizzly Attack," August 13, 2015.

168 **"Normal defensive attacks by female bears":** "Hiker's Death Confirmed."

168 **transferred to the Toledo Zoo:** Associated Press, "Ohio Zoo Takes Cubs of Bear Euthanized after Yellowstone Hiker Killed and Eaten," as appeared in *The Guardian*, August 15, 2015.

168 **financial losses caused by predation:** Albert Sommers et al., "Quantifying Economic Impacts of Large-Carnivore Depredation on Bovine Calves," *Journal of Wildlife Management* 74, no. 7 (2010): 1425–34; Gloria Dickie, "Pay for Prey," *High Country News Magazine*, July 23, 2018.

168 **more than four hundred grizzly bear deaths:** M. A. Haroldson et al., "Documented Known and Probable Grizzly Bear Mortalities in the Greater Yellowstone Ecosystem, 2015–2021," US Geological Survey data release, 2022. https://doi.org/10.5066/P9U1X0KF

169 **the bears will take up full-time residence:** Chris Servheen, author interview, 2021.

169 **killed by wildlife officials for eating cows:** Associated Press, "After Reappearing in Central Montana, Grizzly Killed over Cattle Depredation," as appeared on Montana Public Radio, May 14, 2021.

169 **Jim Laybourn:** Gloria Dickie, "Grizzly Face-Off," *High Country News Magazine*, May 16, 2016.

170 **briefly removed protections:** Cornelia Dean, "Wyoming: A Comeback Worthy of a Grizzly Bear," *New York Times*, March 23, 2007.

170 **took the agency to court:** Matthew Brown, "Feds Sued over Removal of Grizzlies from Threatened List," Associated Press, June 5, 2007.

170 **The judge ruled:** Greater Yellowstone Coalition Inc. v. Servheen (D-MONT. 9-21-2009).

170 **impact of climate change on whitebark pine:** Greater Yellowstone Coalition v. Servheen.

170 **an average of 1.3°C (2.3°F):** USGS et al., "The Greater Yellowstone Climate Assessment," 2021.

170 **where whitebark pine grows:** Janet Fryer, "*Pinus albicaulis*," US Department of Agriculture, Forest Service, Rocky Mountain Research Station, Fire Sciences Laboratory, 2002.

170 **their own investigation:** Frank T. Van Manen et al., "Response of Yellowstone Grizzly Bears to Changes in Food Resources: A Synthesis. Final Report to the Interagency Grizzly Bear Committee and Yellowstone Ecosystem Subcommittee," 2013.

170 **forage at lower elevations:** Van Manen et al., "Response of Yellowstone Grizzly Bears to Changes in Food Resources," 3.

170 **reduced cub survival rates:** Van Manen et al., "Response of Yellowstone Grizzly Bears to Changes in Food Resources," 5.

170 **praised the bears' diverse diet:** Van Manen et al., "Response of Yellowstone Grizzly Bears to Changes in Food Resources," 14.

170 **relied more on meat:** Van Manen et al., "Response of Yellowstone Grizzly Bears to Changes in Food Resources," 4.

170 **without much whitebark pine:** Van Manen et al., "Response of Yellowstone Grizzly Bears to Changes in Food Resources," 13.

170 **too many grizzlies were crowded:** Van Manen et al., "Response of Yellowstone Grizzly Bears to Changes in Food Resources," 35

170 **"We have not observed a decline":** Van Manen et al., "Response of Yellowstone Grizzly Bears to Changes in Food Resources," 35.

170 **recommended that protections be stripped:** Kelsey Dayton, "Will the Grizzly Bear Flourish or Falter after Decades under ESA?" *WyoFile*, December 24, 2013.

172 **black bears and grizzlies in Alaska:** Steve West, author interview, August 2017; Gloria Dickie, "Bear Market," *Walrus Magazine*, May 2018.

172 **Oryx in Namibia:** West, author interview, 2017; Dickie, "Bear Market."

172 **episodes had featured him unloading:** "Steve West Smashes Long Standing Boone & Crockett Grizzly Record with Muzzleloader," *Outdoor Hub*, August 7, 2012.

173 **"I'll buy the first tag":** Steve West, author interview, 2017.

173 **lost federal protections for a second time:** Department of Interior, "Endangered and Threatened Wildlife and Plants; Removing the Greater Yellowstone Ecosystem Population of Grizzly Bears from the Federal List of Endangered and Threatened Wildlife," *Federal Register*, Vol. 82, No. 125, June 30, 2017.

173 **"one of America's great conservation successes":** Colin Dwyer, "After 42 Years, Yellowstone Grizzly Will Be Taken Off Endangered Species List," NPR, June 22, 2017.

173 **opening a trophy hunt:** Ayla Besemer, "Wyoming Announces Grizzly Hunt Near Yellowstone and Grand Teton," *Backpacker*, May 24, 2018.

173 **less than $20:** Todd Wilkinson, "Jane Goodall Joins Wyoming Protestors in Buying Up Grizzly Hunt Tickets," *National Geographic*, July 16, 2018.

173 **Grizzly 399:** "Into the Wild with Thomas D. Mangelsen," *60 Minutes* with Anderson Cooper, May 6, 2018; Todd Wilkinson, "Famous Grizzly Bear 'Back from the Dead'—with a New Cub," *National Geographic*, May 12, 2016.

173 **Thomas Mangelsen entered the lottery:** Karin Brulliard, "A Wildlife Photographer Won a Permit to Shoot Grizzlies. Here's What He's Doing with It," *Washington Post*, August 1, 2018.

174 **seven thousand people entered the draw:** Brulliard, "A Wildlife Photographer Won a Permit."

174 **Mangelsen was one of them:** Brulliard, "A Wildlife Photographer Won a Permit."

174 **isolated Yellowstone grizzly population:** "Groups Challenge Decision to Remove Yellowstone Grizzly Protections," Earthjustice release, August 30, 2017. https://earthjustice.org/sites/default/files/files/2017-08-30-ECF-No1-Complaint.pdf

174 **ignored legal requirements to consult:** Melodie Edwards, "Nine Tribes Sue, Saying Feds Didn't Consult Them on Grizzly Delisting," Wyoming Public Media, August 4, 2017. https://www.courthousenews.com/wp-content/uploads/2017/07/Grizzlies.pdf

174 **signed the Grizzly Treaty:** Gloria Dickie, "Tribal Nations Fight Removal of Grizzly Protections," *High Country News Magazine*, June 20, 2017; "The Grizzly: A Treaty of Cooperation, Cultural Revitalization and Restoration." https://www.piikaninationtreaty.com/the-treaty

174 **"arbitrarily and capriciously":** United States District Court for the District of Montana, Missoula Division ruling on Crow Indian Tribe et al. v. United States of America et al. and State of Wyoming et al., September 24, 2018, 2.

174 **exceeded its legal authority:** United States District Court for the District of Montana, 2.

174 **"simplistic at best and disingenuous at worst":** United States District Court for the District of Montana, 25.

175 **rejoining these island populations and creating:** United States District Court for the District of Montana, 25.

175 **Black Bart is the only bear:** Trina Jo Bradley, author interview, May 2021.

176 **Montana's Grizzly Bear Advisory Council:** Alex Sakariassen, "Grizzly Bear Advisory Council Struggles with 'Herculean' Challenge in Missoula," *Montana Free Press*, December 6, 2019.

177 **have long questioned:** Dickie, "Pay for Prey." In 2019, Wyoming Game & Fish noted said grizzlies killed 176 cattle, per Angus Thuermer, "Grizzly CSI: Cutting to Facts in a Predator-Livestock Whodunit," *WyoFile*, August 4, 2020; "Government Data Confirm That Grizzly Bears Have a Negligible Effect on U.S. Cattle and Sheep Industries," Humane Society, March 6, 2019.

177 **Northern Continental Divide bears:** Nicky Ouellet, "Northern Continental Divide Grizzlies to Lose Federal Protections, USFWS Says," Montana Public Radio, May 10, 2018.

178 **Chris Servheen first laid eyes:** Servheen, author interview, 2021.

178 **national grizzly bear recovery coordinator:** Associated Press, "Only US Grizzly Bear Recovery Coordinator Retiring after 35 Years," April 21, 2016.

178 **under the mentorship of John Craighead:** Servheen, author interview, 2021.

179 **just thirty breeding females:** Servheen, author interview, 2021; "Proceedings—Grizzly Bear Habitat Symposium," IGBC, Missoula, Montana, April 30 May 2, 1985, 3.

179 **he had been adamant:** Dickie, "Grizzly Face-Off."

179 **"The objective of the Endangered Species Act":** Dickie, "Grizzly Face-Off."

179 **fly-fishing in Missoula:** Montana Wildlife Federation, "About Us."

179 **written some guidance:** Servheen, author interview, 2021.

180 **made it his mission to bring attention:** Chris Servheen, "Backward Thinking Targets Bears and Wolves," *Mountain Journal*, March 7, 2021; Chris Servheen, "Scientists Say Gianforte's Anti-Wolf, Anti-Grizzly Policies in Montana Have No Scientific Basis," *Mountain Journal*, October 2, 2021.

180 **"anti-predator hysteria":** Servheen, "Backward Thinking Targets Bears and Wolves."

180 **an unlimited number of wolves:** Montana Bill SB314; Alex Sakariassen, "What Got Signed, and What Got Vetoed," *Montana Free Press*, May 20, 2021.

180 **use of spotlights and bait traps:** Sakariassen, "What Got Signed."

180 **use leg-hold traps and neck snares:** Montana HB 224; "Montana Joins Idaho in Passing Extreme Wolf-Killing Legislation," Center for Biological Diversity press release, May 20, 2021.

180 **spring hound hunting season:** HB 468; Sakariassen, "What Got Signed."

180 **banned in Montana for a century:** Servheen, "Backward Thinking Targets Bears and Wolves."

181 **returned to California:** Laura Zuckerman, "Conservation Groups Demand U.S. Restore Grizzly Bears to Native Range," Reuters, June 18, 2014.

181 **Grand Canyon:** Zuckerman, "Conservation Groups Demand."

181 **Southern Rockies:** Zuckerman, "Conservation Groups Demand."

CHAPTER SEVEN: THE ICE WALKERS

185 **six hundred or so polar bears:** Chris Woolston, "Polar Bear Researchers Struggle For Air Time," *Nature* 599 (November 2021): S16–S17; Andrew Derocher, author interview, November 2018.

185 **first iteration of the Tundra Buggy:** John Volk, "The Bears of Churchill: Magnificence and Beauty in the Canadian Wilderness," *Chicago Tribune*, March 24, 1985.

186 **split off from the grizzly bear:** Shiping Liu et al., "Population Genomics Reveal Recent Speciation and Rapid Evolutionary Adaptation in Polar Bears," *Cell* 157, no. 4 (2014): 785–94; Webb Mill et al., "Polar and Brown Bear Genomes Reveal Ancient Admixture and Demographic Footprints of Past Climate Change," *Proceedings of the National Academy of Sciences* 109, no. 36 (2012): E2382–90.

187 **twenty-six thousand polar bears are believed to exist:** IUCN Red List of Threatened Species Assessment, *Ursus maritimus*, August 2015.

187 **Inuit even purport that the population is growing:** The Canadian Press, "'So many bears': Draft Plan Says Nunavut Polar Bear Numbers Unsafe," as appeared on CBC, November 12, 2018.

187 **climate change has devastated the sea ice:** NASA, "Arctic Sea Ice Extent." https://climate.nasa.gov/vital-signs/arctic-sea-ice/

187 **Henry Hudson:** John Edwards Caswell, "Henry Hudson," *Encyclopedia Britannica*; "Henry Hudson," History.com, updated September 12, 2018; "Henry Hudson North-West Passage Expedition, 1610–11," Royal Museums Greenwich.

188 **the crew mutinied:** Caswell, "Henry Hudson."

188 **unique population of polar bears:** Andrew Derocher, author correspondence, June 2021. The three polar bear groups that live in the region around Hudson Bay—Foxe Basin, Southern Hudson Bay, and Western Hudson Bay—exhibit this behavior.

188 **sea ice breaks up last in spring:** Andrew Derocher, author interview, November 2018. He also notes, in 2021 correspondence, that bears are attracted to the peat banks in the region, which allow them to build their dens before the snow arrives.

188 **only place in North America:** Andrew Derocher, author correspondence, June 2021.

189 **dispersing southward from Nunavut:** Parks Canada, "Grizzly Bears—Wapusk National Park"; Douglas Clark, "Recent Reports of Grizzly Bears, *Ursus arctos*, in Northern Manitoba," *Canadian Field Naturalist* 114, no. 4 (2000): 692–4.

189 **20 percent of its body weight:** World Wildlife Fund, "Polar Bear Diet."

189 **fast for more than four months:** Andrew Derocher, author correspondence, June 2021.

189 **Canada is the only nation that still allows:** Ingrid Margaretha Høie, "International Trade in Polar Bears from Canada Could Threaten The Species' Survivability," Norwegian Scientific Committee for Food and Environment risk assessment, June 25, 2020.

191 **dirt or tannins from the peat:** Derocher, author correspondence, June 2021.

191 **physical size of Western Hudson Bay polar bears:** "For Hudson Bay Polar Bears, the End Is Already in Sight," *Yale Environment 360* interview with Andrew Derocher, July 8, 2010.

192 **live in the Canadian Arctic:** "Polar Bear," Environment and Natural Resources, Nunavut. https://www.enr.gov.nt.ca/en/services/polar-bear

192 **extinguished by the excruciating cold:** Liu et al., "Population Genomics Reveal Recent Speciation."

192 *Ursus arctos sitkensis*: James Cahill et al., "Genomic Evidence of Geographically

Widespread Effect of Gene Flow from Polar Bears into Brown Bears," *Molecular Ecology* 24, no. 6 (2015): 1205–1217.

192 **"Not only had [the polar bear] gone from brown to white":** Charles T. Feazel, *White Bear* (New York: Henry Holt and Company, 1990).

192 **Dorset hunted almost entirely on the sea ice:** Robert W. Park, "Dorset Culture," University of Waterloo; "Middle Palaeo-Eskimo Culture," Canadian Museum of History; "Disappearance of Dorset Culture," Canadian Museum of History.

193 **Inuit were the descendants of the Thule:** "Thule and Their Ancestors," Museum of the North, University of Alaska Fairbanks; "Thule Culture," Museum of the North, University of Alaska Fairbanks.

193 **learned to hunt seals from the polar bear:** This is an often repeated claim, with somewhat obscure sourcing. A blog post from the Scott Polar Research Institute at the University of Cambridge, "Object in focus: carving in ivory of a polar bear hunting a seal," repeats this statement. Bernd Brunner, *Bears: A Brief History* (New Haven, CT: Yale University Press, 2007), 161, notes that Reverend John George Wood, *Nature's Teachings* (London: Daldy, Isbister, 1877), mentions this incident stemming from an 1871 Arctic expedition.

193 **have isuma, a shared way of thinking:** Brandon Kerfoot, "Beyond Symbolism: Polar Bear Characters and Inuit Kinship in Markoosie's *Harpoon of the Hunter*," *Canadian Literature* 230 (Fall/Winter 2016): 162–76; Frédéric Laugrand and Jarich Oosten, *Hunters, Predators, and Prey: Inuit Perceptions of Animals* (New York: Berghahn Books, 2015); Lorraine Brandson, curator of Churchill's Itsanitaq Museum, author interview, November 2018.

193 **the raven:** Frédéric Laugrand and Jarich Oosten, "The Bringer of Light: The Raven in Inuit Tradition," *Polar Record* 42, no. 3 (2006): 187–204.

193 **"the great white one":** Rachel Attituq Qitsualik, "What the Inuit 'Want,'" *Indian Country Today*, November 24, 2004.

193 **"the ever-wandering one":** Stemming from the Inuit word *Pihoqahiak*, used in Inuit poetry and mythology. Christina E. Macleod, "It Takes a Village to Save a Polar Bear," IUCN Governance for Sustainability—Environmental and Policy Paper No. 70, 2008.

193 **Norse travelers were making the acquaintance:** Michael Engelhard, *Ice Bear* (Seattle: University of Washington Press, 2016).

193 **King Haakon of Norway gifted:** Daniel Hahn, *The Tower Menagerie* (London: Penguin, 2004).

193 **rate of 4 sous a day:** Miriam Bibby, "King Henry III's Polar Bear," Historic UK. https://www.historic-uk.com/CultureUK/Henry-III-Polar-Bear/

193 **"Greetings. We commend you":** Hahn, *The Tower Menagerie*.

194 **fish for himself:** Hahn, *The Tower Menagerie*.

194 **he gifted Henry an African elephant:** "The Tower of London Menagerie," Historic Royal Palaces; Hahn, *The Tower Menagerie*.

194 **populate mainland Norway and Iceland:** Engelhard, *Ice Bear*; Michael Engelhard, "Here Be White Bears," *Hakai Magazine*, May 30, 2017.

194 **"a great leane beare":** James Wilder et al., "Polar Bear Attacks on Humans: Implications of a Changing Climate," *Wildlife Society Bulletin* 41, no. 3 (2017): 2.

194 **first account of a polar bear attacking:** Wilder et al., "Polar Bear Attacks on Humans," notes that although Indigenous people had inhabited the Arctic for thousands of years, the 1595 attack was the first recorded (de Veer, 1876).

194 *hic sunt ursi albi*: Engelhard, *Ice Bear*.

195 **heat melts the glossy white Arctic sea ice:** "How Does Sea Ice Affect Global Climate?" National Oceanic and Atmospheric Administration, 2021.

195 **lost roughly one-third of summer sea ice:** The 1979–1990 average September sea ice extent was about 7 million square kilometers (2.7 million square miles). The 2011–2020 average September sea ice extent was about 4.5 million square kilometers (1.7 million square miles). CHARCTIC, National Snow & Ice Data Center.

195 **as early as 2035:** Maria-Vittoria Guarino, "Sea-Ice-Free Arctic during the Last Interglacial Supports Fast Future Loss," *Nature Climate Change* 10 (2020): 928–32.

195 **cannot adequately hunt:** Thomas Brown et al., "High Contributions of Sea Ice Derived Carbon in Polar Bear (*Ursus maritimus*) Tissue," *PLoS One* 13, no. 1 (2018); Kristin Laidre et al., "Glacial Ice Supports a Distinct and Undocumented Polar Bear Subpopulation Persisting in Late 21st-Century Sea-Ice Conditions," *Science* 376, no. 6599 (2022): 1333–38, finds a population of bears able to persist without sea ice; however, as Derocher notes, "Bears in SE Greenland augment sea ice with glacier ice as a platform to hunt but the seals they feed on rely on the sea ice ecosystem to reproduce & for food. No sea ice, no seals, no bears," Twitter, June 22, 2022.

196 **eggs:** Patrick Jagielski et al., "Polar Bears Are Inefficient Predators of Seabird Eggs," *Royal Society Open Science* 8, no. 4 (2021).

196 **around 210 days:** Peter Molnar et al., "Fasting Season Length Sets Temporal Limits for Global Polar Bear Persistence," *Nature Climate Change* 10, no. 8 (2020): 732–38.

196 **starve to death:** Molnar et al., "Fasting Season Length."

196 **breaking up about one week earlier:** Andrew Derocher, "Western Hudson Bay Polar Bears," Polar Bears International blog, October 31, 2018.

196 **fasted for approximately 177 days:** "Polar Bears Returning to Ice," Polar Bears International blog, November 10, 2017.

196 **declined by around 50 percent since 1987:** Nicholas Lunn et al., "Demography of an Apex Predator at the Edge of Its Range: Impacts of Changing Sea Ice on Polar Bears in Hudson Bay," *Ecological Applications* 26, no. 5 (2016): 1302–1320.

196 **from 943 individuals to 780:** Martyn Obbard et al., "Re-Assessing Abundance of Southern Hudson Bay Polar Bears by Aerial Survey: Effects of Climate Change at the Southern Edge of the Range," *Arctic Science* 4, no. 4 (2018).

196 **declined by almost 50 percent:** "Marine Mammal Protection Act; Stock Assessment Report for Two Stocks of Polar Bears," US Fish and Wildlife Service Federal Register, June 24, 2021.

196 **created a time line:** Molnar et al., "Fasting Season Length."

197 **an air raid siren sounds:** Alexis McEwen, "Living on the Edge in the Town of Churchill," Travel Manitoba blog, November 1, 2016; reporting notes.

198 **Brown bears kill 14 percent:** G. Bombieri et al., "Brown Bear Attacks on Humans: A Worldwide Perspective," *Scientific Reports* 9, no. 1 (2019), finds that 14 percent of global brown bear attacks between 2000 and 2015 were fatal. Wilder et al., "Polar Bear Attacks on Humans," finds that polar bears killed 24 percent of those they attacked. From 1960 to 1998, Stephen Herrero found that black bears and grizzly bears killed a higher proportion of those they attacked in Alberta, around 42 percent and 32 percent, respectively, but in a smaller sample size.

198 **mentally ill:** Bryan Holt, "Man Lived Only Two Blocks from Bears," *Baltimore Afro-American*, August 31, 1976.

198 **Lafayette Herbert:** Associated Press, "Man's Body Mauled by Bears in Zoo," as appeared in the *Gettysburg Times*, August 28, 1976.

198 **mauled by three polar bears:** Maryland Zoo registrar, author correspondence.

198 **Hattie Amitnak:** Sean McKibbon, "Polar Bear Kills One, Injures Two Others," *Nunatsiaq News*, July 16, 1999.

198 **Paulosie Meeko:** Canadian Press, "Polar Bear Kills Eskimo Student at Churchill," as appeared in the *Ottawa Citizen*, November, 18, 1968.

198 **Tommy Mutanen:** UPI, "Migrating Polar Bear Mauls Canadian," November 30, 1983.

198 **stuffing his parka's pockets:** Jon Mooallem, *Wild Ones* (New York: Penguin Books, 2013), 31.

198 **throwing whatever they could find:** Mooallem, *Wild Ones*, 32.

198 **"shuttered their homes and stayed inside":** UPI, "Migrating Polar Bear Mauls Canadian."

199 **4,093 polar bear skins:** Lorraine Brandson, author interview, 2018.

199 **Gypsy's, the local bakery:** Carolyn Turgeon, "Victim of Vicious Polar Bear Attack Stuck with $13,000 Bill for Air Ambulance to Winnipeg," *National Post*, January 25, 2015.

199 **Greene was walking home:** Turgeon, "Victim of Vicious Polar Bear Attack."

199 **Halloween is a complicated affair:** "Halloween with the Polar Bears," Frontiers North Adventures blog. https://blog.frontiersnorth.com/halloween

200 **She'd often thought about:** Erin Greene, author interview, October 2020.

200 **She'd had nightmares:** "RAW: Erin Greene on Being Attacked by a Polar Bear," CBC, 2013. https://www.cbc.ca/player/play/2425415449

200 **Greene instinctively knew it would choose her:** Erin Greene, author interview, October 2020.

200 **tried to hide her face:** "RAW: Erin Greene on Being Attacked."

200 **Bill Ayotte was already awake:** Paul Hunter, "He Saved a Woman from a Polar Bear. 'Then the mauling was on for me,'" *Toronto Star*, May 20, 2017.

200 **pajama bottoms, a sweater, and slippers:** Hunter, "He Saved a Woman."

200 **polar bear "wagging":** Hunter, "He Saved a Woman."

200 **flesh behind his knee:** Hunter, "He Saved a Woman."

201 **screaming and throwing shoes:** Hunter, "He Saved a Woman."

201 **drove straight for the bear:** Hunter, "He Saved a Woman."

201 **was only minutes:** "RAW: Erin Greene on Being Attacked."

201 **initially shot the wrong one:** Canadian Press, "Two Polar Bears Shot After Attack in Churchill, Manitoba," as appeared in *Toronto Star*, November 1, 2013.

201 **twenty-eight staples:** Hunter, "He Saved a Woman."

202 **Biologists recently cataloged:** Wilder et al., "Polar Bear Attacks on Humans."

202 **forty-seven attacks:** Wilder et al., "Polar Bear Attacks on Humans."

202 **"We're just getting more reports of bears":** Geoff York, author interview, November 2018.

204 **24/7 polar bear hotline:** Polar Bear Alert Program, Frequently Asked Questions Media Handout, updated October 2015.

204 **burned down in 2018:** Elisha Dacey, "Gypsy's Bakery in Churchill Burns to the Ground," CBC, May 13, 2018.

205 **opened in the early 1980s:** Polar Bear Alert Program, Frequently Asked Questions Media Handout.

205 **Polar Bear Control Program:** Polar Bear Alert Program, Frequently Asked Questions Media Handout.

205 **mandate of shooting and killing:** Andrew Szklaruk, author interview, October 2020.

206 **twenty-three hundred polar bears:** Author correspondence with Polar Bear Alert Program.

206 **air-conditioned:** Polar Bear Alert Program, Frequently Asked Questions Media Handout.

206 **clean wood shavings for bedding:** Polar Bear Alert Program, Frequently Asked Questions Media Handout.

206 **"What are the cells constructed of?":** Polar Bear Alert Program, Frequently Asked Questions Media Handout.

206 **"steel reinforced cinder":** Polar Bear Alert Program, Frequently Asked Questions Media Handout.

206 **transports them by helicopter:** Ed Yong and Robinson Meyer, "Busy Times at the World's Largest Polar Bear Prison," *The Atlantic*, December 16, 2016; Mooallem, *Wild Ones*.

207 **obvious trend since 1999:** Sarah Heemskerk et al., "Temporal Dynamics of Human-Polar Bear Conflicts in Churchill, Manitoba," *Global Ecology and Conservation* 24 (2020).

207 **waste disposal site:** Heemskerk et al., "Temporal Dynamics."

207 **BEARDAR:** Gloria Dickie, "As Polar Bear Attacks Increase in Warming Arctic, a Search for Solutions," *Yale Environment 360*, December 19, 2018.

208 **polar bears attacked and killed two men:** Sarah Frizzell, "Inuit Lives Must Be Protected over Polar Bears, Nunavut Community Says," CBC, November 14, 2018; Darrell Greer, "Naujaat Man Mauled to Death by Polar Bear," *Nunavut News*, September 5, 2018.

208 **killed and left unharvested:** "Several Polar Bears Shot without Tags Near Arviat; Bears Not Harvested," CBC, August 2, 2018; Cody Punter, "Arviat Polar Bear Slaughter Sparks Debate," *Nunavut News*, August 8, 2018.

208 **twelve tags:** Darrell Greer, "Nine of 12 Polar Bear Tags Used So Far in Rankin Inlet," *Nunavut News*, November 19, 2020.

208 **relax hunting restrictions:** Beth Brown, "Don't Deduct Polar Bear Defence Kills from Quotas, Inuit Say," *Nunatsiaq News*, November 15, 2018; Sarah Rogers, "Red Tape Hampers Response to Increased Polar Bear Encounters: Nunavut MLAs," *Nunatsiaq News*, October 29, 2018.

208 **Longyearbyen on the Norwegian archipelago:** Geoff York, author interview, October 2020.

210 **sixteen grizzly bears were harvested:** Jodie Pongracz et al., "Recent Hybridization between a Polar Bear and Grizzly Bears in the Canadian Arctic," *Arctic* 70, no. 2 (2017): 151–160, Table 1.

210 **Wrangel Island:** Ulyana Babiy et al., "First Evidence of a Brown Bear on Wrangel Island, Russia," *Ursus* 33, no. 4 (2022): 1–8.

210 **a grizzly traveling along the sea ice:** Table 1 of Jodie Pongracz et al., "Recent Hybridization": the dates April 23, 2012, and April 25, 2012, note sightings of a grizzly bear and suspected hybrid; Andrew Derocher, author correspondence, June 2021; Ed Struzik, "Unusual Number of Grizzly and Hybrid Bears Spotted in High Arctic," *Yale Environment 360*, July 27, 2012.

211 **Jim Martell:** "DNA Tests Confirm Hunter Shot 'Grolar Bear,'" CBC, May 9, 2006.

211 **chatting on the bush radio:** Andrew Derocher, author correspondence, June 2021.

211 **guide knew instantly:** Derocher, author correspondence, June 2021.

211 **able to interbreed:** Pongracz et al., "Recent Hybridization."

211 **first-ever evidence of a wild hybrid:** Pongracz et al., "Recent Hybridization," Table 1, documented as April 6, 2006, F1 harvest.

211 **several other hybrids:** Pongracz et al., "Recent Hybridization," 153.

211 **unusual sexual preoccupation:** Pongracz et al., "Recent Hybridization," 153, notes that "the polar bear ancestry of these eight individuals traced to a single female polar bear (10960) who mated with two grizzly bears."

EPILOGUE

213 **forested overpasses:** Gloria Dickie, "As Banff's Famed Wildlife Overpasses Turn 20, the World Looks to Canada for Conservation Inspiration," *Canadian Geographic*, December 4, 2017.

214 **Hindu Kush Himalaya:** Babar Zahoor et al., "Projected Shifts in the Distribution Range of Asiatic Black Bear (*Ursus thibetanus*) in the Hindu Kush Himalaya Due to Climate Change," *Ecological Informatics* 63 (July 2021).